DATE D

The
Notorious
Lady Essex

Frances Howard, Lady Essex

From the Woburn Abbey Collection by kind permission of His Grace
The Duke of Bedford

The
Notorious
Lady Essex

Edward Le Comte

The Dial Press, Inc. NEW YORK 1969

Contents

		Preface	vii
		Identifications	ix
1	·	The Child Bride	1
2	·	The Knight from the North	20
3	·	Amorous Pursuit	33
4	·	The End of Overbury	58
5	·	The Annulment Commission Meets	91
6	·	The Countess of Essex Becomes the Countess of Somerset	114
7	·	Murder Will Out	135
8	·	On Trial	155
9	·	Condemned	187
10	·	Aftermath	215
		A Note on Authorities	244

PREFACE

Another book on the Overbury case, when there have been three since 1952? I plead partly guilty, with an explanation. This is the first book to bring the lady to stage center and keep the spotlight on her as much as possible. It is the first to give the other big episode of her life, her first marriage, its admittedly indecent due. One will never understand "the fatal Countess" by averting the chaste eye from the problem that made her fatal: the Essex marriage was the tragicomedy that preceded and gave rise to the tragedy. Also, I have given more attention than my predecessors to the literary and subliterary reactions, of praise and of abuse, that help us to see her as her contemporaries saw her. In short, this is the first biography of Frances Howard, who even lacks an entry of her own in the *Dictionary of National Biography*.

My debt to twentieth-century books on the case, and to Andrew Amos's nineteenth-century book, is considerable, for the material they have ordered and called attention to, and sometimes for their opinions and speculations. These and other sources are discussed in a backnote.

I have twice had the benefit of a summer Faculty Fellowship awarded by the Research Foundation of the State University of New York, and I am grateful to two outside scholars who wrote recommendations: Sidney Burrell, now chairman of the Department of History at Boston University, and Douglas Bush, Gurney Professor of English at Harvard University. Professor Thomas Kranídas of the University of Delaware sent me an offprint of his article on *Epicoene* and set me to reading *The Countess of Montgomery's Urania*. Of my colleagues at Albany, Townsend Rich lent from his specialized library rare or out-of-print books, one of which I kept for four years; Hugh Maclean and David Redding alerted me to certain recent items, and the latter came expertly to my aid in deciphering manuscripts.

E. Le C.

IDENTIFICATIONS

It is not easy to keep track of the Howards. But there are only four who play major roles in this story. *She* was Frances Howard (nicknamed Fanny or Frankie), who became successively the Countess of Essex and the Countess of Somerset. Her first husband, Robert Devereux, the Earl of Essex, had the same name and title as his famous father, Queen Elizabeth's "Robin." Her parents were Thomas and Catherine Howard, the Earl and Countess of Suffolk. Thomas's uncle, her great-uncle, was Henry Howard, Earl of Northampton.

The favorite of King James started as Robin or Robert Carr, was intermediately Viscount Rochester, and finally the Earl of Somerset.

The Child Bride

1

Elizabeth, the Virgin Queen, died in 1603 without having uttered one clear word as to who her successor was to be. That had ever been a forbidden subject with her, like the question in her younger days of whom she should choose for her husband. She had kept many a suitor dangling, and now King James VI of Scotland was kept dangling. He had been looking hungrily south from his poor kingdom for a long while. He was the logical successor, by descent from Henry VII. Others were as closely related but were not monarchs. True, Elizabeth had had to have his mother, Mary Stuart, Queen of Scots, beheaded as a Roman Catholic conspirator against her. But James was a safe product of the Scottish Reformation and could be relied on not to plunge Protestant England back to the martyr-filled days of the other Mary, Bloody Mary, Elizabeth's half-sister, who had actually taken as husband, shared the throne of England with, the hated Philip II of Spain, strategist of the Armada of '88 and other armadas. Fortunately, that pair had had no children.

Elizabeth was one of those mortals who just could not get around to making a will, rendering the succession clear as her father Henry VIII had taken pains to do. As she approached her allotted span of seventy and the forty-fifth year of her reign, she not only did not look death in the face but avoided her own reflection, banning mirrors. Her maids dared to vermilion her nose; but this did not matter. The last favorite had gone, the dashing but difficult Earl of Essex, executed justly as a traitor for his foolish rebellion of 1601. As the Queen lay speechless on her back in the bed in Richmond Palace, after having been more or less forcibly removed from the floor, where she had sat propped for days, her red wig askew, it was thought—perhaps wishful thinking—that she made a gesture of assent when her Secretary of State, Sir Robert Cecil, mentioned James as King. Certainly James had his allies below the border, and when he came into his own— very smoothly, after all—as King James I of England, he was ready to pay off various obligations.

Which introduces a twisted tale that is the stuff of ballads. Frankie and Robbie were lovers, and two other men (not Robbie) did her wrong. On both Frankie worked her sensational revenge. The first to wrong her was her husband, the third Earl of Essex (son of the beheaded favorite): after having been wedded to him for nearly eight years she secured an annulment by deposing that, despite their best endeavors, she was still "a pure virgin untouched." Actually, she was already the mistress of the future Earl of Somerset, Robert Carr. When Sir Thomas Overbury stood in the way of this affair and their plans for marriage, she had assorted poisons sent him in the Tower of London, and he died a loathsome and painful death. This is her second claim to fame.

The nineteenth century's word for her was "disgusting." "Nor shall I dwell upon the disgusting particulars," wrote Lord Braybrooke, when he had to mention this ancestress of his. He preferred to edit—and to censor—Pepys. The 1836 editor of the Loseley Manuscripts said the same: "the details . . . are superlatively disgusting," and was echoed, word for word, by Rimbault, Overbury's 1856 editor. Sir Edmund Gosse likewise regarded her story as too "disgusting" to tell. But many more disgusting stories have been detailed since Gosse's Victorian time. And perhaps to know more of "beautiful little Fanny Howard, of the beautifullest face and figure you would find in all these islands," is to pardon more.

She came from the oldest of the old nobility. The Howards defied William the Conqueror. Their lines of the Earls of Arundel date from 1139, and the Dukes of Norfolk from 1483. It is the oldest dukedom today: the present Duke of Norfolk, the sixteenth, whom newspaper photos recently showed standing beside Queen Elizabeth II at Epsom Downs, impassive in his boutonniere and frock coat and gray top hat, is paid twenty pounds a year, a sum fixed in 1483, as hereditary Earl Marshal of England, in charge of special royal occasions, such as the Coronation and State funerals—if not the Derby. He led the procession at Sir Winston Churchill's funeral.

The fourth Duke of Norfolk was Frances Howard's grandfather. He was beheaded for treason in 1572, whereupon Queen Elizabeth I finished her reign without dukes of any sort. He had got too close to that perpetual siren, Mary Queen of Scots, disregarding the warning of *his* Queen "to be careful on what pillow he laid his head." Other relatives of Frances Howard were also, unfortunately, beheaded: Henry Howard, Earl of Surrey, the poet, and Katherine Howard, Henry VIII's fifth wife. The latter died for love: "I die a Queen, but I would rather die the wife of Culpeper." Frances Howard was also to be sentenced to death for a crime of passion, her murderous hatred of Overbury being the other side of her love for Robert Carr.

The Howards were powerful partly by being prolific, flooding whatever court they were at with sheer numbers. Alex-

ander Pope was to pay sardonic tribute to the family tendency: "What can ennoble sots or slaves or cowards?/Alas, not
all the blood of all the Howards." After all, the practice of
nepotism under, say, King James I, does require that there be
nephews; and Thomas Howard, father of Frances, was to be
partner in intrigue with his uncle, the Earl of Northampton.
Another kinsman, Charles Lord Howard of Effingham, was
Lord High Admiral. Now wizened, with a white sprig of a
goatee, he had been the leader in repelling the Armada, re-
porting at the glorious time: "Their force is wonderful great
and strong; and yet we pluck their feathers by little and
little." Thomas, a generation younger, had also distinguished
himself then; he commanded in the Azores in 1591 and was
admiral of the third squadron against Cadiz in 1596.

At home, he attended to the steady Howard business of
proliferation. Like Job he had seven sons and three daughters. This is just to count those that grew up: there were no
less than fourteen births, all from his second wife. The first
wife, Mary, had died without issue when her husband was
sixteen. The wife that endured was Catherine, daughter and
coheiress of Sir Henry Knevet of Wiltshire, who also brought
a widow's portion to this second marriage of 1583. Frances
—fair but "disgusting" Fanny—was born ten years later—about
midmost of the brood.

Walden was her first home, Saffron Walden in Essex,
bright with that useful flower, the yellow crocus. But Walden
did not suffice for the ambitious Howards. The house was old
and ought long ago to have been rebuilt. It had not even
been the capital residence of Thomas's father, the attainted
duke. The needs of Thomas and his matriarch had expanded.
When he entertained the Queen two months before her death
he had resorted to the ancestral town house, the Charter-
house. How far he had come already, since 1588, when he

4 ·

had been knighted at sea by his relative the Lord Admiral. He had proved that that was not nepotism; the Spaniards had heard from his vessel, the *Golden Lion,* had been made grimly aware of its 500 tons and 38 guns and crew of 250. Unlike the unlucky Grenville, he had brought his squadron safely back from the Azores in 1591, to earn from the grateful monarch the sobriquet of her "Good Thomas." At Cadiz in 1596, in the most brilliant expedition of the decade, he had been one of four commanders, with Essex and Ralegh and Lord Admiral Howard, in that "singeing of the King of Spain's beard." The next year he became Lord Howard himself, as well as Knight of the Garter. He was summoned to Parliament as Baron Howard de Walden. When there was rumor of another Armada in 1599, he was the one relied on to mobilize the fleet.

The temper of the times changed with the coming of James Stuart to the English throne in 1603. The valiant and efficient sailor moved now in another medium. With his wife's and uncle's help, "Good Thomas" looked to be metamorphosed into a good courtier—whatever the ambiguity of that adjective attached to that noun. The new monarch was peaceful, if not homosexual. He signed a treaty with Spain. There was no use for a warrior. But James rewarded the warrior, paid off a debt to the family. The King had looked through his fingers as his mother, Mary (that persistent plotter against the Protestant regime of her cousin Elizabeth), went to her doom, but he did not forget her exclamation during her trial at Fotheringay, "Alas, what has the House of Howard suffered for my sake!" Thomas Howard was created Earl of Suffolk and made Lord Chamberlain. His uncle, Henry Howard, who was pro-Spanish and pro-Catholic, gained equal rank a few months later as Earl of Northampton. For years he had been a busy, flattering letter writer and schemer. William McElwee, author of two books on the period, has singled him out as "probably the most dangerous man in England." He and Thomas were members of the Privy Council, the inmost circle of it. At the old Queen's death he had been one of the first to hurry north "to possess [as a letter writer said] the King's ear," an ear his secret, oleaginous correspondence had made receptive.

One of Northampton's flairs was for architecture, with which he now inspired his nephew. When Frances Howard was ten there began to rise around her at Saffron Walden "that excellent fabric," and vast, Audley End, the most remarkable pile of Elizabethan Gothic (with touches of Doric and Ionic) in the land, with its courts and porticoes, its turrets and countless mullioned windows, its Clock Tower, its Long Gallery (226 feet long, 32 feet wide, and 24 feet high) whose carved oak chimney piece appropriately represented the labors of Hercules, while the ceiling depicted the loves of the gods. But the sailor insisted on another motif for the saloon, which came to be known as the Fish Room on account of its ceiling panels of ships and whales and mermaids and sea birds and sundry monsters of the deep. The palatial mansion was the observed of all observers. Two diarists of a later generation, Evelyn and Pepys, came to stare. The latter liked the cellar best, for its liquor, which he sampled, and for the "excellent echo," which he tested with flageolet and song. A foreign visitor of 1669, who also left a record, was fittingly named Cosmo de Medici (afterwards Grand Duke of Tuscany). A bishop of Frances Howard's own generation, Godfrey Goodman, was moved to cautious but unmistakable awe: "In the first court, there are such pillars as I do not think all Christendom can afford better."

Audley End has to be seen to be believed, but today (government-owned as a national monument) it is reduced from what it was, like so much else of the old Elizabethan and Jacobean magnificence. The King was a guest there in 1610 and 1614, and on the latter occasion, having just appointed Suffolk to a post that could be as lucrative as it sounded (depending on the flexibility of the holder's conscience), he remarked dryly, "By my troth, mon, it is too much for a king, but may do for a Lord High Treasurer." This palace (Charles II made it officially that by purchasing it), pridefully designed to be the largest private house in the kingdom—one would have to hark back to Wolsey and Hampton Court for a comparison—took thirteen years to complete, and 200,000 pounds. That sum was not acquired by simple honesty, and the Latin motto on the stone parapet did not speak of anything so old-fashioned. It broadly hinted that cunning paid: *Prudentis est in consilio fortunam semper habere,* "Good counsel is to a prudent man like gold." The motto of the Garter bordering the other side did not necessarily succeed in counterbalancing for most observers this Baconian advice.

At any rate there was room for any number of children. There were lawns, bowling greens, cherry gardens, stables, a double avenue of lime trees for stately sauntering, and flowing through the middle of the outer court the river Cam.

As we contemplate Winstanley's 1676 drawing of the original Audley End that, with its arched cloisters and studious-looking upper stories, might have passed for one of the larger colleges at Cambridge or Oxford, our thoughts turn to problems of nurture. With our modern stress on environment and our sometimes envious theories of the debilitating effects of wealth on character, we have to ask whether three daughters brought up in Audley End *could* have turned out virtuous and unspoiled. The only answer we shall ever have is that if this was the goal in any Howard mind it singularly failed of achievement. All three daughters went down the primrose path of a marriage that was satisfactory only from the social and material point of view. And it was the parents that led them, indeed pulled them.

Under the date of October 24, 1605, that gossipy letter writer John Chamberlain reported, "The Earl of Essex and the young Lord Cranborne shall marry two of the Lord Chamberlain's daughters at court very shortly. The only stay is for the King's coming, who is looked for the next week." The one wedding as well as the other did take place, but not at the same time and neither so soon as expected. Two weeks later Chamberlain was saying, "The marriages . . . are put off till toward Christmas."

Two reasons for delay developed, neither having to do with the tender ages of the prospective brides. For one, James when he did come to town for the opening of Parliament had very nearly been blown up with both Houses. Outstanding in the investigation of the Gunpowder Plot of November 5th was the Lord Chamberlain. He was eager to demonstrate that no mad Roman Catholicism motivated this Howard, whatever the perennial suspicions directed at his uncle, who outwardly changed his religion five times. Thomas Howard had in fact refused a Spanish pension in 1604. On the other hand he did not stop his wife—and could not stop his uncle—from accepting from Spain 1,000 pounds a year each, for which from time to time they passed on government secrets. However, it is only fair to add that Fanny's mother, Catherine Howard, Lady Suffolk, did something for her king: once she had sized up his besetting weakness, she collected charming young men as candidates for minionship, personally supervising their curling and perfuming. Audley End needed a lot of feathering, with Spanish gold, peculation, alliances with favorites, matrimonial or other.

The other reason for delay was that the eldest daughter

had not been married yet. She had evidently been a problem, not having Frances's beauty, but lightning struck and Elizabeth was, after all, the first—as propriety demanded—to leave home. William, Baron Knollys of Rotherfield Greys, lost his wife on October 31st. He was so used to her or to the married state that he immediately looked for a replacement. Elizabeth and he were wed two days before Christmas. She at eighteen had been withering on the vine, by the quick standards of the time. However, she was not as withered as her husband, who was fifty-eight.

There would be trouble with that forty-year difference, not that such differences were uncommon. Romance was not what counted. Even John Donne, known for his love poems, was to marry one of his daughters to a man of means thirty-seven years her senior. In both cases the husband was older than the girl's father, and in both cases we happen to have record of ill consequences. It is not surprising that these wives, like Sir Francis Bacon's wife, skipped on to younger men as soon as death freed them, if not sooner. Donne to his credit had tried to find a younger man for his Constance, but matrimony was a market where the parent or guardian dared not pass up high bids; the child was the last person consulted, if at all. Chamberlain tells of the furore that broke over a young couple that were so far in advance of their time that they presumed to pick each other. "Young George Beeston shall shortly marry a daughter of the Lady Cave's . . . the young couple having contracted themselves without their parents' privity or consent, whereat the mother doth the more storm for that she had the choice of the heir of the Kingsmills, or of Sir William Cornwallis, who offered her a thousand marks a year to her and her heirs." Dorothy Osborne, who did manage to marry for love, scarcely expected to: "I do not see any great likelihood of the change of our fortunes, and *that* we have much more to wish than to hope for; but 'tis so common a calamity that I dare not murmur at it; better people have endured it, and I can give no reason why almost all are denied the satisfaction of disposing themselves to their own desires, but that is a happiness too great for this world, and might endanger one's forgetting the next."

Her desired husband was Sir William Temple, future diplomat, essayist, patron of Jonathan Swift. The pair corresponded for seven years before the opposition of their families was overcome. Just before the so long awaited Christmas wedding day, her beauty was swallowed up by the smallpox, but they lived happily ever after in a rare storybook, history-book romance, with posterity grateful for the ill wind that blew it Dorothy Osborne's very remarkable, in fact, uniquely personal for the time, letters.

Frances Howard, that jewel in that stupendous setting, was worth an earl. Going on thirteen (her birthday is unknown; in her statement before the Nullity Commission she showed she did not know it herself), her elfin beauty already stunned observers. She had gingery hair and hazel eyes. A friend of the family who had known her from childhood recalled her as "of the best nature and sweetest disposition of all her father's children, exceeding them also in the delicacy and comeliness of her person." Her eyes bewitched, her small mouth beckoned—and forbade. Her décolletage would soon become famous. She was deliciously past the legal age for marriage, which was twelve for females (fourteen for males). New Hampshire is almost that permissive, but in England the Church performed marriages upon infants in arms, their parents agreeing. Child marriages were common among the nobility. Indeed the newborn Mary Queen of Scots was supposed to marry the five-year-old future Edward VI, but the compact was not kept. Louis XIII was told the facts of life at age one, and put them into practice on his wedding night at fourteen.

The husband picked out for Frances was older than is usually noticed, not just fourteen but within a week of being fifteen. Approximately fifteen espousing approximately thirteen—these were the same chronological conditions as attended Thomas Howard's own first union with little Mary Dacre. Poor thing, she had lasted scarcely a year after receiving all her matrimonial rights and privileges. Maybe the present groom could be persuaded to postpone consummation. Probably he should continue his education abroad for a year or two, and the same arrangement would be imperative with Fanny's younger sister. In fact, her wedding to "the young Lord Cranborne" was put off for three years.

The third Earl of Essex was not troublesomely ardent. The only son of a great lover and a dashing general, he was neither. His father had lost his head, figuratively and literally; the son was phlegmatic, prudent and patient. He pocketed his dowry and did as he was advised. Like the Earl of Suffolk and the Earl of Northampton, he had known some lean years in the shadow of an attainted father, and evidently could say with Edward Hyde, "My first inclination to marriage had no other passion than an appetite to a convenient estate." It was a politic match that pleased the King, whose faults did not include ingratitude. The prior Earl of Essex, once Queen Elizabeth's spoiled darling, had worked secretly for James's succession. There had been correspondence; Essex had faithfully destroyed it, burning the little black bag that hung around his neck and under his doublet, before being led to the Tower after his mad uprising. When James came to the throne he took measures to restore the son to his father's title and lands (and released that young co-conspirator Southampton from the Tower). Now the Howard family would increase and thrive in union with the Devereux. No expense should be spared for this gala occasion on January 5, 1606, the night before Twelfth Night. Were there not poets who said that "Devereux" was a contraction of *devenir heureux*—"to become happy"?

Poets were always playing about with words, rather irresponsibly. The poet who wrote the wedding masque made much of the anagram *unio*—union, and *Iuno*—Juno, the goddess of marriage. But it is a fair guess that the girl bride was not thinking of anything so solemn and clever. She knew only that she was going to be the center of attention at the biggest party ever, held in the capital at the royal palace of Whitehall, with the King himself looking on benevolently. All in white except for her jewels, her hair down to her shoulders in sign of virginity, she would dance with the Prince of Wales.

We know unusually much about that occasion, because the poet who wrote the masque published it with footnotes and an appendix, and because a newsletter has been preserved from a spectator who enjoyed himself hugely, although he had a cold. John Pory reported to Sir Robert Cotton: "The bridegroom carried himself as gravely and gracefully as if he were of his father's age. He had greater gifts given him than my lord of Montgomery had, his plate being valued at £3000; his jewels, money, and other gifts at £1000 more. But to return to the masque. Both Inigo [Jones], Ben [Jonson], and the actors, men and women, did their parts with great commendation. The conceit or soul of the Masque was Hymen bringing in a bride, and Juno Pronuba's priest a bridegroom, proclaiming that those two should be sacrificed to nuptial Union; and here the poet made an apostrophe to the union of the Kingdoms. But before the sacrifice could be performed, Ben Jonson turned the globe of the earth, standing behind the altar, and within the concave sat the eight men-maskers, representing the four Humors and the four Affections, who leaped forth to disturb the sacrifice to Union. But amidst their fury, Reason, that sat above them all, crowned with burning tapers, came down and silenced them. These eight, together with Reason their moderatress mounted above their heads sat somewhat like the ladies in the scallop-shell of the last year. About the globe hovered a middle region of clouds, in the center whereof stood a grand concert of musicians, and upon the cantons or horns sat the ladies, four at one corner and four at another, who descended upon the stage—not after the stale downright perpendicular fashion, like a bucket into a well, but came gently sloping down. These eight, after the sacrifice was ended, represented the eight Nuptial Powers of Juno Pronuba, who came down to confirm their Union. The men were clad in crimson, and the women in white. They had every one a white plume of the richest hern's feathers, and were so rich in jewels upon their heads as was most glorious. I think they hired and borrowed all the principal jewels and ropes of pearls both in court and city. . . ." The heron's feathers for the ladies had been sent down by the King from his favorite hunting lodge of Royston.

The great stage designer (and architect) Inigo Jones had never devised more intricate machinery. Jonson, who had not yet quarreled with him as to who should get first billing in their collaboration on court masques, was also pleased with the dance master, Thomas Giles, and the composer and conductor, Alphonso Ferrabosco. Above all he was pleased with himself. He had done elaborate research on Roman marriage ceremonies, and everything in the masque was guaranteed to be authentic, beginning with the *quinque cerei* mentioned by Plutarch ("five pages . . . bearing five tapers of virgin wax"), and including Juno's two peacocks and Order in a blue undergarment, and "Union's *orgies*"—of which a foot-note, giving the word in Greek, explains that it does not mean what is vulgarly thought. The Auspices were not neg-lected: "Auspices were those that handfasted the married couple; that wished them good luck; that took care for the dowry; and heard them profess that they came together for the cause of children." But Jonson's Epithalamion at the end was cut after one stanza. He really was overdoing the union idea, ignoring the children's plan not to be precocious:

> So! now you may admit him in;
> The act he covets is no sin. . . .
> And Venus, thou, with timely seed,
> Which may their after-comforts breed,
> Inform the gentle womb;
> Nor let it prove a tomb:
> But, ere ten moons be wasted,
> The birth, by Cynthia hasted.
> So may they both, ere day,
> Rise perfect every way.

Frances Howard and Robert Devereux, Earl of Essex, were going to suffer imperfection for a while. And Ben Jonson, when in 1616 he published *Hymenaei* (for the second time) with the Epithalamion restored ("I have here set it down whole; and do heartily forgive their ignorance whom it chanc-eth not to please"), no longer cared to say what marriage it had celebrated.

Many a couple just as young or younger had been seen to bed at the end of the wedding party, and the curtains drawn on them, to the accompaniment of customs more English than Roman. The bride was supposed to be bedded first, and it was the function of the bridesmaids to undress her. Her garter or stocking was cut up and there was scrambling among the bachelor guests for the pieces. Then the same guests, with appropriate jokes, untrussed the bridegroom, brought him to the wedding chamber, and nobody left until the couple were sewn naked together into the sheets. James was the sort who would come the next morning to receive personal assurance of consummation: that is what he did when his daughter was married. At a 1604 wedding he appeared bright and early in his shirt and nightgown and lolled in the marriage bed.

So the fun was truncated, despite the expensive show on the night before Twelfth Night, 1606. This may seem humane, considering the ages of the pair and the improbability that they would successfully practice the only form of birth control current, *coitus interruptus* (and that was seldom used, judging by the annual births—or miscarriages: Jonson knew what he was doing when he rhymed "womb" and "tomb"). A pamphleteer of 1615 declared that early marriages produced dangerous births and shortened the life of the mother. But there is something to be said on the other side, especially in the light of what happened in this particular case. It was legally risky not to consummate the marriage immediately: the way was left open for annulment. There are teen-agers today who apparently would not regard the couple as too young for intercourse. And there is the question of whether making love may not make love. The husband left his wife unattached and adrift at an impressionable age. He might have made some sort of effort to win her instead of going off to learn soldiering.

Arranged marriages were not all bad. It can even be argued that they had as good a chance to succeed as romantic love, which turns out to be an illusion—a temporary fire—while the matches settled at the attorney's table with the engrossing of deeds had at least the solid basis of carefully spelled-out property arrangements and similar social background: both parties knew exactly what they were starting with. Money can be a consolation if it has to be. They also knew that divorce with permission to remarry was unheard of. What could they do but settle down and make the most of the contract? Henry Smith in 1591 put it caninely but sensibly: "If they might be separated for discord, some would make a commodity of strife; but now they are not best to be contentious, for this law will hold their noses together, till weariness make them leave struggling, like two spaniels which are coupled in a chain, at last they learn to go together, because they may not go asunder." There was no intrinsic reason why the love that had not come before marriage could not come after. We have instances today where, instead of faith in the parents' judgment, there is a touching reliance on columnists or computers. Some resort to fortune tellers, which incidentally is what Fanny Howard was to do, disastrously.

What moved or failed to move the boy husband, who had seen himself personated as "the longing bridegroom, in the porch"? Jonson had done all *he* could, chorally admonishing, "A minute's loss in love is sin." But Robert Devereux bided his time. He lingered in the porch for years. Never has there been so sluggish a bridegroom. It took him seven years to discover that in letting his wife go by default that night he had lost her forever. He had lost his chance (but how much had he ever wanted it?).

Frances at thirteen had not yet developed into the uncontrollably self-willed creature that a few more giddy years at court would make her. She was passive. A contemporary described her as "too young to consider, but old enough to consent." She was still pliable, and it was a man's world. Women were brought up to obey, and it took time for a few of them to decide not to. If the first Robert had assumed the initiative in asserting his rights, it would at least have been more difficult for her to fall in love with the second Robert—and impossible to marry him without perpetrating a different murder, her husband's (which, it is only fair to say, she did take some bungling measures towards).

Was Essex being kind and considerate, by the advice of his elders? Was he shy? Did he like her, as distinguished from her dowry? Was he impotent, or at least afraid of some humiliating failure? He would not have been the first or last man-boy to be nervous about the wedding night and glad for any respite. Had he had any experience whatsoever with girls? His testimony before the nullity inquiry was that "he believeth that *before* and after the marriage he hath found an ability of body to know any *other* woman" (italics supplied). Such is the version in Howell's *State Trials*. British Museum MS. Titus C. vii., fol. 100, adds an "h," instead of "ability of body," "hability of body," but this settles down as a variant spelling rather than a variant meaning: according to the *Oxford English Dictionary*, "hability" did not acquire the (French) sense of deftness until a later century. We are left, dropped "h" or not, with something feebly put. These and other words of the Earl's have a collusive and defensive ring, in a suit fraught with statements that half the Commission, even under the King's prodding, could not force themselves to believe. Moreover, regardless of whether he was telling the truth, the Earl was not affirming that at fourteen or any other age he had *known* (in the Biblical sense) a woman. He would not have wanted to proclaim precocious looseness before marriage, and any experience afterwards would have been adultery, which would have changed the complexion of the suit and left neither him nor his wife free to marry another. So he went on to clarify: "and hath oftentimes felt motions and provocations of the flesh, tending to carnal copulation." However, he managed not to be overwhelmingly provoked during the at least two-day celebration of his marriage. With his fifteenth birthday coming up January 11, what he wanted to be, what he already partly was, was a cadet—and he became a general, of sorts. The arms that drew him were not a woman's. We have a painting of him looking florid in his breastplate. He was never at ease with women. We have no record that he so much as danced at his own wedding; maybe he did not know how.

His mother, still very much alive and married to her third husband (said to resemble her second), was also named Frances, and *she* had been a child bride (fourteen). Did the son have feelings of ambivalence? He could have seen or read *Hamlet,* which quite possibly was in part a memorial to his father, who had himself been a most vacillating person. Without the benefit of the commentary by Ernest Jones, the psychoanalyst (*Hamlet and Oedipus*), Robert Devereux with other contemporaries could recognize, or half-recognize, a case of mother-involvement (Hamlet and Gertrude) when he saw it projected, if not in himself. How difficult it was to live up to a famous (but also infamous) father, though there might be certain imitations! And his mother's first husband, the receiver of her maidenly best, had been the peerless Sir Philip Sidney. Widowed when that knight fell at Zutphen, she had married the only possible successor, thereby incurring the fierce jealousy of the aging Queen Elizabeth. It was all very complicated, because Sidney's "Stella" sonnets were addressed, even after his marriage, to Penelope Devereux, even after her marriage (to Lord Rich), the great Essex's sister, the present Essex's notoriously wild aunt. Forbears of such sexual and military prowess placed a heavy burden on a scion who was confident of neither and felt he could pursue only one at a time. Interesting as it would have been to get into bed with somebody named Frances, he decided he would rather be shot at.

The child bride was left to dance with Prince Henry, or whom she pleased. "They danced all variety of dances, both severally and *promiscue,* and then the women took in men as, namely, the Prince, who danced with as great perfection, and as settled a majesty, as could be devised, the Spanish ambassador, the Archduke's ambassador, the Duke, etc. And the men gleaned out the Queen, the bride, and the greatest of the ladies."

The Knight from the North

2

Although he danced with her, Prince Henry did not then mount her on his steed and bear her away forever from "a laggard in love." This was out of the question, apart from the fact that he had not read Sir Walter Scott. He was heir apparent to the throne; moreover, he was even younger than she was, eleven going on twelve. Pory's praise of his "settled . . . majesty" was a pat on the head. They would have to develop an interest in each other. As for Lochinvar, he was a Scot.

The Prince and Essex did have a quarrel, but not over her. It was a boyish hot-headed dispute in tennis that led to Essex's being called "son of a traitor," whereupon he struck the Prince "so shrewdly" with his racquet that he drew blood. The King took Essex's side: "He who did strike him then, would be sure, with more violent blows, to strike his enemy in times to come." Charles I would experience the irony of this, when Essex led parliamentary armies against him in the civil war to come. Maybe the fallout at tennis was not trivial; maybe Essex never forgot and never forgave the first Stuart offense. It was just that Henry did not live to be his grown-up opponent.

They were reconciled. Essex went to the continent, having received his M.A. from Oxford, where the time he could spare from military exercises he had expended "in the perusal of books that afforded most profit, not most delight." Dates are uncertain, but within a year or two he was writing Henry from Montreuil. "Most gracious Prince—I do in these few lines present my humblest duties unto your Highness. Being now entered into my travels, and intending the end thereof, to attain to true knowledge and to better my experience, I hope God will so bless me in my endeavors as that I shall return an acceptable servant unto your Highness." Another missive expressed the hope "that his Highness will please to remit all past errors." In the spring of 1608, this earnest young man practiced being a good servant by staying with the King at Fontainebleau. Did he write to his wife in French, as Lord Chesterfield was to do with his little bastard boy?

The sort of thing the virgin bride was exposed to at a court more licentious than that of Paris under Henry IV is illustrated by a report of a masque that followed the marriage one by six months. The account comes from Sir John Harington, who was certainly no prude, although nostalgic for the days of his godmother, Queen Elizabeth. Everybody, that July of 1606, was trying to keep up with the imbibing by a royal visitor, Queen Anne's brother, Christian IV of Denmark.

The sports began each day in such manner as persuaded me of Mahomet's paradise. We had women and indeed wine too of such plenty as would have astonished each sober beholder. Our feasts were magnificent, and the two royal guests did most lovingly embrace each other at table; I think the Dane hath strangely wrought on our good English nobles, for those whom I never could get to taste good liquor now follow the fashion and wallow in beastly delights. The ladies abandon their sobriety and roll about in intoxication. There hath been no lack of good living: shows, sights and banquetings from morn to eve.

One day a great feast was held, and after dinner the representation of Solomon his Temple and the coming of the Queen of Sheba was made before their Majesties. The lady who did play the Queen's part did carry most precious gifts to both their Majesties; but forgetting the steps arising to the canopy overset her caskets into his Danish Majesty's lap and fell at his feet, though I rather think it was in his face. Much was the hurry and confusion; clothes and napkins were at hand to make all clean. His Majesty then got up and would dance with the Queen of Sheba; but he fell down and humbled himself before her and was carried to an inner chamber and laid on a bed of state, which was not a little defiled with the presents of the Queen which had been bestowed on his garments, such as wine, cream, jelly, beverage, cakes, spices and other good matters.

The entertainment went forward and most of the presenters went backward or fell down, wine did so occupy their upper chambers. Now did appear Hope, Faith and Charity. Hope did assay to speak but wine rendered her endeavors so feeble that she withdrew and hoped the King would excuse her brevity. Faith was then all alone for I am certain she was not joined with good works, but left the court in a staggering condition. Charity came to the King's feet and seemed to cover the multitude of sins her sisters had committed. In some sort she made obeisance and brought gifts, but said she would return home again as there was no gift which heaven had not already given his Majesty. She then returned to Hope and Faith who were both sick and spewing in the lower hall. Next came Victory in bright armor and presented a rich sword to the King who did not accept it but put it by with his hand; but Victory did not triumph long, for after much lamentable utterance she was led away like a silly captive and laid to sleep on the outer steps of the antechamber. Now did Peace make entry and strive to get foremost to the King; but I grieve to tell how great wrath she did discover unto her attendants and much contrary to her semblance most rudely made war with her olive branch and laid on the pates of those who did oppose her coming. I did never see such lack of good order, discretion and sobriety as I have now done.

The chaste Queen, the queen of chastity, was dead. Wine, sex, and venality prevailed. One lady lost her maidenhead at the top of the stairs. Even those whose years should have made them safe from the fires of passion caught the spark. Fanny's kinsman, the Lord Admiral, Howard of Effingham, Earl of Nottingham, verging on seventy, danced with a lady in waiting, married her at court, and rushed to the King the next morning to fill that prurient ear with boasts of what he had done during the night, white goatee and all. "But the next day," reported a courtier dryly, "the Lord Admiral was sick of the ague." The bride had been overheard singing on her wedding night. The wags wanted to know, Did she sing to keep him awake—or to put him to sleep?

No influence was worse than that of Fanny's mother, who used her own paedomorphic charms unscrupulously until age and the smallpox caught up with her. The sailor father, out of his element, was a cat's-paw of his wife and his scheming uncle. He was indulgent and helpless, borne on the tide of insatiable ambitions.

This mother, the Countess of Suffolk, kept her stable of perfumed male darlings in vain. Not one of them attracted the King. It was a protégé of James Hay that won out. Hay had come south in 1603 and, like a number of other Scotsmen, received such marked and expensive favor that there were rumblings from James's first Parliament—the first thunder of storms to come. Hay felt he needed reinforcing against the Howard faction by a younger and, indeed, more effeminate man.

The perfect candidate physically—and no menace mentally —was a cadet of the Carrs or Kers (Scotch spelling) of Fernie- hurst on the Border. Slender, with long flaxen hair, Robert Carr was a bonnie sight on a horse—and King James, whose bow legs supported his corpulent body but poorly, passed his days on horses in happy irresponsibility, neglecting matters of state for hunting and the pageantry of tilting. On one of the latter occasions—the date was March 24, 1607, the scene the tournament yard of Whitehall—Hay introduced his young retainer unforgettably. Carr fulfilled the standards of male beauty, as a contemporary described him: "straight-limbed, well-favored, strong-shouldered, and smooth-faced." James was none of this and thus could be presumed to be looking for his opposite. The lad pranced forward on a steed "full of fire and heat"; both showed off their mettle before Carr started to dismount to present to the monarch Hay's shield. Abruptly the horse threw him. He lay prostrate before the lords and ladies with a broken leg.

This was an ideal situation to elicit the half-sexual paternal- ism of James, who was frustrated in his wife and his sons. Anne, gouty, without intellect, Rome-oriented, kept a sepa- rate household. The King and his heir apparent, Henry, were not in sympathy with each other, and Charles was only six. Inquiry brought out that the twenty-year-old youth who had fallen in the line of ceremonious duty had once served the King as a page in Scotland. He had been discharged for saying the Latin grace unbearably badly, but had since been abroad for polish, and the King must have thought it an act of fate—rather than of contrivance—that brought them to- gether again. He assigned his own physician, Mayerne, to him. Always a schoolmaster *manqué,* he tested and deter- mined to improve the young man's Latin, for which the con- tinent had done nothing. The Scotch-haters that abounded at court, already worried, murmured that "someone should teach him English too."

So matters of state were neglected in a new way while the King was closeted alone with his former page for the purpose of conjugation, the conjugation of Latin verbs. All other attendance was forbidden, except the medical. Henry at thirteen had not turned out right. He was independent and martial and gathered a potential opposition around him. James and his queen had wrangled over the boy's upbringing. But this Scots lad was pliant and humble, *tabula rasa.* The pedant felt blissfully masterful as he stood over him with his birch rod and goggled at the red-gold face. It drew him like a pastry.

It was another of Fanny's kinsmen, Lord Thomas Howard, who (in a letter to his old friend Harington), noted that the King "leaneth on his arm, pinches his cheek, smooths his ruffled garment," and even while discoursing to others "looketh at Carr. . . . This young man doth much study all art and device; he hath changed his tailors and tiremen many times, and all to please [the King]." To good looks were added "some sort of cunning and show of modesty." Howard was too jaded to believe in the real thing. He instructed Harington how to flatter his way forward. The young Scot and the King's horse must be equally praised. One noble failed in his suit for neglecting to notice the "good furniture" of the latter; James brushed his petition aside: "Shall a King give heed to a dirty paper, when a beggar noteth not his gilt stirrups?" Harington must alternate between opining that "the stars are bright jewels fit for Carr's ears" and that "the roan jennet surpasseth Bucephalus and is worthy to be bestridden by Alexander."

If the Scotch Alexander could not keep his hands off his Clitus in public, it was a matter for gross speculation what happened in private. James had a record of similar interests when he was merely the beggar king of Scotland. "It is thought," wrote one who knew him well in his younger days, "that this King is too much carried by young men that lie in his chamber and are his minions." Before the year was out Carr was sworn in as, naturally, Gentleman of the Bedchamber. He was also knighted. He had little of the touchiness of Henry Rich, whose career died when, on being favored with a royal kiss full on the mouth, he turned and spat. On the contrary, when the monarch came down with an illness, Carr in his turn proved to be a tender and grateful nurse.

This diamond that was getting smoother needed a guide, a guide to his royal guide and in the intricacies of court ways and politics. Carr was still close enough to being a country bumpkin to stand in awe of brains and education, which he lacked but the benefits of which a gentleman friend was willing to share. Francis Bacon might have been such a mentor, and he made his usual bid, but Thomas Overbury was on the scene first—the worse for all concerned.

Overbury and Carr had met before 1607. A determined careerist, Overbury had gone north in 1601, realizing from what direction power would soon flow. He carried letters of introduction to various Scotch families, among them the Carrs of Ferniehurst, and there he encountered the younger son, truly a fourteen-year-old bumpkin. Overbury was then twenty, a graduate of Queen's College, Oxford, and the Middle Temple, the son of a country justice, whose chief clerk accompanied him. In the intervening years, in addition to acquiring a reputation both for prose and verse, he had served Sir Robert Cecil, the Secretary of State, without, he felt, sufficient reward. An alliance of Carr's peculiar and proven charm with Overbury's savoir faire should bring relatively quick results—and Overbury was twenty-six and in a hurry.

It was not hard work nor mere merit that got anyone ahead any more, as a satirist noted (while also noting that Cardinal Wolsey, the builder of Whitehall, fell):

> Let any poor Lad that is handsome and young
> With *Parle vous France,* and a Voice for a Song,
> But once get a Horse and seek out good James,
> He'll soon find the House, 'tis great, near the Thames.
> It was built by a priest, a butcher by calling,
> But neither priesthood nor trade could keep him from
>   falling.
>
> As soon as you ken this pitiful Loon
> Fall down from your Nag, as if in a Swoon,
> If he doth nothing more, he'll open his Purse;
> If he likes you ('tis Known he's a very good Nurse),
> Your fortune is made, he'll dress you in Satin,
> And if you're unlearned he'll teach you Dog Latin.

James opened his purse wider and wider—or pried open the purses of others. Toward the end of 1607 there was a royal warrant: "To Robert Carr, Groom of the Bedchamber, for a yearly rent-charge of £600, to be paid to him for fifteen years by John Warner and three others, in consideration of a grant to them of certain arrears of rent due to the Crown." This was followed by a gift of the King's picture. Lucky youth, to receive this, not that the monarch was particularly handsome, but the setting of gold and diamonds was worth £300.

Overbury, the minion's minion or "ghost," was given a chance to be industrious when granted September 29 "twenty-five bullaries of salt water, with cribs, stalls, and other appurtenances, in Droitwich, Worcestershire, parcel of the possessions of Robert Winter, attainted" (executed for complicity in the Gunpowder Plot). A bullary or boilery was a salt house, and there was no better spot in England for this manufacture than Droitwich. Overbury got a knighthood too, six months after Carr, and that same June day in 1608 his father was elevated to a judgeship in Wales.

The collaboration of Sir Robert and Sir Thomas, of body and of brains, became an open secret. The Queen, who liked neither, jeered at the pair as "Carr and his governor." It neither was nor is unusual for a "great" man to have a surpassingly clever executive secretary, but the division of functions in this case was so sharp that Overbury not only gave his style to, but supplied absolutely all the contents of, the letters and papers Carr signed. Seldom was an adviser so thoroughly heeded—for a time.

Before Carr could become a peer he had to have an estate. That could be gained only at the expense of someone else. The deprived person this time was Sir Walter Ralegh, who had already lost his liberty and was under suspended sentence of death following a crude trial on charges of treason made by one accuser (the law specified there had to be two), whom he was not allowed to face and who kept changing his tragically unlikely story. The King's mind had been poisoned against Ralegh (who, of course, was anti-Spanish) years before, as the monarch indicated with an ominous pun the first time they met: "On my soul, mon, I have heard but *rawly* of thee." Now a legal blunder discovered in the deed to Sir Walter's property, Sherborne in Dorsetshire, had made it forfeit. Languishing in the Tower, occupying himself with writing a History of the World, this last of the great Elizabethan heroes had counted on Sherborne for the support of his wife and children. What a commentary on the times that the old sea-hawk—"No man but my father," said Prince Henry, "would keep such a bird in a cage"—swallowing his pride, of which he had no small quantity, appealed in vain to the whey-faced favorite! "Sir—After many great losses and many years sorrows . . . it is come to my knowledge that yourself . . . have been persuaded to give me and mine our last fatal blow by obtaining from his Majesty the inheritance of my children and nephews, lost in law for want of words. This done, there remaineth nothing with me but the bare name of lief [lord], despoiled of all else but the tithe and sorrow thereof . . . Sir, seeing your day is but now in the dawn, and mine come to the evening—your own virtues and the King's grace assuring you of many good fortunes and much honor—I beseech you not to begin your first buildings upon the ruin of the innocent, and that their griefs and sorrows do not attend your first plantation."

Lady Ralegh knelt tearfully to the King, others added their voices, but James's invariable answer was, "I mun hae it for Carr." To Carr it went in 1609, not without some payment to Lady Ralegh but well below value. The favorite was willing to—in Ralegh's words—"undergo the curse of them that enter into the fields of the fatherless." It was going to be a perfect morality play, with a highly moral ending, but Robin Carr was as oblivious as the prospering character in the first act always is.

"Many are obscured," said a chronicler, "that he may be graced and dignified. No suit, no petition, no grant, no letter, but Mr. Carr must have a hand in it; so that great rewards are bestowed upon him by suitors, and large sums of money by his Majesty; by which means his wealth increased with his favor, and with both, honors." Another memorialist, Arthur Wilson, waxes sarcastic: "Our Supreme Power works by second causes; the Lords themselves can scarce have a smile without him."

His destined opposite was shining, too. As a married

woman, the Countess of Essex, now sixteen, was under no obligation to hide her light under a country bushel. Jonson had stated in an entertainment he wrote for the second night of her marriage "That the most honored state of man and wife/Doth far exceed the insociate virgin life." Virgin she might be, but insociate she was not. Encouraged by her proud and ambitious relatives, she was free to participate in all the court festivities in London, the masques and the balls and the flirtations and intrigue. She danced, for instance, at Whitehall in the Jonson-Jones *Masque of Queens,* on February 2, 1609. She was pleasantly aware of the effect of her now well-developed charms on others. Even an enemy allowed her "to be a beauty of the greatest magnitude in that horizon. . . . an object fit for admirers, and every tongue grew an orator at that shrine."

There was no point in veiling the shrine excessively. It was enough if she strung her cleavage with pearls. The court world saw and others read about "open breasts beyond accustomed modesty," the purpose of which could only be, moralists judged, "the increase of dishonest appetites." The styles of the day allowed for much, even in Queen Elizabeth's time. It had not been thought unseemly to write of the Virgin Queen, "Her bosom, sleek as Paris plaster,/Held up two balls of alabaster." The French ambassador, in one of Elizabeth's last years, was favored with a glimpse of her Highness' belly, "even to the navel." Virgins were permitted a greater display, in obvious self-interest, than matrons: the nominally married Fanny did not feel very matronly, though she appreciated the freedom her status gave her to leave the feathered nest of Audley End. Let the moralists write epigrams "Of Women's Naked Bosoms." Let them rhyme, "They but invite flesh-flies, whose full spread paps/Like roadways lie between their lips and laps."

More than one accepted the invitation. Henry, the Prince of Wales, "sent many loving glances as ambassadors of his good respects." Another chronicler, Sir Simonds D'Ewes, was more definite. "She was so delicate in her youth as, notwithstanding the inestimable Prince Henry's martial desires and initiation into the ways of godliness, she, being set on by the Earl of Northampton, her father's uncle, first taught his age and heart, and afterwards prostituted herself to him, who reaped the first fruits." Henry was fifteen; he had had "so sweet and bewitching a countenance" before him for three years. The opportunity was blatant, and the husband seemed to have defaulted. Would it not be appropriate to revive an old seignorial custom, the right to the first night? And if the first night, why not the second and the third, there being no obstreperous objection? Henry was no Charles II, no collector of mistresses—he was a proud and somewhat puritanical young man, as interested in learning war as Essex; but his development in every way was speedier than Essex's, and to take possession of this coquette adrift would be a natural but passing phase of growing up, as serious conversation with the imprisoned Ralegh was another. The story of the Countess's first adultery is not so well attested to as her second, but it fits the total picture.

This had thoroughly ceased to be the court of the Virgin Queen. The most extravagant permissiveness reigned. One of the most beautiful, blue-blooded but also red-blooded, patently desirable adolescents in England was not to be kept on ice indefinitely. Her husband abandoned her at his risk as well as hers. Any virgin was on the defensive among these lords and ladies, and a married virgin! Well, Fanny was not amused by the jests that were flung her way. She was driven to assert to the world that she did not deserve this neglect. If Essex did not want her, there were those who did, and she could prove it. In fact she felt more and more like proving it, as she burst from her gowns in full bloom. She was under external pressure, too, from more than one direction. Her ambitious relatives, having sold her once, were not above collecting a little interest on the side. "Making it" meant not only self-indulgence but self-advancement.

If the heir apparent beckoned (he was the other most fit adolescent in the land), what was more appropriate than for her to administer a resounding slap to Essex, whose absence was a daily (and nightly) insult? (Even a woman who wants to say "No" is outraged at the lack of opportunity to say it.) Her nominal husband, as best she could remember, tended toward the plump. Henry was lean and lithe, with a sensitive face. It was a pleasant change, too, that she could play, at sixteen, the older woman—she had a year or so on Henry. It could even be a question as to who was seducing whom. How tiresome it was to be a child—or a grass widow! She was taller than average. She would reach to a future king, explore with him what fruition was, what all the carnal talk and jokes were about. Never send a boy on a man's job, and there certainly were some handsome, full-grown peacocks on view, but, well, let fate decide—or the undertow.

At the beginning of 1610 she was involved with three men. She had stared into Carr's blue eyes and felt something. And her husband, a stranger, had returned to claim her.

Amorous Pursuit

3

Of the three men, Prince Henry soon withdrew, disdainfully. June 1610 was the date for his investiture as Prince of Wales; it was his coming of age, the only coming of age he ever knew, for he died of typhoid fever two years later, at eighteen. He had nothing but contempt for Carr, who had usurped the place in his father's affections that would normally have been his and who was to presume to try to set up a marriage with a Catholic princess for him, him the hope of the Protestant, anti-Spanish party. He respected Essex, a soldier who was on his side in these matters. It was now Carr with whom he fell out at tennis (that inflammable game). When the older man, with smirking arrogance, showed too blatantly that he was letting him win, the Prince struck him "on the back with his racket, or very hardly forbore it." Another time a courtier offered to kill the favorite for him, "for which the Prince reproved him, and said that if there were cause he would do it himself."

Fanny was not sufficient cause. "For dancing one time among the ladies, and her glove falling down, it was taken up and presented to him, by one that thought he did him acceptable service. But the Prince refused to receive it, saying publicly, He would not have it—it is stretched by another."

This was definitely not a reference to her husband. "When I came out of France, I loved her. I do not so now, neither ever shall I" was Essex's summary of three years of attempted cohabitation, the minimum necessary under canon law, after the husband reached eighteen, before an annulment could be sought.

How she staved him off, while luring another on, is a tale of wonder and, in fact, black magic. But she owed no little to her own irreducible sulkiness. Essex expected a wife panting with dammed-up affection. She would enkindle and be enkindled; after the parched years the tinder was ready for the most delightful explosions. He looked forward to being her fireman, the incendiary that doused the flames he had at last caused to flare. Everything comes to him who waits. He had waited; she would come.

Extremes met. She repulsed her husband with the ferocity and ingenuity of a saint defending her chastity. She would not submit to a merely legal bond, when her feelings dictated otherwise. One could call her the first modern woman.

This is not to say that she was a suffragette or an intellectual. It is arrogant of men, and docile of Virginia Woolf, to expect the first modern woman to be a woman of ideas—in other words, to be like the first modern man. The first modern woman would be a woman who broke with the past by having a will of her own and asserting it, blatantly. It might have proved inspiring to read Emerson on "Self-Reliance" but it was not necessary. The sage of Concord arrived at the conclusion that Fanny Howard reached instinctively. "In the Will work and acquire, and thou hast chained the wheel of fortune." A teen-ager with changing notions of what she wanted, Fanny now knew definitely what she did not want. Too many years had passed since it seemed a pleasant party to dress up grandly and marry an Essex. If she paid a great price for being so led, to be deluded, as it were, by a masque, what modern girl thinks more deeply, less impulsively? It had been virtually a prepubescent acquiescence in the ambitious or diplomatic schemes of others. Four additional years, some hormones, some experiences, had made a modern adolescent out of a spoiled child.

We can visualize her stamping her feet and tossing her flaming hair and sulking very easily indeed. Yet her plight had its tragic resemblance to Hamlet's in that for both the times were out of joint and it was their cursed spite to have to set them right, with grave consequences. Both, having been born too soon, lacked the obvious modern solution to their immediate problem. Hamlet was aware of a crime but could not call in the police; she was in a situation she had to fight her own way out of. The law was not, as yet, on her side: so much the worse for the law.

Essex had expected to bear her off to his big cold house in the northwest, Chartley Hall in Staffordshire. This had been the last place of incarceration of the lovely and legendary Mary Queen of Scots before Fotheringay. There she had received and sent out in beer kegs the letters of the Babington plot that cost her her head. The great Essex, off warring in the Low Countries, had expressed his resentment at the use of his manor house as a prison—and a trap. But his son was going to shut *her* up there, a hundred miles from London. She had not the smallest intention of resigning herself to being a wife, much less a country wife. He would have to let her stay for Henry's Investiture ceremonies, at least.

These took place June 4th. On June 5th she acted in Samuel Daniel's masque *Tethys' Festival*. In a transparent blue robe she made the appropriate undulating movements as the Nymph of the river Lee (which bounds Essex!). Henry's mother, who doted on masques, took the part of Tethys, wife of Neptune. We happen to know, from a letter in Winwood's *Memorials of State,* how long the party lasted, in that pregaslit era when 9 P.M. was late. "By that time these [masquers] had done, it was high time to go to bed, for it was within half an hour of the sun's—not setting—but rising. Howbeit, a farther time was to be spent in viewing and scrambling at one of the most majestic banquets that I have seen."

Eat, drink and be merry in a last diversion. Daniel himself pointed the moral of all pleasures, all masques: "Glory is most bright and gay,/In a flash, and so away."

After this gossamer and tantalizing display of her charms, Frances fled from her husband to Audley End. She passed the summer there. It was a retreat to childhood, though she was now seventeen. It was going home to mother with a vengeance. And mother was not pleased, for there were no fruitful politics in this. It meant not seeing Carr, for the Court went on the usual summer Progress through the shires—that is, descended like a cloud of locusts on the country estates and home localities of various lords and gentry for overnight visits and engorgement and entertainment and appropriate presents, often leaving the cupboard and coffer bare before favoring the next host a few miles on. Thus the King made contact with his kingdom at no expense to himself. But Essex (alas!) was not in the retinue of that slow journey of state that ended at Hampton Court in September. He was only forty-two miles away in London and insisted on riding up to Fanny's house for visits for a week or fortnight. You would think they were married! Where was the crowd, any crowd, the safety that numbers would have given her?

At Audley End "they conversed together as man and wife." This nuisance of a house guest importuned to get into her bed. What was worse, he finally succeeded. But that was as far as he got.

He called her Frankie. His advances met with "harsh unseemly words." What words? We have three on record from a later quarrel: *cow, beast* and *coward.* In *other* words, he was clumsy—there are numerous indications of this—and was accused of being brutal and bullying against the weaker sex. It proved a vexing predicament for a man who, lacking the suavity of a courtier, deemed the manly way to take a fortress was by direct assault. It was said that "those who knew him not" found him "somewhat stern and solemn," but "to intimates" he was "affable and gentle." How could he ever get close enough to his wife for her to see his better side? He was wrong by being legally right.

He wooed the father, a person he could better understand. Suffolk gave his daughter instructions in the rights of husbands. She flung petulantly to London, where the only Robin she cared about was. She had a lodging at Whitehall. Her husband followed her there. In October a matron saw them "in naked bed together" at Hampton Court palace. This "Frances Britten, widow," particularly recalled the morning she was asked to search for a ruby earring that the Lady Frances missed. "That thereupon she and the lady's chambermaid turned down the bedclothes and there they saw the places where the earl and lady had lain, but that there was such a distance between the two places, and such a hill between them, that this deponent is persuaded they did not touch one another that night."

The couple were not fanatic about privacy, since they had no love-making to hide. Early one morning, four months later, Fanny's younger sister, Katharine, was with them in the bower while they lay in bed. Moreover, Kathy, seeing the same Frances Britten hesitating on the threshold, invited *her* in. "Then Lady Frances stepped out of her bed [meaning her side of the bed], and left the Earl there." Maybe she thought three company, four a crowd. Mrs. Britten remembered this to have been St. Valentine's Day, for Katharine told her brother-in-law there was a valentine for him. Who would have given the third Earl of Essex a valentine remains one of the smaller mysteries of history.

It was a winter, that of 1610–11, of grave personal crises. His patience had given out and Essex had insisted that she prepare to go to Chartley. He rode ahead to make arrangements. She countered by withdrawing to the house of her wily great-uncle and threatening suicide. Northampton took her part, for reasons of his own. Essex, alone at Chartley, came down with the smallpox, and he almost died. This near-riddance was enough to give her ideas, and the pock marks he presented for kissing the next time she had to lay eyes on him added nothing to his attractiveness. Meanwhile, in London, she had leisure to employ extreme measures to fend off the one man and draw on the other.

Carr was getting more glamorous all the time, and to cooler and more calculating eyes than hers. On March 25 he was created Viscount Rochester. With this dignity had to come some more property—Rochester Castle. May 1 he was installed, along with Prince Charles, as Knight of the Garter. Within a few weeks he was in charge of the Signet; in other words, he was King James's private secretary. Naturally he would have to join the Privy Council. There were such other honors as the Barony of Winwick and being made Keeper of Westminster Palace for life. To help him live in style, on June 26 arrived a "warrant to pay Visct. Rochester £8000, still remaining due to him from sums bestowed on him by

His Majesty." In Chamberlain's correspondence he became, without need for further identification, "the great man."

Overbury, who had been abroad in 1609—on a trip about which he ambitiously compiled a dull book—was at the favorite's elbow, and employing his own in missives, including eventually love letters and sonnets from Carr to Lady Essex. Robin still had not the confidence to speak for himself and the insiders' summary was, "Overbury governed Carr and Carr governed the king." The first sparks between Carr and Lady Essex had presumably arisen during Overbury's absence; but the literary knight had no objection to helping in an affair (he was addressing amorous words on his own behalf to the Countess of Rutland), if it did not become too serious and threaten his own influence. But Northampton saw an opportunity to use his infatuated great-niece as a wedge, separating Overbury from Carr and making Carr an ally of the Howards. Essex, a country clod uninterested in intrigue, was uninteresting to Northampton.

The elevation of Carr to the peerage made him the first Scot eligible to sit in the English House of Lords. However, there was no Parliament for him to take his place in, as that body had been dissolved the month before, after murmurings against him and all his kind, including the King. Thomas Wentworth (not to be confused with the renegade who became the Earl of Strafford) declared to his fellow commoners, "For his part . . . he would never give his consent to take money from a poor frieze jerkin to trap a courtier's horse withal." He inquired, with pointed ambiguity, "For what purpose is it for us to draw a silver stream out of the country into the royal cistern, if it shall daily run out thence by private cocks?" Chamberlain summed up the general knowledge: "The realm grows poor." Although he had failed to wring any financial settlement whatever from the late Parliament, the King proceeded to shower on his favorites £34,000.

Fanny needed help of a different sort, and had jewels to pay for it. She was as prone as anyone to the superstitions of her age. As a child she had seen too much of a friend of her mother's, the wife of the Bishop of Bristol, Mrs. Thornborough, who experimented in palmistry and philters. More dangerous still was a new acquaintance, Mrs. Anne Turner, a widow.

Mistress Turner was a jill of many trades, including mistress. She was the mistress of Sir Arthur Mainwaring, who left his estate in Cheshire to father three children by her. She was reputed to be the mistress of Northampton, Fanny's great-uncle, though she was probably only his spy: the old bachelor loved power more than sex. She was a costume designer employed by Inigo Jones for masques, and Fanny in all likelihood first had her in as a dressmaker. Her big contribution to the world of fashion was enormous yellow ruffs and sleeves. These were all the rage, enough to become the object of satire and moral complaint. The secret of preparing the yellow starch she kept profitably to herself. It was, possibly significantly, the color of her hair. "Of a low stature, fair visage, for outward behavior comely," she did not let any of her charms fade, though she must have known that her best days, her prettiest, lay behind her. Her husband, in his will, had offered Mainwaring £10 to take her over. If this was humiliating, she proved herself not the lowest of the butterflies in this foul milieu. She supported the whole irregular family of five by pandering to the vices and the weaknesses of the court. She catered at parties. She sometimes served as a procuress. Weeks later the same parties might call on her again, for she induced abortions. She dabbled in magic.

Her master in magic was Simon Forman, who had set himself up across the river in Lambeth as a physician, and who
did a thriving business in prophecy and love philters in the
time he could spare from seducing his female patients. Her
husband, also a physician, had known him well, and she had
lately seen for herself what Forman could do. She had gone
to him for magic help after Mainwaring had deserted her.
That weak man was taught a lesson hopefully permanent.
The spells Forman cast "wrought so violently with him that
through a storm of rain and thunder he rode fifteen miles one
dark night to her house, scarcely knowing where he was till
he was there." It was surely the most spectacular happening
in that line since Dr. John Fian, burned as a magus in Edinburgh in 1591, was tricked by a boy whose sister he coveted.
He had ordered the lad to get him some of the girl's pubic
hairs for use in a spell, but the brother brought him some
from a heifer instead. The outcome was that while Dr. Fian
was attending church the heifer broke through the door and
attempted to assault him carnally, and thereafter everywhere
Fian went the love-stricken bovine was sure to go. His reputation as a wizard grew enormously. This was for a while a
fortunate but at last a fatal thing.

Simon Forman, to whom Fanny became so compacted that
she addressed him as "Father," had had his ups and downs,
which he recorded in his curious diary. He first felt remarkable when, as a child, he had hallucinations, visions of "many
mighty mountains and hills come rolling against him: although they would overrun him and fall on him and brust
him, yet he got up always to the top of them and with much
ado went over them." His taste for "science" began with ap-
prenticeship to a grocer and apothecary. At a time when all
physicians were necessarily quacks, Simon Forman quickly
passed the usual bounds by going in for fortune-telling, for

which he was often thrown into jail. Like Dr. Faustus, he was drawn ever more into the forbidden. He discovered in himself the power of prophecy in 1579. In the year of the Spanish Armada, "I began to practise necromancy, and to call spirits." In 1590, "At All-Hallowtide I entered the Circle for necromantical spells. . . . The 22nd day of March, A.M. at 8 we heard music at Circle." The year 1594 saw the completion of his book on the Philosopher's Stone.

It was typical of the corruption that accompanied James to the English throne that in that year of 1603 Forman, who by then had powerful friends and clients, was licensed by the University of Cambridge to practice medicine. Women, citizens' wives and increasingly the aristocracy, flocked to his pentagrams and his clutches. He seduced some, blackmailed others, or did both. We should like to know how far the tongue of Anthony Wood, the seventeenth-century antiquary, was from his cheek when he wrote of this arch-charlatan: "He was a person that in hororary questions, especially theft, was judicious and fortunate; so also in sickness, which was indeed his masterpiece, and had good success in resolving questions about marriage."

So Lady Essex and Mistress Turner took a wherry across the Thames to get a question about marriage resolved. The girl made it crystal-ball clear that she would never, never yield herself to the man that had his legal chain on her. She went on to confide what the sorcerer undoubtedly knew, that she was saving herself for Carr. Such romanticism, together with obvious readiness to pay, had its appeal. She would become a novice in the black arts, she would resort to anything: the only law was her will. He must help her: Anne Turner had said that he could and would.

He prepared two powders, one for her husband, one for Carr. It was important that she not get them mixed up, as so often happened in fairy tales, for one powder would kill desire and the other would stimulate it.

In giving the drugs that were to be mixed with the food of the two men, did Dr. Forman feel that he was practicing medicine, or magic? It is a nice academic question. Was Essex to be administered what was thought to be a natural sexual depressant, according to the pharmacopia, and Carr an aphrodisiac? If so, in Carr's case how could it be made certain that, on being inflamed, he would be inflamed by the right object? Perhaps Fanny was to have dinner with him, slip the white powder into his sauce, and take care that James, for instance, was not present.

But Carr was already at least somewhat interested in her. She just wanted to confirm it. The more pressing problem was to kill Essex's interest, such as it was. Nobody in that darkened room in Lambeth, with its retorts and tripods and cabalistic signs, had any compunction about tampering with an already weakened constitution. What a bore it was that this degeneration from a great father (and a great lover) had struggled stubbornly through, in his bed at Chartley, to convalescence from an illness that so often put people safely under ground! How she loathed him, with his dull blinking eyes and fat face and hands fit to groom horses, whose company he had for years preferred. Frances Howard, Lady Essex, belonged to the new spoiled breed that would elicit from foreigners the epigram, "England in general is said to be the Hell of horses, the Purgatory of servants, and the Paradise of women" (Fynes Moryson, *Itinerary*, 1617). Robert Devereux, third Earl of Essex, belonged with his horse.

And what connection had Simon Forman with Hell? He did not, after all, rely on medicine alone, this gray-beard Faustus among whose papers was found the notation, "This I made the devil write with his own hands, in Lambeth

Fields, 1596." How he would have enjoyed all the horrendous parts of *Macbeth*. In fact he did, at that very time in the spring of 1611 when Lady Essex was sealed as his "spiritual" daughter. His diary entry about his afternoon at the Globe concludes: "Observe also how Macbeth's queen did rise in the night in her sleep and walk, and talked and confessed all, and the doctor noted her words."

This doctor, having heard desperate words, did diabolical things to reinforce the philters. He made obscene "mommets" in wax and lead of couples moving toward the ultimate embrace. The images were grotesquely recognizable. Essex was portrayed in a state of extreme languor; the Carr puppet was the opposite, ardent and successful. And Lady Essex, her double (of which we lack a description) must have been a diptych of revulsion and pleasure, while the Lady herself took cheer at the potential effects of sympathetic magic.

Shakespeare cues us in on the common belief. The father of Desdemona cannot believe the Moor won her fairly, but rather "practised on her with foul charms," "corrupted" her "By spells and medicines bought of mountebanks." Falstaff says of Poins, "I am bewitched with the rogue's company. If the rascal have not given me medicines to make me love him, I'll be hanged; it could not be else, I have drunk medicines." In *A Midsummer Night's Dream,* Puck's juice from the herb love-in-idleness is poured on eyelids both to have the wrong people love—and the right.

A bull of Innocent VIII, issued at Rome in 1484, grieves over those all-too-numerous members of his flock who have given themselves to devils, who "hinder men from performing the sexual act and women from conceiving, whence husbands cannot know their wives nor wives receive their husbands." Aquinas allowed "that demons are something and that they can do harm by their operations and impede carnal copulation." The interest in producing impotence by magical means was so widespread that there was a word for it, *ligature* —a reference to the favorite method, hexing by tying knots in a cord. Of course Forman with his effigies was harking back to the pagans and the primitives. The author of *Truth Brought to Light* knows exactly what it was that finally succeeded in this case. "Many attempts failed, and still the Earl stood it out. At last, they framed a picture of wax, and got a thorn from a tree that bore leaves and stuck upon the privity of the said picture, by which means they accomplished their desires." Manifestly these experts at doing things in reverse noticed, long before the limerick, "That Eros spelt backwards is sorE."

The tragicomedy of the marriage dragged on. In May 1611 Essex, "maigre" after his long winter illness and "la face un peu gâtée de petites verroles," came down to London to carry his wife off to Chartley at last. If he was no Lothario it also turned out that he was a poor Petruchio, and of course he had no idea of his shrew's magic defenses. Arthur Wilson relates how she behaved. "When she came thither (though in the pleasantest time of summer), she shut herself up in her chamber, not suffering a beam of light to peep upon her dark thoughts. If she stirred out of her chamber, it was in the dead of night, when sleep had taken possession of all others but those about her. In this implacable, sad, discontented humor she continued some months, always murmuring against, but never giving the least civil respect to her husband, which the good man suffered patiently, being loth to be the divulger of his own misery."

There was the rub. What was wrong with *him*? What did the servants and his friends and her relations think of a man who could not win—if necessary, subdue—his own wife? He had been trying ridiculously long. What stories went out that were even worse than the truth, what smirks and crude gestures stalked him that he almost, if not quite, turned in time to see, what mocking laughter rolled down the halls of that disturbed and darkened dwelling? He became a byword: "To wish a maid into a mischief was to commend her to grumbling Essex, as they styled him."

As to what the Earl would not do for a maid, Arthur Wilson, who admired him and served him, tells a story. The country home, Chartley, had a moat into which a laundry maid fell and was drowning, while Essex stood on the drawbridge, shouting and indecisive. It was Wilson who jumped in and saved her. Yet the Earl displayed courage in battle. But with a laundry maid—or his wife—it was not so easy to take the plunge.

Pride had to be swallowed in the interest of getting allies. She was wrong; he had said so before and would say so again: he would shout it to the eaves and to the eavesdroppers and to all her family. Meanwhile, in his wounded retreat, he experienced to the quick the wisdom of Solomon's words (Proverbs xxi, 9), "It is better to dwell in a corner of the house-top, than with a brawling woman in a wide house." What good was it to be a laughingstock of an earl? better to be a carl with a sweet, docile, and loving mate.

A generation later, no less a writer than John Milton was to picture the plight of the sober, inexperienced man who wakes to find himself joined to "an uncomplying discord of nature." Such a one may meet "with a body impenetrable"— and no solution offered, no dissolution either.

If Essex had much to complain of, his Lady was equally miserable. We can pick from Milton's divorce tract some vividness to cover her with, too: "a drooping and disconsolate household captivity, without refuge or redemption." But Fanny speaks for herself. Mary Queen of Scots all over again, she sent out rash notes of distress and conspiracy that she asked the recipient to burn. The philters were not working the way they should have.

Sweet Turner,

I am out of all hope of any good in this world, for my father, my mother, and my brother all said I should lie with him; and my brother Howard was here and said he would not come from this place all winter; so that all comfort is gone; and which is worst of all, my Lord hath complained that he hath not lain with me, and I would not suffer him to use me.

My father and mother are angry, but I had rather die a thousand times over; for besides the sufferings, I shall lose *his* [Carr's] love if I lie with him. I will never desire to see his [Carr's] face if my Lord do that unto me.

My Lord is as merry as ever he was, so as you may see in what miserable case I am.

You may send the party [Forman] word of all; he sent me word all should be well, but I shall not be so happy as the Lord [Carr] to love me. As you have taken pains all this while for me, so now do all you can, for never so unhappy as now; for I am not able to endure the miseries that are coming on me, but I cannot be happy so long as this man liveth: therefore pray for me, for I have need, but I should be better if I had yr company to ease my mind. Let him [Forman] know this ill news. If I can get this done, you shall have as much money as you can demand, this is fair play.

Your sister,
FRANCES ESSEX

It was no wonder she took up with those beyond the pale and was driven to irregular methods of self-protection, for all the conventional people were arrayed against her. She was being faithful in her fashion: "I will never desire to see his face if my Lord do that unto me." Whether or not she had any virginity left, she had integrity. She had a heart and was following it; the others, her own family, were insensible, and deaf to appeal. She was fighting for a woman's right not to give herself to the wrong—or unchosen—man.

And in fighting there was no blow she might not strike. This letter was produced at the murder trial: appropriately enough, since it contains a murderous thought: "I cannot be happy so long as this man liveth." That has to be weighed with the concluding words: *"If I can get this done,* you shall have as much money as you can demand, this is fair play." *What* done? The poisoning of her husband? Or does she mean: If I can get to the end of this predicament? Her letters are a maze of vague antecedents and references, the product of cunning and grammatical inexperience and haste and hysteria. Probably at this emotional point she did not care what was done, so long as this disagreeable man vanished, whether by giving up or by dying. We get the right flavor from an entry in the Calendar of State Papers for December 9, 1612, on an examination into the "practices of Mary, wife of John Woods, to poison her husband or be divorced from him." One would do as well as the other, but poison was much more available. This Mary Woods—"Cunning Mary," she was called—comes directly into the picture later on, but the point about Essex's wife is that one does have to give her credit for backbone, even though one would not like to have encountered it, this dagger underneath the flesh. Unlike ordinary folk who merely fantasied the opposition dead, she acted out her wishes, conspired to make them a reality. It was only a narrow chain of circumstances that dictated who the victim was ultimately to be. She practiced against her husband's health long before another man got in her deadly way. The longed-for road was the same, only the obstacle was to change.

Essex, having recovered from the smallpox, was displaying,

if not an iron will, an iron constitution; he perversely seemed to be *enjoying* the powders that were spilled, ever more frantically, into his food. "My Lord is as merry as ever he was," in Fanny's words.

So another missive went out, to the doctor, asking for more "Galls":

Sweet Father,

I must still crave your love, altho' I hope I have it, and shall deserve it better hereafter: Remember the Galls, for I fear, tho' I have yet no cause but to be confident in you, yet I desire to have it as it [Essex or his condition] is yet remaining well; so continue it still, if it be possible, and if you can you must send me some good fortune, alas, I have need of it.

Keep the Lord [Carr] still to me, for that I desire; and be careful you name me not to anybody, for we have so many spies that you must use all your wits, and all little enough, for the world is against me, and the Heavens favor me not, only happy in your love; I hope you will do me good, and if I be ungrateful, let all mischief come unto me.

My Lord is lusty and merry and drinketh with his men; and all the content he gives me is to abuse me, and use me as doggedly as before: I think I shall never be happy in this world, because he hinders my good, and will ever, I think, so remember (I beg for God's sake) and get me from this vile place.

Your affectionate, loving daughter,
FRANCES ESSEX

P.S. Give Turner warning of all things, but not the Lord [Carr]: I would not have anything come out for fear of the Lord Treasurer [Robert Cecil, Earl of Salisbury], for so they may tell my father and my mother, and fill their ears full of toys.

"Keep the Lord still to me" indicates that she has at least had the consolation of reassuring love letters from Carr (composed by Overbury). The favorite, through Mrs. Turner and bribery, was regularly receiving Dr. Forman's medicaments, and *he* got sick: on September 1 the King's principal physician, Dr. Mayerne (who had once seen to his broken leg), attended him for dyspepsia.

But something more drastic had to be tried on Essex, according to the relation of Wilson. "These instigations made him [Forman] active, and the man, being skilful in natural magic, did use all the artifice his subtilty could devise really to imbecilitate the Earl; for no linen came near his body that was not rinsed with their camphire compositions and other faint and wasting ingredients, and all inward applications were foisted on him by corrupted servants, to lessen and debilitate the seminal operations. Which *veneficium* is one great part of witchcraft, destructive to nature and horridly abominable to be practised. And this in time wrought such effects upon his person that he found himself unable with her, though she permitted him; yet when he had been from her some reasonable time, to renovate his spirits by shaking off those artificial applications, then his abilities made her unwilling and refractory. Though some are of opinion that he was not much debilitated, but that she got (by her *virtuous agents*) an artifice too immodest to be expressed, to hinder penetration."

Thus we have accumulated a full range of conjectures as to why Essex failed: natural impotence, lack of enthusiasm, drugs, hexing by effigy and spells, nimble or sulky evasion by the wife, secret artificial obstruction by same. Nothing is wanting except Ben Jonson's speculation about Queen Elizabeth: impenetrable natural obstruction ("That she had a membrana on her, which made her uncapable of men, though for her delight she tried many"). Had not Prince Henry proved that not to apply? Or was not Carr proving it? Essex, in self-defense, gave some encouragement to this hypothesis, and Sir Edward Peyton repeated it, while admitting the contradiction inherent in accusing a woman of adultery while denying that she was capable of coition. Indeed, in the later fury and indignation, there were those who asserted that the Countess was a public highway—*regia via*.

In September 1611, she came down to London with her husband to rejoin the Court. The intolerable imprisonment was over for a season. She would see Carr, now Viscount Rochester, publicly, and without doubt there could be private appointments, too. But her spiritual father, Forman, her dear and diligent quack, departed beyond reaching, unless by seance. Whatever his failings (though an astrologer, he did not even get dates right, as his diary of play attendance shows), he came through with foresight at the end. On Sunday, September 8, "his wife and he being at supper in their garden-house, she being pleasant told him that she had been informed he could resolve whether man or wife should die first. 'Shall I' (quoth she) 'bury you or no?' 'Oh Trunco,' for so he called her, 'thou wilt bury me, but thou wilt much repent it.' 'Yea, but how long first?' 'I shall die,' said he, 'ere Thursday night.' Monday came, all was well. Tuesday came, he not sick. Wednesday came and still he was well; with which his impertinent wife did much twit him in the teeth. Thursday came, and dinner was ended, he very well. He went down to the waterside and took a pair of oars to go to some buildings he was in hand with in Puddledock; being in the middle of the Thames he presently fell down, only saying, 'An impost—an impost—,' and so died, a most sad storm of wind immediately following." Was the dying man endeavoring to pronounce "impostume" (an abscess or tumor)? Or was he using "impost" in its architectural sense—the foundation of an arch: in other words, the arch of his life had been spanned. Having had his grievous errors during fifty-nine years, and taunted by his wife for them, did he die to prove himself spectacularly right at last?

Mrs. Forman had been justifiably jealous, since, as the *Dictionary of National Biography* charmingly puts it, "Women figured largely among his patients, and his treatment of them was very unprofessional." (His diary for 1607, at an age when he should have been thinking of his immortal soul, was so obscene it has never been printed.) His second wife, Jane, had proved no better than the first, only more enduring—a lasting nag. She was a sore trial, but then what wife was not? Was it any improvement to have the grim prediction come from the distaff side, as happened to Sir John Davies the poet? Lady Davies gave her husband his "doom" "in letters of his own name—John Daves—Joves Hand," and told him "within three years to expect the mortal blow; so put on my mourning garment from that time." Every day, for all the days that remained to him, Sir John had to face his wife in black, and it is not surprising that when, three days before his death, she "gave him pass to take his long sleep," he burst out, "I pray you weep not while I am alive, and I will give you leave to laugh when I am dead." Forman had at least kept the man's role, knowledge or pretense of knowledge, and this alone was reason enough for his wife not to be admitted into his consulting room.

The day after he had been right for the last time, however, that sanctuary was anxiously searched. A certain amount of vile and incriminating material found in his study was committed to the flames by his widow, aided by Mrs. Turner and "trusty Margaret, the toothless maid." But not everything damaging was destroyed: someone was careless, or had a keen eye for blackmail, or felt that the best defense against possible accusation would be counteraccusation.

To carry on with the black arts in her client's behalf, Mrs. Turner turned to a Dr. Savery—most unsavory—and "one Gresham," who had nothing in common with the famous financier. But Fanny was not doing badly on her own, now that she was back in town: she continued to rebuff her husband and in a series of assignations nailed down Carr. It was not too difficult for one of the fairest women of her time to show she had certain points of superiority to slabbering James. But the moralists did not look on the cheerful heterosexual side; they saw only the fall of man, for the millionth time: "New places of meeting are assigned, amongst the rest one at Hammersmith. In the meantime the Viscount makes dispatch of his business, leaving things half done, half undone, to the intent he might meet her, who had now stayed for his coming above two hours. And, being met, they solemnly saluted each other, fall into divers discourses, and insinuating phrases, from words to deeds, and from speaking to acting the sin of venery. The Countess having obtained what she desired, and the Viscount caught in the net of adulation, the more he strives to be loosed being caught the faster, lust having by this means got liberty, being covered with greatness, like a fire long concealed in a pile of rotten wood, burst forth with all looseness and licentiousness; places of more frequent and private meetings being concluded between them, and persons fitting for their purposes being acquainted with their proceedings; watchwords are given. All things, having relation to a certain end, make them more boldly and safely to accomplish that which both time and memory cannot demonstrate in former history. . . . Surfeiting thus upon pleasure, having been before accustomed unto hardness, causeth him to fall into all manner of forgetfulness; letting all things go to wreck, careless in attendance, neglecting state affairs, ignorant of his own worth, and subjecting himself to the lustful appetite of an evil woman, accounting no time so well spent, nor hour deemed so happy as when dalliance and pleasant discourses passed between them." More briefly, there was passed around an anagram: "Frances Howarde: Car finds a whore."

And bad morals went with (or in) showy clothes. He became a peacock. "Nothing so costly, no tire so uncouth, but at all costs and charges he obtains it for the increase of favor. New fashions are produced that so he might show more beautiful and fair, and that his favor and personage might be made more manifest to the world."

This is in retrospect. It was some time before the affair was "manifest to the world." So assiduous a gossip as Chamberlain did not know of it until the divorce scandal in the spring of 1613. Others began gasping only with the greater scandal of 1615–16. Of course, some courtiers were early with their suspicions—and their malicious wit. Of course, the infatuated pair were torn between their desire to see each other very frequently and a need, which Overbury was more and more insistent on, to be discreet. Mrs. Turner proved an invaluable go-between and made available her home in Paternoster Row. They also used, as reported above by the author of *The Five Years of King James,* a house in the suburb of Hammersmith. When Essex wanted to pull his wife back to Chartley in the summer of 1612 she gave him so much resistance that, although she had seen hope dim with the sending ahead of her baggage, he ended by riding off in a huff alone. She happily rented a house in Hounslow that was advertised to stand "commodiously for many purposes." One time they gave a fillip to the King himself: while Carr was at Hampton Court with him, he received a note from Mrs. Turner's man, hurried out with the messenger, caught up with Lady Essex's coach, and the lovers sneaked into the equivalent of a motel for the afternoon—a farmhouse off the road. This must have been very upsetting to Overbury, for whom the King's favor was more important than any woman's. He had hitched his wagon to a star that was now wantonly blinking—and might go out for good. "Great spirits and great business do keep out this weak passion" of love, wrote Sir Francis Bacon in 1612, as if the essayist foresaw, with beady eye, the downfall of the increasingly distracted favorite.

Meanwhile, and through 1612, the husband and wife continued to be seen in situations of intimacy by various servants and retainers. At least, such was the testimony at the annulment hearing, testimony that calls for some salt. For, as Philip Gibbs points out, "No doubt these witnesses were well paid to conceal any quarrels they may have seen or heard; for at the time they made their statements it was essential to both parties . . . to prove that Lady Frances had not been guilty of resisting the authority of her husband, and had actually lived with him as his wife." Whether Essex was still trying, or whether he was just keeping up appearances, he was seen in bed with his wife in sundry places, according to eleven depositions. We may take as typical the first by "Katharine Fines, daughter of Thomas Lord Clinton, aged about 18 years": "That from midsummer last to All-Hallowtide the Earl of Essex and Lady Frances remained and kept company together as man and wife: first in the Countess of Leicester's house at Drayton in Warwickshire, and after at the Earl's own house at Chartley in Staffordshire. And that for two nights they lodged at Drayton, being on a Sunday at night and on a Monday at night, they to her knowledge lay together in one chamber: she seeing the Earl go into the said chamber undressed and ready for bed; and she verily believes they did lie together in the same bed those two nights, for that she knows there was but one bed in the said chamber. That before Christmas last the said Lady Frances lying at Salisbury-house in the Strand, the Earl came thither and went into the chamber where Lady Frances was in bed, and went to bed to her, and there was no other bed in that chamber; and this deponent heard the earl and lady Frances talking together a good part of that night."

The list of places where they were seen in bed, begun here with Chartley Hall, Drayton, and Salisbury House in the Strand, took in Audley End, her elder sister's house at Cawsham in Oxfordshire, Durham House in London, "the Lady Walsingham's at the Tilt-yard," "Lady Corbett's house in Derbyshire," and the royal precincts of Hampton Court, Whitehall, Greenwich, and Kensington. It was a well-documented marriage—except that nobody knew what went on. Despite all the references to "naked bed" and "naked in bed," despite all the peeping and hovering, no one could say that they did other than talk and sleep—and, yes, eat: several thought it helpful to report that they supped together. Sometimes the testimony was pathetically peripheral, as when Benjamin Orwell stated: "Hath seen the earl come out of the lady's lodging-chamber in his pantables [slippers], having nothing on him but his shirt: and verily believes he at such times came out of bed from the said lady Frances."

The Archbishop of Canterbury doubted, but passed on, a story that at Christmas 1612 "my Lord of Essex, being in bed with his lady," did "labor a quarter of an hour carnally to know her, and in the end [did] say, 'Frankie, it will not be,' and so kissed her and bid her good-night."

Whoever had it first—maybe she did from the very beginning—both ended up with the thought that they would be eligible to apply for an annulment after three years of this armed, or naked, neutrality: that is, in 1613. Non-consummation became the goal of both, as they lay on their separate sides of the curtained four-poster. Against the chill, a warming pan and blankets sufficed. Non-consummation was by now easy: they had had a lot of practice.

When Essex found out about Carr remains in doubt, as husbands often do.

The End of Overbury

4

Of human traits, arrogance—though quite harmless—stirs a remarkable degree of resentment. It is as if the Adlerian psychology were right: our sensitive egos cannot stomach an air of superiority in others. That this was true even before the surge of egalitarian democracy is illustrated by the case of Sir Thomas Overbury. Thrown without due process of law into a dungeon, unrealizing victim of betrayal and poison, after five months of racking illness and waning hope, he perished without a friend to speak up for him, and all because of his "thrasonical" aptitude for giving offense. He aroused the jealousy of the King; he offended the Queen; he treated Carr with unbearable effrontery; he stood recklessly in the way of the schemes of Northampton; he insulted Lady Essex. Any of the five had provocation to poison him, and perhaps more than one of the five did so.

His spadelike chin dug into people. His tongue was sharper than his pen. His literary reputation rests on his *Characters*, epigrammatic sketches of English types, such as "An Affectate Traveller," "An Old Man," and "An Amorist." A mildly interesting, if not long-lived, branch of the essay, the Overburian characters connect with the late Elizabethan and Jacobean drama, particularly Jonson's comedy of humors, and the future novel. The book was a posthumous publication that cashed in on the growing scandal of Overbury's death, going through nine ever enlarged editions between 1613 and 1616. Many of the best *Characters* are now attributed to other writers, Overbury's name serving only as the bait on the title page. The most famous, fondly recalled by Izaak Walton, was "A Fair and Happy Milkmaid," who lives rurally pure, "and all her care is that she may die in the springtime, to have store of flowers stuck upon her winding-sheet"; this is now assigned to the dramatist John Webster. Overbury was less keen than his notable successor among the character writers, John Earle: Overbury's satire does not crackle and his praise is flabby. He was more adept at vexing living people who wished him dead.

His contemporaries were in heartfelt agreement on the descriptive "insolent": "insolent and thrasonical," "a witty gentleman but truly insolent," "infected with a kind of insolence." He bothered less and less to hide the megalomaniacal feeling that he was the brain behind the throne, especially after the demise of the Principal Secretary, Robert Cecil, Lord Salisbury, in May 1612. It looks as if he leaped to the conclusion that he was indispensable. He certainly thought he was to Carr. In self-regard he had but one rival, Sir Walter Ralegh—"damnable proud," and damned for it. Aubrey reported that "it was a great question who was the proudest, Sir Walter or Sir Thomas Overbury, but the difference that was, was judged on Sir Thomas' side." The Tower swallowed up both. Both walked stiffly, their natural blinders on, into cunning traps, having made the fatal mistake of all their conceited kind: underrating the opposition.

Experience should have warned Sir Thomas, made him at least a moderately doubting Thomas, since he had twice found it expedient or necessary to quit the court. His trip abroad in 1609 may have been the consequence of having offended Queen Anne. There are different versions as to what was his misdemeanor. She naturally took a dim view of Carr and all his tribe. It was on seeing him and Overbury strolling together in the garden at Greenwich that she made her famous remark, "There goes Carr and his governor." Whereupon Overbury, as if out to prove Bacon's description of him as "impudent," guffawed. A Queen may be a trifle insulting, but a subject may not even wordlessly retort. An explanation of the rude laughter was demanded, and duly found by the two men: namely that Carr had been passing on one of His Majesty's irresistibly funny (and bawdy) stories. Another version of Overbury's offense is that he kept his hat on, although he knew the Queen was looking down from her window. In any case, the trouble did not subside without long diplomacy, and probably absence. Two years later Chamberlain was writing about a new disgrace: "Sir Thomas Overbury by much suit is restored to the court, and there is hope in time to the Queen's favor." The banishment lasted for five months, and was probably occasioned by Overbury's speaking too openly of the Queen's debts, in the regulation of which he had a part, after her demands went through channels from King to favorite to him. Overbury had to beg Salisbury "to be witness of the submission both of myself and cause to the Queen's mercy." She on her part sent a note to the Principal Secretary, making it clear that something would have to be done about "that fellow." But this tempest blew itself out, too, and Salisbury died, and Overbury came sailing back, since how could Robert Carr, Viscount Rochester, Keeper of the Signet and to some extent keeper of the kingdom, do without him?

With the passing away of the only real statesman that the reign had seen or was likely to see, there was shameless jock-

eying for power. Overbury-Carr and the Howard family
backed opposing candidates for the Secretaryship. James
put off decision. The Suffolks, Fanny's family, who had
thrown one daughter into the court arena to be on the right
side of Cecil (Fanny's younger sister was now the Countess
of Salisbury), by now regretted that they had wasted another
on Essex. Perhaps, as she was herself urging, she could be
used again. Maybe her husband was really no man, and could
be lawfully dropped. Carr would be their man by firm matrimonial alliance, Overbury ousted, uncle Northampton the
new brain. It sounded beautiful—to everybody but Overbury. He knew what an unscrupulous family it was. Frances's
mother had personally made up so shamelessly to Cecil
(hunchback though he was) as to draw heavy jokes from the
King.

No one knows why, or even how much, Overbury had ac-
quiesced in the love affair with the Countess of Essex. Possibly it ripened while he was away, or unaware, and he was
presented with a *fait accompli* he could not believe would
last or turn serious. Composing poems and love letters for the
favorite was another way of showing how useful he was, and
a pleasant diversion from opening despatches and phrasing
diplomatic declarations and calculating how low the exchequer was. There may have been malicious satisfaction that
one of the proud Howards had been drawn into frantic adultery. He had helped. There may have been vicarious satisfaction in feasting on, or where necessary imagining, the details:
a pleasure not unknown to readers, writers, listeners, and
pimps.

For a while the full extent of the involvement was kept
from him. When he saw later the man that had been employed as a messenger between the lovers, he did not recognize
him. When it was too late, Overbury accusingly reviewed the

duplicity that Carr had found necessary: "You, . . . long intending in your thoughts long ago a marriage with that woman, denied it, sent me to inquire of her; would speak ill of her yourself." Another reading is: "After you had won that woman by my letters, . . . then you concealed all your after-proceedings from me."

Sir Anthony Weldon loftily presents Overbury as "that John Baptist that reproved the Lord for the sin of using the Lady and abusing the young Earl of Essex." Virtue is never louder than when it coincides with self-interest. A poll taken recently by a women's magazine shows that the average person considers divorce a more virtuous alternative than infidelity. By this admittedly rough and anachronistic yardstick, the good impartial councilor should have welcomed the wholesome news that the guilty couple planned to marry. But that word "marry" signally failed to soothe the prophet. "Against this then did Overbury bellow louder," as Weldon taurinely puts it.

Overbury guessed that the Howards were out to dislodge him from the position of power and influence that he had worked so hard to win. Like a jilted lover he began bickering with his Pythias. They may really have been lovers. A 1965 commentator, Beatrice White, observes: "It should not . . . be forgotten that in those days a friendship between two men often—and openly—involved emotional and sexual attachment. James himself set the tone—and an example—for inverted relationships; and there can be little doubt that the friendship between Carr and Overbury was of this nature. Both of them were strikingly handsome; of Carr especially it can be said that his face was his fortune—though Overbury, who never married, may have been more naturally homosexual."

The homosexual and heterosexual triangles thus opened

up dizzy the mind: Essex—Lady Essex—Carr; King James—Queen Anne—Carr; King James—Carr—Overbury; Carr—Overbury—Lady Essex. If jealousy poisoned the body as well as the mind, six personages—not just one—would have dropped dead. A final twist was divulged later: that Overbury guaranteed Carr the "unlawful love of the greatest woman in this kingdom." One can imagine the resentment of plain, pursy Anne (who had surely long since sublimated any sexuality she may have had in dancing in masques) at such an approach or rumor. Approaching forty, she was not drawn to anyone, except maybe priests—least of all her husband's cronies, or the cronies' cronies.

Although a selfish adviser, Overbury could make one telling point: that Carr's absorption in heterosexual love was causing him to neglect the King and the King's affairs. There was danger that the King would turn to someone else just as good-looking, if not more so. In reality James was more jealous of Overbury than of Frances Howard and ready to obliterate the first half of the all-too-common saying that "Overbury governed Carr and Carr governed the King." But the knight tried to stir fears of being supplanted, fears that he sincerely felt: for if Carr were ousted from favor, he would be out too. He knew, furthermore, there could be no compromise with the insatiate Howards. What he did not know was how far some of that family were prepared to go to "overbury" any obstacle in their path (the pun is a seventeenth-century one).

In fact, the King listened complaisantly to the idea of nullifying the marriage he had once blessed when Carr approached him with "humble submissions to the King's great wisdom, who (he acknowledged) had not only raised him to what he is, but may yet make him more happy, by uniting him to a lady of so much honor and virtue." Carr's mentor—

or scriptwriter—got more strident. Power-drunk, Overbury blabbed and boasted and bullied. Petitioners came to him, as they had to, and he treated them with contempt. He did not conceal his low opinion of that body of which he was the brains. He did not seem to care who knew that he was in on the secrets of State, that he wrote Carr's letters, that the Privy Council was taking his advice, that the Kingdom turned on him. He was the puppet master, and the pretty popinjay could not move without him. He would give a little lesson right now by cutting off the supply of love letters. Literary to the last, he could not suppose that a love affair could proceed without this elegant assistance.

But the two lovers were far past the stage of billets-doux, and in prison the author had to admit as much: "When you fell in love with that woman, as soon as you had won her by my letters and after all difficulties being passed, [you] then used your own for common passages." In other words, Carr was literate enough to make appointments—and that was all that was needed. As for Fanny being won by letters, we again have to make a large discount for auctorial pride. This man, who thought he could write about human nature, lived in a dream world, shortly to turn into a nightmare. Typically, power behind the scenes did not satisfy him; he wanted the show of it: there had to be style, his style, his mark, for everybody to see and identify.

They quarreled at Huntingdon. They quarreled at Newmarket. Overbury roundly declared to Carr that "Lady Essex was a strumpet and her mother and brother bawds." A servant (always those ubiquitous servants!) overheard what passed between them one night at Whitehall. Overbury, waiting with some papers for Carr, cooled his heels and warmed his temper till 1 A.M. Nor was his patron, when he at last came down the gallery, overjoyed to encounter his faithful attendant. "How now, are you up yet?"

"Nay, what do you here at this time of night? Will you never leave the company of that base woman? Well, my Lord, if you do marry that filthy base woman, you will utterly ruin your honor and yourself. You shall never do it by my advice or consent; and if you do, you had best look to stand fast."

"My own legs," Carr, the new Viscount, shouted, "are straight and strong enough to bear me up. But, in faith, I will be even with you for this."

"And so flung away in anger," testified the eavesdropper.

The talk about standing and legs was symbolic enough (not to say Freudian). The favorite's rise began with a broken leg, and he had been a dependent (as Overbury never stopped boasting), but now he flattered himself he could proceed well enough on his comely own. Exasperated, nagged, pushed to *hybris*, he was digging his own grave, as was Overbury: the head was never meant to be separated from the body.

"Strumpet," "filthy base woman," such words came round to the ears of Lady Essex. Overbury also circulated a poem, "The Wife," that she took as a calculated insult, since it praised all the qualities that she lacked. It served up, in forty-seven stanzas, the conventional virtues. Its only neat line among 282 was, "He comes too near that comes to be denied," but others were arrows meant to pierce her soul, such as, "God to each man a private woman gave," or, "For wand'ring lust, I know 'tis infinite." Overbury, man of his time, believed in the unquestioning submission of women to their husbands. The concluding couplet of this bachelor read: "For when by marriage both in one concur,/Woman converts to man, not man to her." He was dull on this subject in prose, too, as in his "character" of "A Good Wife":

"She frames her nature unto his howsoever: the hyacinth follows not the sun more willingly." "A Good Woman" was another picture of Fanny in reverse: "Now she is given fresh and alive to a husband, and she does nothing more than love him, for she takes him to that purpose." This was just a paraphrase of the marriage service. But Fanny, a much more deadly plant than a hyacinth, thought it time to swallow up a fly. Call her a Venus's-flytrap.

Moreover, this pest was threatening revelations that would wreck all her hopes—and Carr's and Northampton's too. If the facts about adultery came out, there might be a divorce, yes, but there would be no new marriage, ever. Overbury, who had already been dropping nasty hints, had to be shut up. He could document his charges, especially as he had composed some of the documents. With one well-aimed volley down would come cock Robin and all who had counted on soaring with him. There were distinct limits to what even the King —being God's anointed representative on earth, for all his foibles—could and would sanction.

Fanny's methods of getting rid of those who stood in her way were less refined than her great-uncle's. No slow politic maneuvers for her. In February 1613 she was accused of trying to poison her husband. The charge came from a most dubious source, one of the shadiest of the low characters to whom, in these desperate years, Lady Frances had been turning. The accuser was Mary Woods, "Cunning Mary," a palmist from Norwich, who, sent for by the Countess, promptly absconded with a diamond ring and some money. On being caught and haled before a judge, she claimed that the ring and money had been given her to induce her to provide a slow-acting poison for the Earl of Essex. The gossips were in possession of the story by April, "upon which scandal and slander," Chamberlain the letter writer inferred, Fanny's father "and other her friends think it not fit to proceed in the divorce."

Is the story to be given any credence? With such a headstrong woman it cannot be ruled out. She certainly was capable of throwing caution to the winds. Had Essex had a mood of raising difficulties about the divorce, threatening not to cooperate? Had she drawn the gloomy conclusion that Overbury would spoil everything? Did hatred for her stubbornly hale husband overwhelm her?

Still, with some around her optimistic about the possibility of legal freedom, it was an odd moment for this last resort. Besides, Mrs. Woods had a record: this record had been heard before. As a neighbor testified, she was in the habit of "deluding simple women and threatening, if they prosecuted her, to accuse them of trying to poison their husbands." When her property was taken, Fanny did not act like a woman open to the charge of conspiracy to murder. She did not act guilty at all; she acted indignant: she sent a pursuivant after the thief. No doubt, though, the two women had met for no good. The real reason may be contained in another entry in the Calendar of State Papers, that Mrs. Woods "gave a powder to Lady Essex to wear round her neck, because she wished to have a child." That is, with an eye on the annulment trial, the injured wife was fabricating evidence as to what lengths she had gone to help her defective husband bless her with issue. The petition for annulment was to read: "The said Frances Howard, in hope of lawful issue and desirous to be made a mother, lived together with the said Robert at bed and board, and lay both naked and alone in the same bed, as married folks use: and desirous to be made a mother, from time to time, again and again yielded herself to his power, and as much as lay in her offered herself and her body to be known. . . ."

On the other hand, if we attribute to this ultimately enigmatic woman enough folly and infatuation, the Mary Woods incident shows that she was going all out for both death and life, for widowhood—and a baby by Carr!

It is certain that she decided to get rid of Overbury as the ever more obstreperous obstacle to getting rid of her husband. She made approaches to "a boisterous, atheistical soldier. . . . an ill-looked, red-bearded Scot," Sir David Wood, who was nursing a grudge. This Wood was to explain later that he had won the King's consent to a suit for which he was a petitioner, but that Carr and Overbury stood in his way. The latter was so rude and arrogant that Wood planned to give him a good "bastinado." Although £2200 was at stake in the suit, Carr demanded £1200 to let it pass. Lady Essex stepped forward with an offer of £1000 toward Wood's deficit, if he would do what he should have felt like doing. She "told him, she understood that he had received much wrong from Sir T. Overbury, and that he was a gentleman that could revenge himself; and that Sir Thomas had much wronged her; and Sir David answered, That Sir Thomas had refused him the field. She persuaded him to kill him, and promised him £1000 for his reward, and protection from his enemies; which he refused, saying, He would be loth to hazard going to Tyburn upon a woman's word; but she still persuaded him he might easily do it as he [Overbury] returned late home from Sir Charles Wilmot's in his coach." But the most Wood offered was "some knocks"—and then only if Carr, before a witness, promised him immunity. The condition was impossible, and a mere beating was not what Lady Essex had in mind.

The blow that fell on Overbury was of a different sort, as announced by Chamberlain to his correspondent, Sir Dudley Carleton, under the date of April 29, 1613:

I doubt not but you have heard of Sir Thomas Overbury's committing to the Tower the last week. The King hath long had a desire to remove him from about the Lord of Rochester [Carr], as thinking it a dishonor to him that the world should have an opinion that Rochester ruled him and Overbury ruled Rochester, whereas he would make it appear that neither Overbury nor Rochester had such a stroke with him, but that he would do what he thought fit and what he intended without acquainting either of them with his purposes. And so caused the Lord Chancellor and the Earl of Pembroke to deal with Overbury and to tell him the King's good meaning towards him, whereby he had an intent to make use of his good parts, and to train him for his further service and therefore they offered him his choice to be employed either by the Archduke or into France or into Muscovy (upon which place we have now new projects).

He excused himself as incapable of such places for divers wants and specially of language. They answered that he was young enough and with little labor might attain that in short time, or otherwise he might be assisted and supplied by sufficient secretaries and other fit persons about him. Then he alleged indisposition of body and want of health as being much subject to the spleen, whereto they replied that change of air might be a special remedy for such infirmities.

But he stood stiffly upon it that he was not willing to forsake his country, and at last gave them a peremptory answer that he could not yield to go, and that he hoped that the King neither in law nor justice could compel him to leave his country. With which answer the King was so incensed that he willed the Council to consider what it deserved: who upon this contempt caused him to be sent to the Tower.

It is not necessary to elaborate on the imprisonment plot, for it was none of Fanny's doing. Rather, Northampton secured Carr's cooperation in this scheme to "shut up" Overbury by shutting him up until the marriage nullity could take effect. "The Scab," as Northampton called him, would be held incommunicado. Northampton knew his man, his tragic flaw, that would lead him into the trap. As Chamberlain said, Overbury "stood stiffly upon it." If he had any inclination at first to accept the apparent advancement of an ambassadorship, which in fact would take him away from the center of power, Carr would treacherously encourage his refusal. And the refusal would be sure to be offensively put, for Sir Thomas was, as another letter writer had just remarked of him, "violent and open" and had "irritated and provoked almost all men of place and power by his extreme neglect of them and needless contestation with them upon every occasion." The King would forthwith hold this arrogant subject in contempt of Court. It was Moscow or the Tower.

Sir Henry Wotton, himself an ambassador, had a premonition such as may come to one who was also a poet. He happened to be one of the bystanders when Sir Thomas was led off under guard "about six o'clock at evening." The "suddenness" of it was "like a stroke of thunder," especially as that very personage, "but two hours before," had boasted to this witness that he never esteemed "better than at present of his own fortunes and ends." After commenting on the stiff-necked attitude toward diplomacy that "I should for my part esteem an eternal disgrace to our occupation," Wotton added: "In the meanwhile, I dare pronounce of Sir Thomas Overbury that he shall return no more to this stage."

Nearly everyone else seems to have felt differently, including Overbury. Every effort was made to delude the victim into thinking that his release and restoration to favor were imminent. He had only to be patient while Carr worked to free him. He was being held on a most unusual charge, and surely he could not be confined more than a week or two.

Had he not himself "insisted that the King could not in law nor justice force him to forsake his country"? Meanwhile he must do nothing, say nothing (even if he could) to alienate his patron, whose first letter was signed, "Your assured loving friend." He had to learn to be quiet about any damaging things he knew, to repress rancor.

A new and more servile Lieutenant was put in charge of the Tower, Sir Jervis Elwes, who would allow the prisoner communication only with Carr or the Howards's agents. Northampton wrote Carr: "I spent two hours yesterday prompting the Lieutenant with cautions and considerations; observing with whom he is to deal, that he might the better act his part for the adventure in which he dealeth." So jealously was the prisoner guarded that he had been there scarcely a fortnight when, as Chamberlain reported, "Sir Robert Killigrew was . . . committed to the Fleet from the Council Table for having some little speech with Sir Thomas Overbury, who called to him as he passed by his window, as he came from visiting Sir Walter Ralegh." "Some little speech," the sound of one possibly friendly voice—not even this was vouchsafed the once proud peacock sickening in his cage.

The new Lieutenant, however, the very day he took over approached him and walked up and down with him in his cell, questioning him, in order to report back his attitude. Sir Thomas protested his innocence on the Bible. What did "they" mean to do with him? "They mean to refine you," Elwes responded dryly, "that your pureness may appear a little better." This was after two weeks of solitary confinement, already a depressingly long period considering that, as Overbury was to point out, "contempts never use to have above a week." Elwes recommended cooperating in the match between the Viscount and the Countess, Carr and

Fanny, whereupon the caged bird "grew hot" and tongue-lashed the two he regarded as his principal enemies, Fanny's great-uncle and her mother: "If I am the Countess of Suffolk's prisoner, then let her know that I care as little to die as she to be cruel." The pitiable fact was that nothing in this statement was true.

He never divined who was his deadliest enemy. He had not given much time or effort to understanding the inferior sex, least of all this particular specimen. Now he would be paid back for his scorn, his calumny, his supercilious ignorance. Searching in the darkness for clues to his plight, he had fastened his suspicions on the conventionally ambitious and resentful mother. It had not occurred to him that the daughter might have to be reckoned with as having the motive and the cue for passion and, unlike some oversensitive men, the "will and strength and means/To do 't." Already she had been busy, undeterred by the Mary Woods accusation that had just become public property.

The result was that Overbury found he had a new under-keeper or personal attendant. If the knight had known as much about the love affair as, for his own self-preservation, he should have, he would have identified this man, Richard Weston, as one who had often carried messages between the lovers in the early days. He had been Mrs. Turner's man, had once been—sinister thought—an apothecary's assistant, and now (for the time being) he was Lady Essex's man.

On the evening of May 9, in the third week of Overbury's confinement, the new Lieutenant of the Tower encountered in a corridor the new underkeeper. The latter had a bowl of broth in one hand for the prisoner's supper. In the other hand was a two-inch phial of greenish-yellow liquid.

"Sir, shall I give it him now?" Weston inquired.

"What shall you give him?" countered Elwes, coming closer.

"As if you did not know, sir."

But Elwes really did not know. He was not in on any poison plot. Instantly, both were in consternation, the one realizing he had given something away. "Why, sir, know you not what is to be done?" He was left holding the phial, helplessly.

Elwes, a weak, complaisant man, saw he had got into something deeper than he had bargained for when he had hopefully paid £1400 for the privileges and perquisites of his honorific office. He could not be sure who wanted—and similarly he did not know who did not want—the murder of his prisoner, but he was not going to cooperate in a capital crime. At the same time, he dared not offend "the great" on either side. Therefore, he failed to do the only right thing: put the villain before him under arrest. Instead, he got him to pray. "When Weston had told me that it was poison which he meant to give, I reproved and beat him down with God's judgment; nay, I humbled him so that upon his knees he thanked God and me, and told me that he and his had cause to bless God for me, for that I withheld him from doing that act."

That sounded fine; only Weston happened to be a canting hypocrite who would do anything for money. And neither God nor Elwes was offering him gold.

However, that particular phial was set aside, and Elwes saw it dashed in the gutter the next morning. The Lieutenant worried lest dogs lick it.

By Elwes's astonishing admission, he "drank to him," toasted the would-be poisoner to strengthen his reform.

According to Weston, the interview trailed off weakly after

the spurt of piety. Weston paid glum tribute to the strong will of his employers. "They will have me give it him, first or last."

The Lieutenant was accused by Weston of answering, "Let it be done so I know not of it."

To gain some time, it was agreed between the two men that Weston would report back to whoever sent him that he had administered the water, which was supposed to work but gradually. Deciding that since he was telling a story he might as well tell a good one, he claimed that the immediate aftereffect was "above sixty stools and one vomit." He demanded his reward of Mrs. Turner, who put him off. "The man is not yet dead. Perfect your work, and you shall have your hire." He went back discontentedly to his prisoner, while Sir Jervis tightened security to foil new attempts.

Although Weston had had some experience with medicine, the supplier of the poison was another of Anne Turner's underworld acquaintances, "Doctor" James Franklin, apothecary. Franklin came from the sinister northern moors, was "crook-shouldered" like Richard III, "of a swarthy complexion and thought to be no less a witch than the two former, Forman and Gresham." Maybe it was on account of deformity that he let his blond hair grow extra long, to form an "elf-lock" on his back. On being cured of the pox by a chirurgeon, he had aroused suspicion by asking what was the strongest poison. He had survived rumors that he had poisoned his wife, who had certainly died suddenly. He declared stoutly "that he would never be hanged for a whore." Little did he know.

The tale he eventually told was, "That in a house near to Doctors-Commons Mrs. Turner did first come unto him about the poisoning of Sir T. Overbury, and prayed him to provide that which should not kill a man presently, but lie in his body for a certain time, wherewith he might languish away by little and little. At the same time she gave him four angels, wherewith he bought a water called *aqua fortis* [nitric acid] and sent it to Mrs. Turner, who, to try the operation thereof, gave it to a cat, wherewith the cat languished and pitifully cried for the space of two days, and then died."

In this way he earned an interview with Lady Essex herself, who, sending for him through Mrs. Turner, "told him that *aqua fortis* was too violent a water."

"But what think you," she inquired, "of white arsenic?"

"Too violent."

"What say you to powder of diamonds?"

"I know not the nature of that."

She called him a fool, she, newly an authority on poisons, and "gave him pieces of gold and bade him buy some of that powder for her" from a diamond cutter. (Actually, ground glass would have done as well, and this was what was often called "powder of diamonds"; it must not be ground too fine, lest it fail to cause a hemorrhage, but it had to feel not too gritty in the mouth!)

At this point, Franklin asked—and posterity must be grateful—her motive. What was her reason for wanting to do away with Overbury? "She told him, He would pry so far into their estate, that he would overthrow them all." Another phrasing in the State Trials is, "would pry so far into their suit, as he would put them down."

She was still the great lover and the great hater, determined to mash any impediment to having Robin Carr full-time and legally—whether her husband or this impertinent upstart knight. Pests had to be exterminated. Overbury alive was Overbury slanderous, and even from his cell he might put a spoke in the nullity proceedings, which were moving very, very slowly and most uncertainly.

A pamphlet, delayed in its publication till the Great Rebellion of the 1640's, may still preserve some of her actual words: "To Mrs. Turner she must go and there renew her complaints with tears (hardly found in a woman of her disposition), protesting she was never so defamed, neither did she ever think that any man durst be so saucy as to call her Whore and Base Woman—and that to Rochester, her only hope, and with an impudent face." It seemed that Overbury, "that scum of men, that devil incarnate, he might do anything and pass either unregarded or unpunished. This moves pity in this pitiful woman Mrs. Turner, who frets so fast to see her fret so that there is such storming between them as is incredible. At length, as we see two clouds, after long strife in the air which shall have priority in place, join in one: so these two women, after they had fulfilled their frantic humor, join in this, to be the death of him." They were good hysterical criminal friends, Frances and Anne, unfurling unhesitantly the flag with the snake, "Don't tread on me."

A list of eight potentially useful poisons was drawn up: realgar, *aqua fortis,* white arsenic, mercury, powder of diamonds, *lapis causticus* (potassium hydroxide), "great spiders" (their venom was overrated), and cantharides. It was realgar that Weston was bearing in the phial on the evening of May 9. Realgar is red arsenic, but its color had been disguised.

After a week or so, Anne and Frances realized that their first attempt had somehow failed, despite Weston's claims of digestive disaster.

The next opportunity arose in connection with the clandestine correspondence that Overbury and Carr began to have. Officially, it was forbidden for messages to be given the prisoner. The standard subterfuge in such a case was to smuggle letters in with food. As a supplement to Tower diet, the Viscount sent the friend he was so carefully betraying a steady stream of jellies and tarts, pastries and wine. Concealed each time was a missive rich in false promises and assurances. Overbury, the master mind, would answer back with complicated plots to secure his release. It needed extra ingenuity to convey these replies, and he openly worried as to whether they were getting through. "I pray you let me know tomorrow before dinner whether that in the scurvy greasy bottle were legible." The device was for the prisoner to send some of the delicacies, as being more than he could consume, around to Lady Elwes's kitchen, for her and the children, but in fact a servant of the Viscount's or the Countess's would pick up the hidden letter.

Nothing makes more pathetic reading than Overbury's letters from the Tower to his false friend. "Do somewhat like an honest man and a friend; though you never do more, get me from hence. For the opinion of this deed, alas! you bid me have a good heart. You must know that the best hearts can ever worst bear shame and victory; and so, for my part, I wonder to hear that you are abroad and are seen in the world, I being here; for God refuse me if I be not so ashamed of staying here so long that now I never dare open the windows to look out."

Doubly, triply in the dark, he fancied he could deceive others. One scheme was to get sick so that Carr could plead to the King for his release on grounds of health. He wrote for and finally obtained a powder that would make him vomit. He had boils on his legs: these could be shown. Carr should likewise take an emetic, giving the King to understand that he was sick for want of his friend. Meantime, the prisoner cunningly assured Elwes that he was receiving no communications. "Yesterday he and I talking of news, I told him how ignorant of all things I was since I came in; he said: 'Nay, you have received wine and tarts.'" The omnipresent

Bible was produced for a solemn round of perjury. Overbury swore that the food was food only, and the Lieutenant, tit for tat, swore that he never suspected otherwise.

Elwes's problem was to let the delicacies in, those that contained letters, but at the same time to protect his prisoner from being poisoned. Fanny's problem was to poison Overbury without poisoning the Lieutenant's family or anyone else. To this end, on one occasion, she sent Elwes a letter in which she outdid herself in flurried ambiguity and scrambled syntax. "Sir, I pray you deliver not these things before supper. I would have you change this tart in the place of his that is now come, and at four o'clock I will send you jelly, one pot, for I had but one sent to me. I was bid to bid you say that one pot was broken after the man had delivered. If he should know there came two pots he must be answered so, if need be, which I think will not, for he cannot tell what is come now. This much more I was bid to tell you, that if he should send this tart and jelly to your wife, then you must take the tart from her, and the jelly, but the wine she may drink it if she will, for in that there are no *letters* I know, but in the tart and jelly I know there is, as you shall know, and from whom when we get the answer as that we shall too." Elwes suspected that "letters" was code for poison.

On laying some of Fanny's gifts aside, he found that the jellies became "furred" and the tarts "black and foul." He had his cook prepare duplicates, and sent these innocent dishes around to the prisoner. But he never could be sure what was eluding him, and there was still the problem that letters from Carr and Northampton were supposed to get through. There were unpleasant accidents along the way. One messenger scooped up some syrup with his finger and licked it: within a few days his hair came out and later his fingernails. The wife of one of the Tower warders guzzled some broth that Overbury had left: she turned wretchedly ill. The Lieutenant must have been nostalgic for the morning when he had worried merely about an unwary dog. *He* had been an unwary dog. He rued the day he was coaxed into buying the office; had not William Shakespeare (now in comfortable retirement at Stratford) said something about "ill-weaved ambition"?

Not being versed in poisons and alone against several conspirators, including Weston, who could dash something into the food after it reached the cell, Elwes had his back against the wall. The list of eight deadly substances had not been drawn up haphazardly; each had its tasty occasion. When Sir Thomas wanted salt, it was mixed with white arsenic. Once he asked for roast pig—and got it with *lapis causticus*. When two partridges were sent him from court, onions with water being the sauce, Mrs. Turner put in cantharides instead of pepper. Mercury sublimate did well in the tarts and jellies.

And still the prisoner lived on, issuing missives to Carr, even to Northampton and Suffolk, full of pleas, protests, and schemes. He gradually lost touch with reality. He weakened in mind and body both. It showed how little he comprehended Carr's involvement that he repeatedly referred to the woman in the case as "Your catopard" (leopard). He was not being tactless, just ignorant. That spotted animal had long been the symbol, as students of Dante knew, of sensuality. But Carr was uninterested in medieval moralizing. When Overbury at last changed his tune it was too late. Three weeks before he died he was writing to Northampton: " 'Tis true, my very good Lord, that I have heard from many, yea and from my Lord of Rochester [Carr] himself, with what bitterness her Ladyship would often speak of me, and out of the sense of that 'tis possible I may have spoken with less respect of her than was fit; but that ever I touched her in point of her honor far be from me, for I profess 'twas never in my words nor in my beliefs; and this I will profess to all the world." He was ready to reach for that Bible again. "For my Lady of Essex, if I might be only freed from her ill-will for time to come, there shall be no man readier to respect and honor her than myself."

She could not understand why he was not dead. Weston had assured her that he had received enough to kill twenty men. Perhaps the doses had been too small, and like the Pontic king Mithridates, he had built up an immunity. Maybe there had been some cheating or thwarting somewhere along the line, the line going back from Franklin and ending with Weston past the barrier of Elwes. Her marriage was still up in the air, easy prey, and this ridiculous peacock still had feathers for his pen, feathers that could still turn to barbs as they had before.

On June 14th, Overbury was sick enough for Carr reluctantly to authorize a visit by one of the King's physicians, Dr. Craig. Craig diagnosed consumption, which was a relief to Elwes. There followed several visits by the great Dr. Mayerne, who began treating the prisoner for "consumption and *flatus hypocondriacus*." As he was feverish, cooling baths were prescribed.

Overbury wanted to be ill, to play on (non-existent) sympathies. He had ordered another white powder, to produce convincing symptoms. He got it—white arsenic—but it came from Fanny. The sad "story" he instructed Carr to pass on was much truer than he had planned.

This morning (notwithstanding my fasting till yesterday) I find a great heat continue in all my body, and the same desire of drink and loathing of meat, and my water is strangely high, which I keep till Mayerus comes. The distemper of heat, contrary to my constitution, makes me fear some fever at the last, and such an one, meeting with so weak a body, will quickly, I doubt, end it. And in truth I never liked myself worse, for I can endure no clothes on, and do nothing but drink. This is the story.

Symptoms poured out like the blood that the doctors were taking.

My fever is relapsed, my water as high as ever, therefore this is the time to strike. . . . I was let blood Wednesday ten o'clock. To this Friday my heat slackens not, my water remains as high, my thirstiness the same, the same loathing of meat, having eat not a bit since Thursday was sennight to this hour. The same scouring and vomiting. For yesternight about eight o'clock after Mr. Mayerus was gone, I fainted and vomited. The very same dryness.

Weston showed one of the messengers "the loathsome stuff" that the knight had vomited, and the latter immediately wanted to take it around to Carr. But Weston would not allow that. He had too much respect for the aristocracy. "It is an unfit sight to show him," he said.

Carr, who had taken the stance that the prisoner was crying wolf, stopped another letter carrier, Harry Payton, and cross-examined him.

"He is sick," Payton answered.

"How sick?"

"Very sick."

"Very sick indeed?" the Viscount persisted.

"Yea, my Lord, in great danger of death."

Then, according to Payton, "My Lord cried 'Pish!' and so turned him away."

The worried parents came down from Gloucestershire in hopes of seeing their son, and were told by Carr, "Your stay here in town can nothing avail your son's delivery; therefore I would advise you to retire into the country, and doubt not, before your coming home, you shall hear he is a free man." On July 20 a brother-in-law, Sir John Lidcote, succeeded in getting through on a warrant to take Overbury's will. He felt he had come none too soon; he "found him very sick in his bed, his hand dry, his speech hollow. . . . Now being ready to depart, the Lieutenant going out before, Overbury asked me softly this question, Whether Rochester juggled with him, or not? But I then told him, as I believed, that I thought not."

Even this bit of whispering upset the Lieutenant, who by now wished nothing for his charge but a natural-appearing end. As for Lidcote, he changed his mind about Carr, "perceived he dealt not plainly." He prepared a letter of new advice, urging equivocation upon Overbury in his turn. Once, as Lidcote was observing him, "my Lord," while pretending to sigh about the situation, failed to conceal a smile.

Overbury had written prophetically:

Is this the fruit of my care and love to you? Be these the fruits of common secrets, common dangers? As a man you cannot suffer me to lie in this misery; yet your behavior betrays you. All I entreat of you is that you free me from this place, and that we may part friends. Drive me not to extremities, lest I say something that you and I both repent. And I hope to God that you may not repent the omission of this my counsel in this place where I now write this letter.

Now he was too weak for further outpourings. Ironically, one of his excuses for declining the embassy had been that his health did not permit him to write long letters!

August 29 it was reported: "Sir Thomas Overbury is like to run a short course, being sick unto death. The Lieutenant of the Tower, together with the physicians that were there with him, have subscribed their hands that they hold him a man past all recovery." Elwes may have secured this verdict to protect himself. Actually the amazing prisoner had gathered enough strength to launch further epistles—elaborate apologies to Fanny's great-uncle, Northampton, and to her father, Earl of Suffolk, that he had been misunderstood, and was, in fact, ready to serve them. (In replying they concealed *their* smiles.) The Court was in progress, and Lady Frances was thus deprived of an excuse for sending goodies.

After a summer of doubt, the dawdling and divided divorce commission was scheduled to hold its decisive meeting on September 18. The Court was back at Windsor in the last week of August and would soon go to Whitehall. In the first week of September Elwes put his prisoner under extra close guard. This was either to expedite his death—or, on the contrary, to make it more difficult for poison to reach him. One cannot be sure of Elwes's motives. Franklin quoted him as writing of Overbury's latest improvement, "The Scab is like the fox: the more he is cursed, the better he fareth." But this piece of evidence is very dubious hearsay, Franklin being even a bigger liar than Weston and the letter from which it was supposed to come never being produced. Elwes was alleged to have written it to Lady Essex, and, Franklin being there when it came, Franklin read it for her, he said "because she could not read it herself." What have we here, a Countess who can write but cannot read? How could such an outrageous statement be allowed to go into the State Trials without some addition to make it a little bit plausible? Usually these records have been carefully fixed up to make the government look good. For example, was Fanny suffering from eye trouble? (A common price of fairness. Persons with light eyes are more apt to need glasses: a dark iris deflects light better; opticians prefer blondes.) Even if Elwes did tell Frances this, it proves only that he was servilely adopting the contemptuous tone he knew she would like. A more ominous (but possibly doctored) reading is in British Museum Additional MS 28640: "The more the fox is banned [cursed], the better he fares, but be he never so crafty, he shall eat of this sour crab [apple] at the last." It is a very ugly fact that two days before the prisoner passed away, the Lieutenant sent around for his best furnishings, which were his perquisite, just as an executioner is entitled to the victim's clothes.

Besides Weston, only Mayerne's brother-in-law, the apothecary de Loubell, and his assistant, William Reeve, were admitted.

Cooped up more tightly than ever, with only the wizened underkeeper to stare at, sick in body and mind, suffering every effect of "five months miserable imprisonment," knowing that he had been tricked though ignorant of the details (he never suspected murder), Overbury gave way to final despair. His true nature erupted for the last time. Flattery had got him nowhere. He lashed out desperately and at length, aflame with the injustice of it all. It was not the least of his galls that the clever man had been duped by one of no mind, a mere puppet that he had been the voice and brain of.

This paper comes under seals and therefore shall be bold to speak to you as I used to do myself. I understand that you told my brother Lidcote that my "unreverent style" should make an alienation betwixt you and me hereafter, at least such a one as we should never be as we had been. With what face could you tell him that you would be less to me, to whom you owe more than to any soul living, both for your fortune, understanding, and reputation? . . .

And now to make so poor a pretence to say you will alter toward me for the style in my letters! Alas! this shift will not serve to cover your vow, your sacrificing me to your woman, your holding a firm friendship with those that brought me hither and keep me here, and not make it your first act of any good terms with them to set me free and restore me to yourself again.

84 ·

And you bid my brother keep your intent secret, that you might steal away with your wickedness. But that shall not be; you and I will come to a public trial before all the friends I have. They shall know what words have passed betwixt us heretofore of another nature than these.

Then came a brilliant sarcasm, almost worth dying for:

I pray you, keep my letters that they may see how much I forgot your Lordship in my style!

And the muses, as well as the avenging goddesses, saw to it that more of Overbury's letters than Carr's survived.

I shall be upon the rack, you at your ease negligent of me, and I must speak calmly!

. . . When I heard how, notwithstanding my misery, you visited your woman, frizzled your hair never more curiously, took care for hangings, and daily were solicitous about your clothes . . . held day-traffic of letters with my enemies, without any turning it to my good; sent me nineteen projects and promises for my liberty, then at the beginning of the next week sent me some frivolous account of the miscarriage of them and so slip out of town.

He moved on to particular threat:

By God, since I came in I have not found the advantage of a straw, by not so much as a servant in my extreme sickness, nor my friends free to speak my last words to. When I had observed this, the bitterness of my soul cannot conceal itself in letters: and that this wickedness may never die, I have all this vacation wrote the story betwixt you and me from the first hour to this day. What I found you at first, what I found you when I came; how I lost all the great ones of my country for studying your fortune, reputation, and understanding; how many hazards I have run for you; how many gentlemen, for giving themselves to you, a stranger, are now left to the oppression of their enemies; what secrets have passed betwixt you and me. . . . All these particulars I have set down in a large discourse, and on Tuesday I made an end of writing it fair, and on Friday I have sealed it up under eight seals and sent it by a friend of mine whom I dare trust (taking his oath not to open it). I send to him; and then to all my friends, noble and gentlemen and women, and then to read it to them and take copies of it; and I vowed to have wrote the truth. This I think you will not deny a word. So thus, if you will deal thus wickedly with me, I have provided that, whether I die or live, your nature shall never die, nor leave to be the most odious man alive.

As so often happens, education failed in emotional crisis, else Overbury, who aspired to the Privy Council, would have remembered Tacitus's precept, "Men are more ready to repay an injury than a benefit, because gratitude is a burden and revenge a pleasure." And especially he should have recalled Machiavelli: "I hold it to be a proof of great prudence for men to abstain from threats and insulting words towards any-one, for neither the one nor the other in any way diminishes the strength of the enemy; but the one makes him more cautious, and the other increases his hatred of you, and makes him more persevering in his efforts to injure you."

In sending this threatening letter, Overbury completed his doom. The eight-sealed narrative referred to—which would make fascinating reading and shed light on matters still dark—has never been found. It probably never left the Tower. Of what sort were the "words" that "passed betwixt us heretofore of another nature than these"? What were their joint secrets? Could Overbury tell, had he in his last extremity confided to paper, things that would ruin more than a marriage? Later it was said that what Carr really feared was Overbury's revealing "secrets . . . of a dangerous and high nature." State secrets? King's secrets? For James was to show that he was afraid, too. Ben Franklin opined that two may

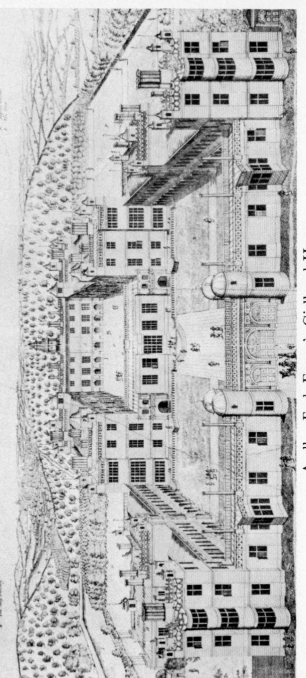

Audley End, Fanny's Girlhood Home

Robert Carr
National Portrait Gallery

The Famous Bosom

Sir Thomas Overbury
Curators of the Bodleian Library, Oxford

keep a secret if one of them is dead. But if three have a secret, and the third is a highly vulnerable monarch, he may well find the second poses a danger, even though the first is safely dead.

Lady Essex remained single-minded, untroubled by politics. She was less inclined than ever to take chances, with her marital future teetering on the brink. She got a last thrust through Elwes's defenses, if he was still making any. She heavily bribed the boy William Reeve, the apothecary's assistant. According to the charge, "The said Weston and another man being an apothecary . . . upon the 14th of September feloniously did get a poison called mercury sublimate (knowing the same to be deadly poison) and put the same into a clyster mingled with the said poison; and the said clyster the said apothecary, for the reward of £20 promised unto him, did put and minister (as good and wholesome) into the guts of said Sir Thomas." Sir Thomas died in agony the next morning. He was thirty-two.

The Overbury case will always be something of a mystery. There is no doubt that Frances Howard meant to poison him. But two major questions remain. Was she acting entirely on her own, for herself, or was there someone else, highly placed, working, with (or even without) her knowledge, to the same end? The crucial letter to Elwes about the "letters" in the tarts contains such provocative expressions as "I was bid to bid you," "This much more I was bid to tell you." Was this just subterfuge (fitting her pattern), or was she letting a little of the truth out?

The other question is whether Sir Thomas actually died of poison. Reeve never testified; he absconded abroad. Cheating was very common in the poison game, since it was easy and profitable and constituted a good defense in case of being caught. Ignorance was even more common. That was Wes-

ton's defense: he did not know for certain what he was pur-
veying. Who indeed did? Franklin did not make up his poisons; he bought them. He could have been passing on harmless or relatively harmless substances. His employers had
asked for something slow. Who was being tricked—or incom-
petent—when a process envisioned as lasting a week or two
went on for five months? And how much of whatever it was
did Elwes succeed in deflecting?

None of the physicians gave any sign that they suspected
poison (but there is a question of whether they were paid to
cooperate). Their diagnosis, it will be recalled, was consumption, and, in view of the gastric symptoms, they added *flatus
hypocondriacus*—or, as we say, "nervous stomach." The knight
could have died of natural causes. (And, incidentally, been
resistant to poisons because his system was too deranged to
absorb them!) He was not well when he entered prison, and
though the Tower, once a royal residence, had for inmates
more favored than Sir Thomas some aspects of a hotel or
comfortable apartment, no Elizabethan or Jacobean prison
was a particularly healthful place. Donne's brother died in
one, in the prime of life, and Donne himself got so sick, after
he had been put in one for eloping with Anne More, that he
had to be released after three or four days, lest he perish.
"Gaol-fever" (typhus) carried off many. Overbury had a suf-
ficiency of reasons besides poisons to die. He was denied
exercise, sunshine, fresh air, and friends. He gave as one of
his grounds for refusing to serve as ambassador that he was
"exceedingly troubled with the spleen," and years later his
servant confirmed that "for ease thereof, he had by the advice
of his physician an issue made in his left arm"—that is, he
kept a vein open with a gold pellet to let the spleen out! In
the Tower he asked Carr for and got white powder for a
sympathy-arousing emetic. When he became ill, he admin-

istered remedies to himself, such as *aurum potabile,* in addition to those the overconfident doctors recommended. (Sir Theodore de Mayerne was notoriously fond of mercury as a treatment; thus he may have furnished the *coup de grâce* to the man he was sent to cure. This eminent Frenchman had been having bad luck with his patients lately, and accusations had flown. It was said he killed Cecil by bleeding and Prince Henry by purging. Overbury was fortunate if he received only his unguent for hypochondria, his famous "balsam of bats," prepared from adders, bats, earthworms, sucking whelps, hog's grease, the marrow of a stag, and the thighbone of an ox. One must in passing—or in passing away—ask: Had the First Physician to the King, like Dr. Forman, attended a performance of *Macbeth*?)

After five months the clinical picture had a possible range from the toxicological to the psychogenic. It was cloudy—or all the colors of the rainbow. Weldon says that the two apothecary's assistants became so exasperated with the prisoner's stubborn longevity that they smothered him. He was awesomely hard to destroy, like the monk Rasputin, who sat calmly eating poisoned cakes and drinking poisoned wine and asking for more until his panicky assassins, convinced he bore a charmed life, started firing bullets into him, and then, when he got up, bludgeoned him and threw him into the Neva River. A modern archetypal critic, like Northrop Frye, might see Overbury (a fated name suggesting overkill) as the sacrificed god, who, having once been an oracle—Sir Francis Bacon called him Carr's "oracle of direction"—now underwent the role of "the *pharmakos* or sacrificed victim, who has to be killed to strengthen the others."

The crowning irony was that it was given out (there being sores on his body) that the prisoner died of venereal disease. In due course Bacon, speaking for the prosecution, corrected this, pointing out that it was rather the irascible part of the soul that dominated Sir Thomas. He had been against venery.

Chamberlain set down words truer than he knew, at the news of his death: "He was a very unfortunate man, for nobody, almost, pities him, and his very friends speak but indifferently of him."

Among the many who did not pity him was the woman who was free of his threats. All the signs are that she felt only joy and relief. Her legitimate happiness was one step nearer. A clear and present danger had been removed. Dwell not on the manner. She looked ahead, not back. Tears for those we have destroyed is a virtue saved for later times and later consciences. She was not *that* modern. Hypocrisy and beating the well-rounded breast did not come natural to her, though she would do whatever her advisers told her to get out of any fix she was in.

The Annulment Commission Meets

5

Under the Emperor Constantine, a husband could divorce his wife for being "a preparer of poisons." He could divorce her for adultery also. It is likely that by the spring of 1613 word had reached Essex of his wife's interest in Carr. But they were not living under Roman law: rather, the Roman Catholic attitude prevailed, despite the objections of some Reformers. Holy wedlock was indissoluble.

The ecclesiastical courts could grant a separation *a mensa et thoro,* from bed and board, for adultery or cruelty. This judicial separation might be ordered for either a limited or an indefinite time. But the parties were still married and could not marry again.

It will be remembered that Essex came from a famously adventurous family, what with his father having been beheaded and his mother having married thrice. Pertinent now was the scandal of his aunt's latter years. She had flouted canon law when he was fourteen, providing present inspiration for his wife, if not for him.

Aunt Penelope Devereux's arranged marriage to the rich

Lord Rich had been a failure, as Sir Philip Sidney lost no time in proclaiming in his sonnets and songs. This was so despite the fact that she bore her husband seven children and, in 1600, during a serious illness nursed him better than Lady Frances Devereux did Robert Devereux. He ceased to have anything to do with her after her brother's execution in 1601, providing maintenance only. "Is it not evil that such a devil wants horns?" rhymed Sidney. Penelope, a lover of literature, took care of that in the most unmistakable way. Even before she had kissed Sidney, her childhood playmate was Charles Blount; he was her great love, and the five children she had after 1595 Blount acknowledged as his (making her total from the two men an even dozen). Her open adultery was accepted by easygoing King James, who wished the whole Devereux family well.

But at last Lord Rich, patient man, secured a separation *a mensa et thoro*. Then he remarried—which was not permitted even the innocent party. Next, and far worse, Lady Rich married her lover. The offense this caused was beyond anything in a Restoration comedy or *The Beggar's Opera*. One hears the shocked voice of Peachum: "Married! . . . Do you think your Mother and I should have lived comfortably so long together, if ever we had been married? Baggage!"

Blount, a very able soldier who had succeeded in Ireland against Tyrone after the great Essex had failed, had risen to be Earl of Devonshire, and, having a chaplain, got him to perform the ceremony the day after Christmas, 1605. The tide of criticism was not walled off by a statement that the lady had protested against her first marriage "at the very solemnity," that it had in fact been forced upon her, that she had lived in constant fear afterward, that not only had she been subjected to mental torment but Rich had sought to rob her of her dowry and would have gone on to physical assault had it not been for his dread of her swashbuckling brother. But the King and Queen were adamant in barring them from their hypocritical court, and the moralists were encouraged to note that the couple did not long outlive the sinful ceremony. In March 1606, Devonshire and Rich, meeting in the House of Lords, exchanged "foul words," and days later Devonshire died of a burning fever in his wife's arms, and, after moping in a corner of their bedroom, she followed him the next year. The chaplain who had officiated marked off December 26 annually as a day of repentance: he called this blot on his conscience, this youthful mistake, "My cross." He was William Laud, destined to be Charles I's historic Archbishop of Canterbury. He had said it would have been better if he had been martyred, and he was, in 1645.

Although the disgraced pair could not have put in an appearance at her January 1606 wedding party, Fanny had at least heard about and probably seen the determinedly gay divorcee. Penelope was only in her mid-forties when she died, with, obviously, still enough of the blonde, black-eyed beauty that Sidney had sung to draw a lover into marriage. It was no mean feat, and eluding the ecclesiastical prohibitions was no mean feat either. It showed that love did find ways in a hostile world.

But annulment was a better way. The marriage tie was binding, yes. Those whom God hath joined together let no man put asunder. But the knot had to be a proper one. That could be searched most microscopically. There were a delightful number of technical grounds for finding a marriage invalid—and, therefore, as if it had never been, no matter how many children had been born (bastards they). A marriage could be pronounced null and void for such reasons as mistaken identity, prior contract, certain conditions known to one party but not to the other, solemn religious vows, membership in holy orders, differences of religious faith, fear caused by threats, criminality, impotence, relationship within the forbidden degrees of consanguinity or affinity. The last was interpreted most liberally, even unto the eighth generation, keeping genealogists busy.

Fanny, though no great reader, was familiar of course with the case of Henry VIII's first marriage. It well illustrated the intricacies of canon law and had plenty of relationship, since the beckoning third party was still another Howard, Anne Boleyn, whose mother was Elizabeth Howard, daughter of the second Duke of Norfolk, the prolific peer from whom the present family sprung. In the first place, Catharine of Aragon had been married to Henry's older brother and heir presumptive to the throne, Arthur. At any rate, there had been a wedding, in St. Paul's cathedral, and they lived together afterward under the same roof for four and a half months. Then Arthur sickened and died, and Henry became heir. For the same political and dynastic and financial reasons, it was expedient for the Spanish princess to become the bride of Henry. But it was incestuous to marry your former brother-in-law. (Thus Hamlet, father and son, could and did call Queen Gertrude's second marriage "incestuous.") It went against Leviticus xviii, 16 and xx, 21 (though those passages were contravened by Deuteronomy xxv, 5: the basis of levirate, which says a man should take care of his brother's widow by marrying her). But had Catharine ever really been Henry's sister-in-law? That is, had the marriage between her and Prince Arthur been consummated? Or had she kept the frail fifteen-year-old boy at a mystic distance those four and a half months? The English were inclined to believe she was not a virgin; the Spaniards believed she was, and she swore she still was. Just in case, before Henry acquired his first wife, a dispensation was obtained from the Pope.

Then, when he felt his ungovernable passion for Anne Boleyn, the King's conscience commenced to prick him over having married his brother's widow. Was it not a sin, and had not the Pope exceeded his authority in allowing it? The testimony of bystanders at Arthur's wedding night was sought. The very sheets, which had been sent to Spain, were recovered and exhibited. Arthur's boast of the next morning was recalled by more than one: "Willoughby, give me a cup of ale, for I have been this night in the midst of Spain." After twenty-four years Queen Catharine (who had never been a beauty) was permanently cast off, the only surviving offspring, Mary, rendered illegitimate. It was not a divorce in the modern sense. (The Church of England still views marriage as indissoluble.) What the King failed to wrest from Pope Clement and what he secured from his own Archbishop Cranmer was an annulment—on the grounds of his tender, if somewhat slow-working, conscience.

And in the six years these proceedings took, the usual steely Howard will was never far from making itself felt, like a spring coiled behind Henry's will. Anne Boleyn was not to be balked of legitimacy, even if it meant a split in the Christian Church. There was even some poisoning on the side. Just as Fanny came close to accidentally doing away with the family of the Lieutenant of the Tower, so a cook set out to poison Bishop Fisher, who opposed Henry's annulment. But the soup never reached the bishop: instead it killed a dozen of his household and a beggar woman who was in the kitchen. The cook confessed, and was boiled alive. Nothing happened to Anne—until she proved no more capable than Catharine of bearing the King a male child.

Lord and Lady Essex had duly gone through the prescribed triennial period of probation. They were ready to show that, for a reasonable length of time, they had attempted to cohabit. The stage was set for proclaiming non-consummation. Fanny was still, to her shame and sorrow, *virgo intacta*. The reason was her husband's impotence. She felt unmarried and she wanted a pronouncement that she was.

Innocent of the long history of aphrodisiacs, we may think of untimely impotence as a modern malady, or at least a modern topic of·discussion. Those strenuous Elizabethans? Ah, but the effete Jacobeans! The subject was bandied about freely in the ecclesiastical courts—often by men whose ignorance of sex was supposed to be complete. Also it entered into real-life conversations of which we have record. For instance, James at forty-nine confessed this much of himself to the Spanish ambassador, Gondomar, upon receiving a like admission from Gondomar. As a boy, James had had an aunt, the Countess of March, who had got free of her husband on this basis, though she was pregnant at the time, having been seduced by the Earl of Arran, whom she married—to become chief lady at the King of Scots's court. Thus James's rather uneven standards got off to an early start. The husband of Lady Margaret Hoby, first English woman diarist, was said to be impotent—though that never quite found its way explicitly into her record of the years 1599–1605. She consoled herself with strenuous religious exercises, just as if she had read William James, and "Mr. Hoby" was often obliging enough to walk with her between prayers.

Essex was tender of his reputation. He might want to marry again. The most that he would allow to be declared was that he was impotent *toward her*. His potential in other directions was not to be impugned. Once Overbury had been decoyed to the Tower, representatives on both sides met for collusion, Suffolk and Northampton for Fanny, Lord Knollys and the Earl of Pembroke for Essex. These were not well-trodden paths, as in a New York divorce. The preparation could not be too careful—and it was not.

Northampton sent off a note to Carr:

Sweet Lord,

Now all is concluded about the form of the nullity. The counsel on both sides is agreed and the libel is approved sufficient and good in law. I doubt not but God will bless the next bargain. I hope hereafter to find better pen and ink in this lady's chamber. Be still happy.

HENRY NORTHAMPTON

Using in eager anticipation her maiden name, the Lady subscribed, "I am witness to this bargain—Fra. Howard." Thus she sealed her love, while not boggling at her great-uncle's commercial word, "bargain."

The next-to-last sentence is taken literally by modern authorities: "I hope hereafter to find better pen and ink in this lady's chamber." Unfortunately, the manuscript does not survive to be examined for inferences about the writing equipment on hand. But let us not innocently overlook the Howard penchant for obscene metaphor. Suffolk remarked contemptuously of the husband "that it was truth, that the Earl had no ink in his pen." Northampton purred in another letter to the favorite that it was unfair to say that his scrawl (now that he was on his own) was a torture to decipher: "Your characters are no more pain for me to peruse, being as well acquainted with your hand as my own—the pain is no more than the cracking of a nut for the sweet kernel, or my niece's pain in the silver-dropping stream of your pen." *This* was not literal; in court the Lord Chief Justice "left off reading for the bawdiness of it." Apparently such language did not wait on the invention of the fountain pen. Both missives belong to May 1613. It seems the old bachelor, Northampton, Lord Henry Howard, "tall, black, and cat-faced," was running over with a vicarious eagerness of his own.

By this time we can see that Fanny, her parents having failed her, had resorted to various replacements. Mrs. Turner, for example, replaced her mother. The Countess of Suffolk, the heartless harridan, had reached the greedy age, deadeningly out of all sympathy with such romantics as her daughter and the mistress of Sir Arthur Mainwaring. As for Dr. Forman, he had offered to do for Fanny what a father should have done; she addressed *him* as "Sweet Father." (He was the father-lover to many a patient.) Her parents had got her into a grotesque marriage when she herself was too young to have a voice. When she found her voice, they remained deaf to her cries for help. In fact, they sided with her husband: "I am out of all hope of any good in this world, for my father, my mother, and my brother all said I should lie with him." Her father was not mean, just passive, a nonentity, dominated— it was common talk—by his wife at a time when it was much clearer than today who should wear the pantaloons. So the great-uncle stepped into the breach, licking his lascivious chops, a grandfather figure. It was said to be Uncle Harry that pushed her toward Prince Henry in 1609. In any case, he now had an ascendency over her that lasted for the rest of his life. He smiled and smiled, and she did not think of him as a villain. He had solutions for her difficulties. Uncles, as father substitutes, can be most seductive, coaxing-voiced, leading little nieces on, with due gradualness, to naughtier and naughtier things. As easily as undressing, they show how to take away obstacles, one by one—and scarcely ask a kiss. Overbury off. Essex off. All the nasty men.

On May 16 the King appointed a commission of ten to act on the annulment—four bishops and six lawyers. Apparently ignorant of the true complications, he expected a favorable and speedy decision. He now spoke out against arranged marriages of children. In fact he recalled a girl in Scotland who had gone so far as to poison the husband that had been forced on her. The Essexes were miserable, and the knot should be cut. This is what the petition asked, in all simplicity. "She requireth, since this pretended matrimony is but in fact, and not in right, it may be pronounced, declared, and adjudged as none, and of none effect; and she may be quit and free from all knots and bonds of the same, by your sentence and authority." But the Commission (not knowing that a man's life hung in the balance) seemed to be out to illustrate Hamlet's complaint of "the law's delay." And the more testimony and arguments the judges heard the more doubtful some of them became.

The chief ecclesiastic on the panel, George Abbot, Archbishop of Canterbury, was a man of integrity. True, he had been guilty of hyperbolic praise of James in a pamphlet, but that had been some years before. His appointment as Archbishop in 1611 had stirred surprise. He was a stout anti-Catholic, with Puritan sympathies. He had seen to the burning of two Arminians, and clashed with Lord Chief Justice Coke over *habeas corpus* for an adulterer who had failed to support his wife. In 1612 he boldly challenged Northampton at the council board, producing evidence of the Lord Privy Seal's dealings with Spain and belief in papal doctrines. Naturally the Howards were convinced of his prejudice against them, and the Archbishop joined the Queen in opposing Carr. But he repeatedly declared his impartiality during his long agonizing over the case before him: "that it was nothing to me whether she remained wife to the Earl of Essex, or were married to another man; but that I might not give sentence where I saw no proof; that I had lived 51 years, almost, and had my conscience uncorrupted in judgment; that I knew not how soon I was to be called before God, and I was loth, against that time, to give a wound to mine own soul." Others felt as he did. He begged to be allowed to withdraw from this "matter of great difficulty," or "at least, give no sentence in it till I were a married man and so might better understand the business."

The Archbishop had "heard before of some discontentment between that noble couple" but never imagined "that matters were come to that head." He was amazed to find interested parties, beginning with the King and the Lady's father and great-uncle, hurrying and pressuring the judges. More than once the King took him aside about the matter, while the two relatives impatiently watched at the end of the gallery—or prodded him in their turn. It became clear to him, also, that two of the commission, Sir Julius Caesar (yes, that was really the name of this LL.D. who was Chancellor of the Exchequer) and Sir Daniel Dunne, were barefacedly acting for Lady Essex. And they told tales outside of school—outside of the executive sessions. In happier times, justice was managed differently.

By June, the depositions were in—all that peeping and hovering over the couple naked in bed in a dozen different castles and mansions. The Earl of Essex put in his answer July 5. Questioned as to whether his wife was "virgo incorrupta," he smiled. "She saith so, and she is so for me." Mostly he was as reserved and reticent as the examiners would allow him to be, clearly uneasy, which was no help to the Archbishop's conscience. Of course the subject was embarrassing, but so would be—to a man in the habit of telling the truth— false testimony. A reference by the Archbishop to the case of his aunt and the Earl of Devonshire was not well received.

The Archbishop was rather too fond of awkward analogies. To Suffolk he had mentioned the repute of Essex's father as a lover.

After doing his minimum, Essex was glad to leave town for the summer. No man ever experienced more sorely or with greater humiliation the truth enunciated by his contemporary, the great lawyer John Selden: "Of all actions of a man's life his marriage does least concern other people, yet of all actions of our life 'tis most meddled with by other people."

It was decided to examine the Lady—to examine her physically. Four gentlewomen and two midwives were picked as a panel of inspection to determine: "1. Whether the Lady Frances were a woman fit and apt for carnal copulation, without any defect which might disable her for that purpose. 2. Whether she were a virgin carnally unknown by any man." "After some convenient time" they came back from the next room with an affirmative to both questions.

How had she passed? Who cared to delve deeply? An adverse finding would have brought on the enmity of powerful people—and pleased no one. The Bishop of London, the Archbishop's stanchest ally on the commission, heard from the gentlewomen that they "knew not well what to make of it; that they had no skill, nor knew not what was the truth; but what they said was upon the credit of the midwives, which were but two, and I knew not how tampered with." One story is that Fanny, requesting that she be veiled to hide her blushes, got a virgin of the same stature to stand in for her. Authors differ as to where a virgin was found at King James's court but agree that she was very young.

The claim was impotence as regards one woman, and one woman only. Archbishop Abbot had never heard of that.

General disability, yes, but that? Was it possible? Were there any precedents? He asked the lawyer Dunne, the colleague who most unabashedly "was a stickler for the nullity."

"Yes," Dunne replied readily, "there be precedents thereof. In Anne of Cleves' case we have an example, and another in one Bury, which I have here in my book."

He read passages from a notebook that he was carrying. This preparation showed that he was acting not as a judge but as a *parti pris* advocate.

"I did not think that King Henry's separation from Anne of Cleves was for any such matter," the Archbishop objected, "but upon a precontract." Besides, he added, "King Henry VIII was a strange prince in that kind. He put himself into many marriages. . . ."

Nevertheless, though he "much suspected the conscience of the man [Dunne], knowing him reasonably well before, both out of mine own estimation of him and out of the judgment of my two predecessors, the Lords Whitgift and Bancroft, who held him for a man most corrupt," the Archbishop promised to do the recommended reading. But he could find nothing pertinent in the Anne of Cleves case. "Good lord! thought I, how doth this man deceive me!" Everyone knew that Henry freed himself from the German princess because she was ugly—and beheaded Thomas Cromwell for having recommended her. It was possible that in the six months that he was supposed to be her husband Henry had left the Rhine-maiden a maiden. When Cromwell had nervously asked him, the morning after the wedding night, whether he did not like her better, he had been hit by the blunt reply, "Nay, my lord, much worse, for by her breasts and belly she should be no maid; which, when I felt them, strake me so to the heart that I had neither will nor courage to prove the rest." (In casting doubts on his bride's virtue Henry was clearly and unfairly ignorant of the flabbiness which can weigh down a Rhine-maiden of thirty-four, despite or even because of unblem-ished chastity.) Some time later the Queen related that she was but kissed each night and was "contented I know no more." But the King, at forty-nine, was supposed to have been rejuvenated by his next wife, Katherine Howard, seventeen (Anne Boleyn's cousin). Had this not been, then, a case of special impotence? The Primate of England shrank from such a so-called precedent. If all wives were to be shunted aside for such frivolous reasons!

In fact the Archbishop was beginning to suspect that Essex's *"Non potuit* was for lack of love, and not for want of ability." The commission had no authority to separate a couple merely because they did not love each other. The remedy for that was prayer.

The Archbishop next studied the Bury case. John Bury, of the county of Devon, married Willimot Gifford, and they lived together for the three-year probationary period. In 1561 she sued him on the ground that he was unable to con-summate the union. He admitted this, and she on examina-tion was pronounced a virgin. The cause was a shortage of— as the transcript discreetly puts it—"s——s" (stones: testicles). He had been kicked by a horse, and the effects of this were sadly apparent to all who examined him. A nullity was granted. Afterward Bury took to wife one Philippa Monjoy, his first wife being alive, and a son was born. That was con-sidered suspicious; more suspicious still, Philippa afterward forsook Bury and—without a divorce—married one Langeden. The question was, how long had Langeden been her lover? Was he the father of the Bury boy? This was not just of gossipy interest; a question was raised in the common law courts about the inheritance of John Bury's land, long after John Bury was dead. It was decided that his son was illegitimate, because the nullification of the first marriage was founded on a claim that turned out to be false! (Of course, if the claim was true, the son was also illegitimate.) The marriage between Bury and Willimot having been restored to validity by the courts, Philippa had never been married to Bury, which meant that she *was* married to Langeden, but no matter how you looked at it her son was a bastard, which was a good lesson to slippery women.

This case, like the Anne of Cleves case, left Archbishop Abbot as uninstructed as ever. There *were* no precedents. "We are now to act a novelty, a thing strange, and unheard of in the Church of England, whereof let other men be the managers, I may have no hand in it." Some of the commissioners—perhaps half of them—were still holding fast. Others, summoned individually to Whitehall Palace, came back with their original opposition altered.

The counsel for Lady Essex expanded on the *impotency toward her* plea to hint at *maleficium,* witchcraft. Naturally, they did not mention Dr. Forman. The truth not being known, *maleficium* seemed to be an idle conjecture more appropriate to France than England. Across the channel, "the common sort" were so superstitious that they resorted to marriages at night and in secret places lest they be hexed. Let that "be cast away as a rotten rag of popery." "I hope that those who have embraced the Gospel should be free from this *maleficium,* especially since, amongst a million of men in our age, there is but one found in all our country who is clearly and evidently known to be troubled with the same."

The stubborn prelate dispatched to the King a memorandum bristling with doubts and citations. Scripture contained no precedent. The ancient Church councils were equally silent. Besides, even supposing Essex *were* bewitched, "I demand what alms hath been given, what fasting hath been used, and what prayers have been poured forth to appease the wrath of God towards him or his wife; or what physic hath been taken, or medicine hath been applied for three years together?"

A half dozen paragraphs of Latin quotations followed. The great systemizer of Luther, Philipp Melanchthon, was shown to have recommended that during the three-year trial all possible remedies be explored. Melanchthon also remarked that really virtuous women did not complain; they kept decently quiet about their husbands' weakness till death parted them. One woman endured married virginity for eleven years; only as a widow—and to her second husband—did she admit it.

Hemmingsen, the Danish theologian, pointed out that only if the impotency preceded the marriage and was unknown to the prospective bride could there be an annulment. If it developed afterward, that of course was one of the hazards—in sickness and in health—for which there was no legal remedy. But Theodore Beza, Calvin's eminent successor at Geneva, did allow that if paralysis struck between the marriage ceremony and the first conjugal embrace, this was like the voice of God ordering a separation.

The King returned in his own hand a still longer answer to the Archbishop. He prided himself on being a scholar and a theologian, though he admitted at one point that more research into the Fathers and Councils would be desirable. Let the Primate know, however, that to say that Scripture was a guide "to decide all controversies" smacked of Puritanism. Besides, had not God made King Abimelech impotent as regards Sarah, Abraham's wife? And what God could do, "the devil, being God's ape," could do. Whether it was an old trick of the Devil's or a new one did not matter. That he had new ones—"look [in] my *Daemonologie*" (1597;

reprinted 1603). The fact remained that, whatever the cause, marriage without copulation was no marriage. How did the Archbishop know that remedies had not been tried? Besides, "no such cure . . . is likely to succeed well except the parties' own hearts and desires be set thereupon." Brushing aside the Latin excerpts as immaterial or on the side of annulment, James sounded pragmatic—and therefore modern. Why grudge the two marrying others, "wherein they may have the satisfaction of their hearts, and enjoy the blessing of procreation of children?" If "they shall be forcibly kept together," they will "live in perpetual scandal, or misery, or both." The Archbishop was just raising obstacles where none existed.

James's benevolence (mixed with guilt feelings) toward the young couple and his complaisance toward a third party waiting in the wings did make the Archbishop look like a malevolent obstructionist—which is what the Howards said he was. They had the King's ear, both ears. Also, my Lord of Canterbury in his written memorandum had got lost in peripheral matters instead of hammering at the feebleness and shiftiness of the particular evidence. Of course the Archbishop would then have been implying fraud and collusion, which would probably have been a waste of courage, taken as further evidence that he was carrying on a personal feud.

Still, he might as well have been hanged for a sheep as a lamb. All he received for his present pains, besides the monarch's formal refutation, was a sharp accompanying letter questioning his motives. "I must freely confess," James rapped, "that I find the grounds of your opposition so weak as I have reason to apprehend that the prejudice you have of the persons is the greatest motive of breeding these doubts into you; which prejudice is the most dangerous thing that can fall in a judge for misleading of his mind." Thus spoke the unprejudiced monarch, who modestly concluded: "it should become you rather to have a kind of faith implicit in my judgment, as well in respect of some skill I have in divinity, as also that I hope no honest man doubts of the uprightness of my conscience; and the best thankfulness that you that are so far my creature can use towards me is to reverence and follow my judgment, and not to contradict it—except where you may demonstrate unto me that I am mistaken or wrong informed. And so farewell."

From the very first the Archbishop had warned the counsel for the Lady, "That they had laid a very narrow bridge for themselves to go over." But it was tough and embarrassing for the more honest of the judges. As Weldon noted, "the discourse would have better befitted the mouths of bawds and ruffians than the grave divines." Chamberlain, who liked scandal as much as the next man, was nonetheless shocked that "a churchman in open audience" should have to ask of a husband "whether he had affection, erection, application, penetration, ejaculation, with a great deal of amplification upon every one of these points." Good honest people were disgusted by the whole proceedings—and smelled a rat or two.

What James was blithely ignoring was that if the traces were down many would flee. Chamberlain, though a disinterested bachelor, grasped that point: "if such a gap be once let open, it will not be so easily stopped but that infinite inconveniences will follow." The Archbishop was cogent on this *in camera* at Lambeth Palace, his executive seat: "Every man who is discontented with his wife, and every woman discontented with her husband, which can have any reasonable pretence, will repair to me for such nullities. If I yield unto them, here will be strange violations of marriages; if I do not, I must not tell them that it was fit for my lord of Essex but it is not so for you; for the law knoweth no persons, but is indifferent to all."

By the end of August, despite a thinning under pressure in the ranks of the righteous, there was still not a majority in favor of the annulment. In fact, the Commission was deadlocked, five to five. It was useless to threaten the Archbishop by reminding him that his predecessor, Grindal, was suspended for not sanctioning the bigamy of Dr. Julio, Queen Elizabeth's physician. They could shear him of his power in "temporalities": he had not asked for it, least of all in this case. Worrisome it was that the King acted his displeasure at the delay and the obstruction. The old prelate threw himself on his knees before His Majesty, and his eyes filled with tears. He did what he could, not to antagonize Majesty, turning away wrath with soft answers, but ultimately he feared his conscience more: that was the only ultimate. Sir Daniel Dunne was merely fatuous in fretting, "What a disgrace will this be to my Lord Chamberlain and his daughter, if it should not now go forward." Dunne drew on himself the riposte: "They should have looked to that before they did begin it. We were not the men that set the matter on foot. If it were a disgrace, they put it on themselves." If Fanny's father "was so passionate . . . that he lay as on a gridiron, broiling till the matter were accomplished," he was not the only one, but John King, the Bishop of London, assured the Archbishop that "the eyes of the whole Church of England were upon" him and that he felt if he himself, John King, yielded, "the devil would that night fetch away his soul."

And there were devilish things to remember. The Archbishop recalled something Overbury had said. The Lady had a new husband awaiting her. Besides, he "heard many strange stories of the Lady's carriage." Had she not taken the law into her own hands—what with the Mary Woods accusation, the rumors of adultery (or fornication)—before relaxing it into theirs, or rather, expecting them to relax it for her? Hell was literal, and there was more than one Christian who had no mind to go there to accommodate a tart and a minion.

The King was still insisting that he had no doubts of Essex's inadequacy. "Some of the Earl's friends had put a woman to him, and he would not touch her." Also, James had heard that the Earl had once intended to go to Poland to be "unwitched." But the Earl, feeling by autumn pressures of his own, chose a strange moment for a display. "That Sunday morning, having five or six captains and gentlemen of worth in his chamber, and speech being made of his inability, [he] rose out of his bed and, taking up his shirt, did show to them all so able and extraordinarily sufficient matter that they all cried out Shame of his lady, and said, That if the ladies of the court knew as much as they knew they would tread her to death." This got back to the Archbishop. No one made any allowance for the fact that it was early in the morning: the boast could have been inflated. It could be that the Earl had not yet resorted to a certain domestic vessel under his bed.

The Archbishop wanted to call back Essex for further questioning. The King sent word that this would not be permitted. The self-conscious husband had been working himself up in a variety of ways, even to the point of a duel with Henry Howard, his wife's brother. Insults had been exchanged, and the two had set sail separately for the Continent with seconds, dueling being severely forbidden in the Peacemaker's domain. But the men were intercepted before they could cross swords. The seconds, at least, were still belligerent. The total scandal by now was a very mixed and seething pot, with no assurance that there would not be a serious and irreparable explosion.

Events rushed to a climax in September. No honest man could dam them further. The Earl of Essex became reckless, Overbury was silenced forever, and the King packed the court.

Two servile bishops were added to the deadlocked Commission. They would vote "right," for Bishop Bilson desired a seat on the Privy Council and Bishop Buckeridge wanted to be translated from Rochester to a more lucrative see. This kind of bribery had not worked with the Archbishop, although the King had tried looking "merrily upon me" and "gave me promise of the bishopric of Lincoln for my brother, as I understood it." There was not even a pretense of a proper review of the case so that Bilson and Buckeridge could seem to render impartial judgment. They came in, Caesar and Dunne and Lady Essex's counsel gave them instructions, and their minds were made up.

Archbishop Abbot's mind was made up, too, with that last straw of being debarred from asking one of the principals a few appropriate questions. The Howards were going to have no more sifting of dirt. "If that be denied us," the Primate avowed, "and we have no further proof, I shall never give sentence for the nullity. As good declare my mind at first as at last, and I pray you so acquaint His Majesty." There were things he could not bring himself to do, even for his own brother.

"When I went homeward, I much revolved this in my heart, thinking, Good Lord! What a case is this? Shall any truth be kept from us? Are they afraid to have all out? Do they only look to attain their own ends, and care not how our consciences be entangled and ensnared?"

The decisive meeting was supposed to have been that of September 18. But they adjourned, at odds on procedure. The sitting did not break up in memory of Overbury— though it should have, for the news of his death had just reached Lambeth, along with "the sound of some fearful apprehensions thereupon bruited about the city." Poor knight! He could have assisted the conservative members enormously, had they only been able to get together.

The following Wednesday a peremptory message was delivered to the chairman that "His Majesty desired a speedy end of this business, that it had hung long, and the world was in expectation of it; that the term grew on, which would be full of business." Decision *had* to be rendered on Saturday, September 25. The King was to meet his Queen at Windsor on Monday. It was understood that, she being against the nullity, he wanted to be able to give her the news that the matter was settled, once and for all. Or rather, not for all—just for Lord and Lady Essex. It was a very special case; let no one else entertain loose notions.

One of the two new judges, Bilson of Winchester, was outrageously pert that Wednesday. Among other misdemeanors, he rounded on John King of London with the question, "How many times in a year was a man bound carnally to know his wife?" Did not every theologian know that Luther had answered that: two or three times a week. These licentious opponents were rebutted by the steadfast Archbishop that day, and the next day too, but he noted wryly that even if St. Paul had been present he would not have prevailed.

For the final battle on Saturday the Archbishop had prepared, in writing, an eight-thousand-word speech giving six reasons against the nullity. Two weaknesses of the Earl's testimony worth airing were that he had admitted that his wife sometimes refused him, and that he had given up long before the probationary period had ended. (Their quarrels were public property; on the matter of refusal, it sifted down to Chamberlain that the Earl "grew to that impatience that he prayed God to damn him if ever he offered her any such kindness till she called for it, and she in the like heat wished to be damned if ever she did.") It still sounded to the prelate like an ordinary case of lack of love:

Between a lady and her husband there is some discontentment, which time and God's grace may easily remove: there is then an end of that controversy. Or, if the disagreement shall never be appeased, it is no more but one lady doth want that solace which marital conjunction would afford unto her—which many a good woman is enforced to endure, and yet commits no sin, neither labors to violate the laws of the church. For suppose the husband be sick of some long disease or languishing weakness, must not the wife sustain it with patience and quietness? Suppose the husband be captive in some foreign nation or prisoner in his own country, whereby occasion of marital connection is taken from the wife: no divine will pronounce that a separation is in this case to be sought.

Let a woman do that in modesty which others are enforced to do out of necessity. And let her expect God's leisure, in fasting and in prayer, and in other humiliation.

Given the smallest acquaintance with Frances Howard, the Archbishop must have smiled as he wrote this. "Modesty"? "Humiliation"? What sort of sauce for the goose was this? But he was concerned, rightly, about all the other geese and ganders eager to fly the coop. In his own latest words, "For if the gap be open, who will not run in?"—into court. Not just lords and ladies; ordinary folks, unless there was to be a different justice for them. He called out, like the town crier: "Whatsoever couple, therefore, have no children, and live discontented: come presently to take part of this general jubilee."

Equipped with a more forceful argument than he had offered the King, he would bring up in the rear, after the other judges had announced their opinions. "Leave it to me," he told the faithful four who sided with him, "I doubt not, in Almighty God, but to batter their nullity to dust."

Alas, he had tipped his hand. The King conveyed an order that there was to be a vote only: no reasons, no speeches.

The vote was seven to five, as expected. The case was over. The Archbishop did not live to read Weldon's encomium in 1650: "The Archbishop of Canterbury, to his everlasting fame, mainly opposed all the proceedings and protested against them, for which he ever after lived in disgrace, excluded from the council table, and died in the disgrace of the king on earth, though in favor with the King of kings."

Of course the Archbishop's brother did not get the see of Lincoln, which went to one of the bishops who had voted "right." Bilson's son was knighted, only to be nicknamed for the rest of his life "Sir Nullity Bilson." The son-in-law also was the butt of humiliating jokes that drove him to another town, jests to the effect that he only *"thought* he had a wife": a nullity might descend upon him any time—from his father-in-law.

So, after difficulties that an ordinary woman would have sunk under, Fanny was returned to the state of being a certified virgin and unaffianced. The slate, which was very black and much scribbled upon, had at last been wiped clean. It had been a lengthy, irritating, and messy struggle, but she was getting the second chance that other married people, miserable and envious, would never have and perhaps did not deserve, because they had not wanted it enough to do whatever was necessary to secure it. A second chance? That sounded too much like a chance to go wrong, to substitute her own mistake for her parents'. There was nothing chancy about this: she was marrying a sure thing this time, a thing she already knew and doted on, and that now was to be duly blessed, in God's holy church. Dearly beloved, we are gathered together again, and whose death?—none but Robin's or mine—can part us.

The Countess of Essex Becomes the Countess of Somerset

6

Excited beyond all control by the prurient annulment proceedings, a helpless moth drawn to the flickering hair and hazel eyes and public cleavage of Lady Frances, now a luscious twenty, Lord Norris made overtures to the Lord Chamberlain for his daughter's hand. It had to be admitted that there was one small obstacle, apart from the fact, unknown to the suitor, that the Lady had other plans. Francis, Lord Norris, was already married. But marriages were easily severed these days, were they not, and there would be the immeasurable advantage that the new couple would be able to call each other "Frankie." This young man came, inevitably, to an impetuous end nine years later. Sent to the Tower for quarreling with Lord Scrope in the passageway of the House of Lords, he took his disgrace so hard that he committed suicide with a crossbow.

The decree did not presume to give Lord and Lady Essex

advice: "We do free and divorce her, leaving them as touching other marriages to their consciences in the Lord."

But a viscount cannot expect to be loved, honored, and obeyed by a countess, who outranks him. It was necessary that Carr be elevated further. On November 4, 1613, Viscount Rochester became the Earl of Somerset—his final title, the title by which he is best known to fame or infamy. His more adroit successor as royal favorite went on to a dukedom, but Robin Carr was doing phenomenally well for a country bumpkin, although the central administration's inefficiency detectably increased once Overbury was no longer at his side. Overbury had said he would be missed—and he finally, reluctantly, was, impersonally, as one misses a good advocate.

There had been trouble, incidentally, in the disposition of Overbury's cadaver, though Northampton bothered about that more than Carr and it was of no concern at all to Lady Essex, who was interested in only one body. Overbury died at five in the morning. Instantly his corpse, as viewed by Weston, was as if it had lain unburied for days. Swarming with issues and sores, it cried to Heaven—and stank to Hell. Elwes was in another of his quandaries. If he yielded to his natural impulse to huddle it at once into the grave, suspicion would be aroused that there had been something to hide. It was proper procedure for relatives and the coroner's jury to take over. Elwes and Northampton had to act as if they welcomed an investigation, while doing everything possible that it be quick and superficial and fervently hoping that it would allay—not increase—suspicion. After all, there was that testimonial from the physicians that the prisoner had been "sick unto death."

Noble Lieutenant,

If the knave's body be foul, bury it presently; I'll stand between you and harm; but if it will abide the view, send for

Lidcote and let him see it to satisfy the damned crew. When you come to me, bring this letter again yourself with you, or else burn it.

NORTHAMPTON

The old fox dispatched no fewer than four letters that day, September 15, two more to the Lieutenant and one to Carr. He admitted his "post-haste" and was in such a dither that he lapsed into overt Catholicism: "let the priest be ready." At seventy-three, he should have been worrying about his own funeral, which was imminent. If not guilty himself, Fanny's great-uncle is a man sitting on the lid of that which he does not want to boil over: "If they have viewed, then bury it by and by [right away]; for it is time, considering the humors of that damned crew, that only desire means to move pity and raise scandals." The apothecary de Loubell came to the Tower and found on the body plasters which he had not provided. A hastily summoned coroner's jury of six warders and six others "found the body so bare as in effect it was consumed away, having nothing but skin and bones." A black ulcer festered between the two shoulder blades, "and in the brawn of the left arm he had an issue kept open with a little bullet of gold, and had a plaster on the sole of one of his feet, and on the belly of him two or three blisters of the bigness of a pease, as yellow as amber."

The twelve good men and true rendered a verdict of "death from natural causes," although it is a fact that mercury poisoning produces sores. Northampton wrote with malicious glee to his "Sweet Lord," Carr:

Overbury being viewed, there was found in his arm an issue, and on his belly twelve kernels likely to break to issue, each as big as three pence; one issue on his back with a tawny plaster on it; this was strange and ugly. He stank intolerably, insomuch as he was cast into the coffin with a loose sheet over him. God is good in cutting off ill instruments from off the factious crew. If he had come forth, they would have made use of him. Thus, sweet Lord, wishing you all increase of happiness and honor, I end,

Your Lordship's, more than any man,

HENRY NORTHAMPTON

One must admire the clever contrast of the sentence showing that Overbury was so noisome that no one could approach him to wrap around a winding-sheet, followed by the Te Deum to obliging Deity. Overbury was laid away in the Tower chapel the afternoon of the next day, thirty-four hours after he died —a reasonably speedy burial, and certainly a timely one. Elwes was apologetic: "I kept it overlong, as we all felt." The brother-in-law, Lidcote, was on hand; in thrifty protest he refused to pay Elwes for the coffin.

Carr tried to pacify the father with a letter wet with crocodile tears.

Mr. Overbury,

Your son's love to me got him the malice of many, and they cast those knots on his fortune that have cost him his life; so, in a kind, there is none guilty of his death but I: and you can have no more cause to commiserate the death of a son than I of a friend. But, though he be dead, you shall find me as ready as ever I was to do all the courtesies that possibly I can to you, or your wife, or your children.

In the meantime, I desire pardon from you and your wife for your lost son, though I esteem my loss the greater. And for his brother, that is in France, I desire his return, that he may succeed his brother in my love.

Sir Thomas would have composed a more ornate epistle on such an occasion, and Northampton would have laid on the sentiments sickly thick. Carr wrote more simply, and in the modern view better, because he had *not* gone to Oxford or Cambridge. But neither Carr nor Northampton could still the rumors that began to fly about, birds of doubt. Overbury's first cousin petitioned the King for an investigation of the death by the law courts. But the premature demise of every prominent person regularly gave rise to stories of foul play, and the rumors that the knight's relatives circulated and encouraged had little to fasten on. History was on the side of suspicion, for Overbury was the first prisoner in the Tower to die (who was not supposed to) since the two little princes vanished in the time of Richard III. (Who would have guessed even the sex of the new villain? No hump on the back? No beetling brows, at least? It was the Puritans, that growing party, that, following Spenser's tradition of the false Duessas and the snowy Florimells, distrusted the fair exterior. The old view was that a villain somehow looked like one.)

So Overbury, without so much as a shroud, was shoveled under in the hope that dead men tell no tales, the annulment was pronounced nine days later, and preparations went ahead for the wedding. Fanny gave no signs of feeling anything but blissful. The main decision (as so often, but particularly acute in this case) was whether to have a small wedding or a large one. Considering the circumambient scandal, there was much to be said for an absolutely secret ceremony. Chamberlain wrote of "the great man" in October: "There is no certainty of his marriage: but either it is done, or is thought will be shortly, though without show or publication till they think good." The Queen's opposition seemed to rule out anything at a palace. The November plan called for having the wedding at Audley End, with the King present. But he was in the habit of getting his wife to change her mind; her in-

Essex

King James I

National Portrait Gallery

Fanny's Mother,
Countess of Suffolk

Fanny's Father,
Earl of Suffolk

Henry Howard, Earl of Northampton

dignation melted, and she agreed to grace the festivities (she loved festivities) with her plump presence, so they were switched to Whitehall and the Chapel Royal and the Christmas season. Everything would be bigger and better than eight years before, even as the new husband was.

Her affianced had plenty of money. Partly it was Scotch thrift, in contrast to the normal financial recklessness of English noblemen. Chamberlain was open-mouthed: "Either his comings in are very great, or else he is a good husband and careful keeper, for it is observed that within this twelvemonth he hath made show of above £90,000." In fact he sometimes lent—and sometimes gave—to the monarch. But Fanny was hard-pressed. Her dowry had not yet been returned by Essex. He had spent it long before. To meet his current obligations Essex had to give up his estate of Benington in Hertfordshire to Sir Julius Caesar for £14,000. She could hardly ask Carr, especially as they were not yet married, for certain sums she had promised to certain shady characters for unmentionable services. Weston, unpaid, groaned to Franklin that "now the Countess's turn is served, she used him unkindly and that they should all be poisoned."

Franklin, whom we may call the Countess's pharmacist, was more patient, but more dangerous because he was given to boasting. One fall day he encountered Mercer, an old acquaintance who had served Essex's father. The two, as servants of opposite factions, thereupon did a more peaceful version of the opening scene of *Romeo and Juliet*.

"What news?" asked Franklin, passing the time of day.

"I hear ill news," Mercer responded. "I am sorry that my old lord and master's son is found insufficient and not able to content the lady."

"I have a hand in that business," Franklin crowed. "I have

a great friend of my Lady of Essex. She allows me half a crown a day for my boat hire and ten shillings a week for my diet. I could have any money I would."

The other did not react as expected. "But, Cousin, how can God bless you in this business?"

Franklin rode roughshod over that. "Let them talk of God that have to do with Him. My Lord of Somerset and the Countess will bear me out in anything I do. If you have any suit wherein you may do yourself any good, and I may gain by it, I will warrant you I will get it."

Still, it was a good question for more reflective moments, such as were to come to all the conspirators. "How can God bless you in this business?" Mercer had a point. At least, if caught, they would feel it.

The wedding was—to coin a phrase—what God could do if He had a lot of money. Fanny's affair became an affair of State, with the King footing the bill when he could not foist it off on someone else, and courtiers giving what they hoped they would get back with interest. Sir Frances Bacon, for instance, spent £2000 on a masque. Newly the Attorney General, he looked to become Lord Chancellor. He refused an offer by another ambitious lawyer, Yelverton, to help out with the costs to the extent of £500. Bacon's calculation was wise, his investment prudent. He became Lord Chancellor as soon as the elderly incumbent died, but Yelverton had to sweeten the King with £4000 for the reversion of Bacon's present office.

It was James's intention to spend £10,000 on jewels for the bride, although his guards and messengers were fruitlessly petitioning him for back pay, and more and more of the Crown lands were having to be sold. Carr was collecting sixteenth-century Italian paintings, glowing canvases by Titian, Veronese, Tintoretto, to light up the eyes of his bride, although Overbury's father was never able to collect from him £1500 he owed the son at the latter's death. Gold and silver were showered on the pair in unprecedented profusion. Among the gold articles were cups, pots, a warming pan, basins, and ewers, some set with gems. There were two complete sets of fireplace equipment, everything silver but the coal. Sir Thomas Lake—with a secretaryship of state in view (he eventually got an associate secretaryship) "gave six goodly candlesticks that cost above a thousand marks." Northampton behaved like a man with a long future. His "present was plate to the value of fifteen hundred pound, besides a sword to the bridegroom, the hilts and all the furniture of gold curiously wrought and enameled. The very workmanship cost a hundred mark, and the sword five hundred pound." We have to stop to estimate that £2000 means not less than $60,000 in today's money (a mark was worth one-third less.). Another Howard elder, Lord Admiral Nottingham, contributed "a very rich basin and ewer of gold set with stone" that had been a present to him, oddly enough, from the King of Spain. One had to learn to distrust Spaniards bearing gifts. On closer examination, the gold turned out not to be pure.

All the City Companies gave plate. The Lord Mayor and sheriffs received back fine gloves. The City had been more or less coerced—after claiming no house was big enough—into offering a banquet at the Merchant Tailors' Hall that lasted till three in the morning. Service was by the comeliest members of the City Companies "in their gowns and rich foins [furs]," and the entertainment, after a torchlight procession through the streets, consisted of two masques, a wassail, and a play, besides incidental poetry and music. London was a stronghold of Puritans and other decent-thinking bourgeois, who were not going to trip it lightly to any piper's tune of bigamy and adultery. There was an Old Testament parallel for everything: Numbers xxv was pertinent here. Fanny was to be called "this Moabitish woman," one of those sent by Balaam's advice to seduce the Israelites to whoredom. She deserved to be stabbed in the same part of her anatomy that Cozbi was. (The recently issued King James version said "belly," but close students of the original knew better.)

Sir Ralph Winwood, who had *not* been Carr's candidate for Secretary of State, was a Puritan. Like other court opponents of the Carr-Howard ascendency, he made the most of a bad situation—and bided his time. Black was the color of the doublet, hose, and cloak he wore at the wedding—they had cost him £80—and black his mood, for he foresaw political and religious whoredom with Spain and Rome. But, after having sent around a basin and ewer (did *everyone* think the couple urgently needed washing?) from the Low Countries that the goldsmiths had offered him a little fortune for, he was asked by the Countess if she could borrow four of his sleek horses to draw her coach in the torchlight procession. He rose to this like a gallant and a millionaire, insisting that the horses be accepted as a present, for it was inappropriate "for such a Lady to use anything borrowed." Carr "made some difficulty at first . . . but in the end took them in very good part." In due course, Winwood would be the first gatherer of evidence—and initiator of murder charges—against the pair. Sir Edward Coke, prosecutor and judge at the trials to come, was, Chamberlain noted, "more moderate" in his giving: "he gave but a fair basin and ewer of silver and gilt, and his lady a cup of fourscore pound value." Among opposing earls who danced at the wedding were Dorset, Montgomery, and Pembroke. Even Archbishop Abbot turned up. Since the annulment pronouncement, cunning maneuvers had been directed at the Archbishop to make it *appear* that he approved—surely he should bow to the prevailing winds—but he avoided every trap, and his grim, quiet, unofficial presence at the wedding was his only concession to tact.

The actual ceremony took place on December 26, St. Stephen's Day, ten days short of being the eighth anniversary of Fanny's first marriage. (It happened to be, if anyone gave it a thought, exactly the anniversary of that bygone disgraced couple, Lord and Lady Devonshire.) Fanny had a sense of history repeating, for there she was in the same Chapel Royal again as she had been as a girl, with the same minister officiating, Dr. Montague, Bishop of Bath and Wells, and most of the same spectators, from the King and Queen down. If this struck some (such as Chamberlain) as a needlessly insensitive arrangement, it had logic. Dr. Montague had not tied (it had been officially found) a good knot the first time: he was being given a second chance, in the spirit of Christian charity, as indeed was she. She appeared in white and "in her hair," that is, with her auburn hair down upon her shoulders in token of virginity. One little change was noticed. The first time it had been the King who gave her away. Now, perhaps feeling unlucky, James left that honor to her father.

With a soldier's or sailor's simplicity, Suffolk had taken any opposition to the annulment or the remarriage as a personal affront. He had given a stern dressing-down to a gentleman who had lately been loose-tongued at Eton. The maze of ecclesiastical and legal argument was more than he could follow. He knew what was convenient and just. "What a matter is this," he murmured in honest surprise, "that men should be of such contrary opinions!" Ever the hale and hearty take-the-bull-by-the-horns type, when he succeeded his uncle, incongruously, as Chancellor of Cambridge University and had to sit through Latin compliments and formalities at his installation, he took the earliest opportunity of rising to say that he had not understood a word but proposed that they now proceed to one language that everybody understood—dinner. If his daughter, brazening it out as an innocent virgin, was self-conscious, he was not.

The sermon was in good flattering English. It was delivered by the Dean of Westminster. Not content with commending the young couple, he branched out to praise Fanny's sister, the Countess of Salisbury, and even went so far as to have unctuous words for that unscrupulous old harridan, "the mother-vine" (as he called her), the Countess of Suffolk. Clever with words was he, George Montaigne (pronounced "mountain"), and obviously not without a sense of humor. He had worked himself up from humble Yorkshire origins to the archbishopric of York, which he won from King Charles with a witticism. He suggested to him, "Hadst thou faith as a grain of mustard seed, thou wouldst say unto this mountain"—laying his hand upon his breast—"be removed into that sea" (see).

Afterward they all had wafers and hippocras, the traditional spiced cordial. Mrs. Thornborough, the Bishop of Bristol's superstitious wife, who had planted the first seed of Fanny's interest in magic, wheeled in a bridal cake that cost the equivalent of $150 at a time when labor was cheap.

But the festivities, which went on for days and nights, are not to be measured in money only. Frances Howard is importantly connected with English literature—and not only because she poisoned an author. The best poets of the day celebrated her second marriage without stint. Previously, as we know, Ben Jonson had done two masques for her, and in the intervening years she had danced in a masque by Samuel Daniel and another by Jonson. Now she had the services of Jonson again, Sir Francis Bacon, John Donne, George Chapman, and the poet and musician Thomas Campion.

The Masque of Flowers, Bacon's contribution, drew up in the rear of the twelve days of Christmas, being presented on

Twelfth Night, January 6, 1614. The budding lawyers of Gray's Inn, masquerading as hyacinths and daffodils, came forward "to show their good affection towards so noble a conjunction." On their first approach—by barge to Whitehall—the crowd and disorder were such they were unable to do their corantos and galliards, and Bacon's £2000 nearly fell into the Thames, so to speak. But the King ordered a second try, and this time the flowery young men, their left arms wound in white scarves sent by the bride, their embroidered gloves a gift of the groom, succeeded in chanting:

> Receive our flowers with gracious hand,
> As a small wreath to your garland.
> Flowers of honor, flowers of beauty,
> Are your own: we only bring
> Flowers of affection, flowers of duty.

If Bacon wrote these lines, they are sufficient evidence that he did not write Shakespeare. But it is probable that he only commissioned the masque, which was published anonymously; no original verse known to be his has come down. He started his essay "Of Masques and Triumphs" with a sentence that almost stopped it: "These things are but toys, to come amongst such serious observations." Though a lavish spender, he neither had a light mind nor *joie de vivre*, and he called poets liars. (What, then, were sycophants?)

The masque for the wedding evening had been by Campion, a versatile lyricist and composer who had given up law to become an M.D. Serviceable to men in power in the way that poets were expected to be, he had literally been the bagman in Sir Jervis Elwes's costly and ill-fated acquisition of the Lieutenancy of the Tower. Sir Jervis had been told that to secure the appointment "he must bleed," and Dr. Campion had been the go-between that carried the £1400, partly in gold, that Elwes paid.

Chamberlain said of the December 26 entertainment, "I hear little or no commendation of the masque made by the lords that night, either for device or dancing: only it was rich and costly." Campion proudly published it, nevertheless, with a Miltonic (or Jonsonian) motto in Latin that he preferred a fit audience, though few, to the ignorant multitude. There was the usual scene of ornate pillars that turn into men, the sea, moving ships and clouds, forest, garden, scallop shell. There was more than conventional reference to "Deformed Error," "Wing-tongued Rumor," and the "sorceresses" Curiosity and Credulity. The four known continents appeared, crowned, *"America* in a skin coat of the color of the juice of mulberries, on her head large round brims of many colored feathers." Most interesting was the criticism of homosexuality:

> Some friendship between man and man prefer,
> But I th'affection between man and wife.

> What good can be in life,
> Whereof no fruits appear?

> Set is that tree in ill hour,
> That yields neither fruit nor flower.

> How can man perpetual be,
> But in his own posterity?

Due allowance being made for what was conventional here too—the Renaissance literary *dubbio* of love versus friendship, the epithalamium tradition of praise of fecundity (pursued by Jonson eight years before), Dr. Campion was presumptuously lauding the change in—or broadening of—Carr's tastes, as well as taking a swipe (the "tree" was priapic) at unfatherly Essex. One can see the courtiers looking nervously in the direction of the King and holding back their "commendation."

Campion did not get into wonted lyric stride until the last speeches of the Squires.

The First Squire

All that was ever asked, but vow of Jove,
To bless a state with—Plenty, Honor, Love,
Power, Triumph, private pleasure, public peace,
Sweet springs and autumns filled with due increase,
All these and what good else thought can supply
Ever attend your triple Majesty.

The Second Squire

All blessings which the Fates, prophetic, sung
At Peleus' nuptials, and what ever tongue
Can figure more, this night and aye betide
The honored bridegroom and the honored bride.

All the Squires together

Thus speaks in us th'affection of our knights,
Wishing your health and myriads of goodnights.

Of the twelve noble Squires or maskers, four were Howards and another was a brother-in-law.

After that performance in the great Banqueting Hall of Whitehall (not yet redesigned by Inigo Jones), the couple were seen to bed in the usual bawdy way. The next day was Ben Jonson's turn. He offered prose, *A Challenge at Tilt*. The challenge was given by two cupids—Eros and Anteros—pages of the bride and groom. The tilting took place on New Year's Day, on each side ten gentlemen—one of them Lord Norris, resigned to monogamy. "There were two handsome chariots or pageants that brought in two Cupids, whose contention was whether were the truer, his or hers, each maintained by their champions, but the current and prize, you must think, ran on her side. The whole show (they say) was very fair and well set out." Hymen gave the dismissal:

Come, you must yield both. This is neither contention for you, nor time fit to contend. There is another kind of tilting would become Love better than this: to meet lips for lances, and crack kisses instead of staves—which there is no beauty here, I presume, so young but can fancy, nor so tender but would venture. Here is the palm for which you must strive; which of you wins this bough is the right and best Cupid.

December 29 brought another entertainment by Jonson. He tried his hand at brogue in *The Irish Masque at Court.* The first of four outlandish "footmen" got the hilarity off to a roaring start with, "For chreeshes sayk, phair ish te king? Phich ish he, an't be? Show me te shweet faish, quickly. By Got, o' my conshence, tish ish he! Ant tou be King Yamish, me name is Dennish." There was such suspenseful dialogue as,

DENNIS.	Peash, Dermock, here ish te king.
DERMOCK.	Phair ish te king?
DONNELL.	Phich ish te king?
DENNIS.	Tat ish te king.
DERMOCK.	Ish tat te king? God blesh him.

It was Suffolk's pleasant duty as Lord Chamberlain to authorize payment of £200 from the King's treasury for *The Irish Masque,* which might seem an exaggerated sum, but the audience was so smitten that it came back for a rerun on January 3. Chamberlain, conservative listener that he was, knew of those who regretted this "mimical imitation of the Irish" (Shakespeare had done it with Captain Macmorris in *Henry V*), it being "no time (as the case stands) to exasperate that nation by making it ridiculous."

But that was nothing compared to the feelings of Fanny, now at last Lady Somerset, on reading a wedding-day poem from Jonson to her "virtuous" husband that Somerset thought so much of that he copied it out on the fly-leaf of one of his books. Overbury's "The Wife" had just been printed for the first time—whether with malicious intent, no one can say. What blunderbuss Ben did—too ivory-towered to have heard court gossip—was indite (or indict):

> May she whom thou for spouse today dost take
> Out-be that Wife in worth thy friend did make.

It speaks wonders for the toughness of Carr's conscience that he did not omit this couplet, at least.

In fairness to the tactless poets it must be remembered how difficult it was to steer an innocuous course. Who could say anything at all without risk of offending? The parties were so vulnerable, including the absent but still to be reckoned with Earl of Essex. There were so very many tender toes. To boost love over male friendship was to reflect on Carr's relationship with the King and Overbury. Overbury was an altogether forbidden allusion, since he had died in the Tower, where he should not have (ugly rumors aside). Praise married love— and in this situation you sounded sarcastic. Mention virginity —and you seemed to be snickering over Lady Frances's inspection by the matrons, or her various legal statements. Speak of fertility—and Essex might come after you with drawn weapon. (He was continuing to give evidence of overwrought nerves. At a wedding a few weeks later he was narrowly prevented from dueling with a young knight who had already lost one hand in a duel.)

George Chapman got into so much trouble that he had to issue an apology or defense. Yet he meant well (as he did in dedicating his translation of the *Odyssey* to Somerset later in that same year of 1614). In direct address to Lady Frances he deplored (but might it not have been more tactful not to notice?) the "forked tongues" that "would fain your honor sting." He wanted "amongst others to offer up my poor mite to the honor of the late nuptials." The poem that he published, which was entered in the Stationer's Register on March 16, was subscribed to by Suffolk and Sir Julius Caesar. It was in his customary obscure style. But he was in hot water, beginning with the very title, *Andromeda Liberata, or the Nuptials of Perseus and Andromeda.* Liberata? Liberated from whom? In the myth, as in the poem, Andromeda was a princess bound to a rock, waiting to be gobbled up by a sea monster—but Perseus rescued her in the nick of time. "And now came roaring to the tied the tide," fanfared the poet, getting in homonymic paranomasia and Pearl White in one blow. It appeared inescapable, by all the laws of allegory, that Essex was either the rock or the monster. Chapman made matters worse by designating the rock "a barren rock." He tried to squirm free later by pointing out, in effect, that after all he had not said sterile, only barren.

> As if that could applièd be to man!
> O barren malice! Was it ever said
> A man was barren? or the burthen laid
> Of bearing fruit on man?

Still more unfortunate was a digression (for didactic purposes) into the myth of the love of Mars and Venus. For there was the triangle again, but full-fledged adultery this time, since Venus was married to Vulcan, who caught them in the act. Moreover, the cuckold was lame, or—shall we say, since he could not hold his wife—defectively masculine; in a word, impotent.

Chapman crowned his indelicacy by associating the Lady

Frances with homicide. Toward the end of his long poem he pushed the argument that a couple that wilfully do not have children are no better than murderers.

> For he no less a homicide is held
> That man to be born lets [hinders], than he that killed
> A man that is born. He is bolder far
> That present life reaves [takes], but he crueller
> That to the to-be born envies the light
> And puts their eyes out ere they have their sight.

Incidentally, Chapman was being hyperbolic about a fruit-less marriage. Accidentally, he was the first to send a public charge of "homicide"—he used the word three times in five lines—in the right direction. In *A Free and Offenceless Justification of a Lately Published and Most Maliciously Misinterpreted Poem entitled "Andromeda Liberata,"* he sought to still "the violent hubbub" with indignant prose followed by indifferent verse. He has Pheme (Rumor) quiz him:

> But who are those you reckon homicides
> In your racked poem? I swear that divides
> Your wondering reader far from your applause.

The Earl of Essex and his former Countess had their different reasons for not being amused. Carr, widely suspected of having let his friend rot, at least, also did not care to have that word "homicide" thrust under his nose again and again: twice more now in the so-called "offenceless justification." It looked as if he who had a poet working for him did not need an enemy.

Bacon, Campion, Jonson, Chapman, Donne: only John Donne came through with consistently good poetry, only he showed what fine flowers can spring from fetid soil. With a sickly wife and a large brood of children, he was assiduously seeking patronage and court preferment, not yet having realized—been forced to realize—that his destiny was the church. His humble, wildly adulatory letters currying Carr's favor make embarrassing reading today, but are not unusual for the time. He first applied to him through Lord Hay, who had been the Highland lad's original patron. Carr gave Donne money for something—probably for a brief in favor of the nullity that Donne prepared (Donne had been trained as a lawyer at Lincoln's Inn). "My poor study having lain that way," Donne told a friend, "it may prove possible that my weak assistance may be of use in this matter in a more serious fashion than an epithalamium." At the same time, "I deprehend in myself more than an alacrity, a vehemency to do service to that company, and so I may find reason to make rhyme." He was too sick to be on the scene in person that jolly season.

In the "Epithalamion," which was enclosed in an "Eclogue," Donne stared down the sneerers by spelling out that the bride and groom's confrontation on their wedding night was their first: "Their souls, though long acquainted they had been,/These clothes, their bodies, never yet had seen."

As was usual with this kind of poem, there were stanzas escorting the pair from the morning of the wedding to bedtime. Donne began by duly noting the season, "The Time of the Marriage": "Thou art reprieved, old year, thou shalt not die;/Though thou upon thy deathbed lie . . ." Every stanza ended with the rhyme-word "heart," which appropriately became "hearts" with the union of the last stanza:

The Good-Night

Now, as in Tullia's tomb one lamp burnt clear,
   Unchanged for fifteen hundred year,
    May these love lamps we here enshrine,
  In warmth, light, lasting, equal the divine.
     Fire ever doth aspire

> And makes all like itself, turns all to fire.
> But ends in ashes, which these cannot do,
> For none of these is fuel but fire too.
> There is joy's bonfire, then, where love's strong arts
> Make of so noble individual parts
> One fire of four inflaming eyes and of two loving hearts.

It would have been hard for any couple to deserve such poetry.

These poets were after fortune and fame, in that order. But there began to circulate underground, anonymous rhymes that cynically doubted the lady's claims to virtue. The satirists did not really get busy until the two publicly fell, but a brief sample is appropriate in this place.

> There was at court a lady of late
> That none could enter, she was so strait.
> But now with use she is grown so wide
> There is a passage for a Carr to ride.

Donne at the time of the wedding was suffering from eye trouble, blurred vision—symbolically enough. When he pictured the bride's day he would have had no use for a detail that came out at the trials for murder. On the very day of the happy consummation of all her dreaming and scheming, Fanny sent around by Mrs. Turner £20 to James Franklin—for services rendered.

After all, how can a careful wife go to bed with good conscience while the druggist's bill remains unpaid?

That Overbury, he had received at last his just desserts. He was only passingly on her mind. She and her new husband had acted like many a modern couple: tried each other out thoroughly before marriage. After all, you did not buy a pig in a poke, and a bride and a groom—who knows what defects might lurk underneath the silks, not discovered until too late? More's *Utopia* of a hundred years before had reduced the hazard by arranging that relatives on the opposite side be given a chance to inspect the sweethearts nude. She had gone through something like that herself, but at long—at longing—last the right Robin was legally hers. They felt they knew each other: the wedding night would hold no unpleasant surprises. Doubtless it did not: there were no surprises of any kind. Did that mean less thrill? Not necessarily, for it was, after all, their first night as man and wife, and she had gone to a lot of trouble to bring that about, more trouble than (she hoped) anybody would ever know. She might well have felt like a virgin bride, which her lovely hair down upon her shoulders had been saying all day she was, as she turned, in familiar but ever marvelous nakedness, to the only man who had ever proffered her a proper wedding night, her one true love, the love that she broke down all barriers to possess: Essex, Overbury, homosexuality, the Church. Paradise was now exquisitely official.

Murder Will Out

7

The next morning, James, according to his custom, visited the newlyweds in their bed. He made himself especially welcome by dangling a rich jewel before them—their morning-after present.

The wheel of fortune had swung them to their pinnacle. She had her legal lover, and the erstwhile Scots bumpkin was begged for favors by lords with royal blood in their veins. There was competition as to whose mansion would be graciously accepted as the Lady's temporary residence (and the King, before the wedding meats were cold, revisited her childhood home). At the Council table the new earl made a becoming show of modesty, "but afterwards the King resolveth all business with him alone, both those that pass in Council and many others wherewith he never maketh them acquainted." So reported the ambassador from Spain, Don Sarmiento, the future Count Gondomar. This was the time when it came to James's knowledge that some of his most trusted courtiers had been receiving pensions from that country. It was appalling to think what they had given or promised in return. On the list of well-paid double-dealers—as slowly spied out by the English ambassador at Madrid—were the Countess of Suffolk, the Lord Privy Seal Northampton, and even Queen Anne's first Lady of the Bedchamber. But the favorite was clear of this discouraging web of Roman Catholic intrigue, his hands were clean. Carr had not even accepted a £300 wedding present from Gondomar without asking the King's permission. He did take bribes, like the other Court officials, but never without conscientiously first telling his master. James, having a Privy Council he no longer trusted, turned all the more to this candid Scot. Here was one loyal servant. And a good husband: when Frances came down with an illness in May 1614, she had two men at her side: "such care and tender respect had of her by her Lord and the King."

A writer has conjectured that her conscience made her sick. The fact is, she had been wining and dining at Kensington in celebration of the wedding of her brother Thomas to one of the Cecils. She looks sufficiently self-possessed in a print of the time that depicts her stepping out with her new husband, he as close to her as her bumptious farthingale allows. Is it a sapphire with pendant pearl that crowns her forehead? It would have become a monarch and probably came from one.

Despite his manifold needs, that monarch was not voted any funds that spring by the so-called Addled Parliament, which was dissolved without having passed a single bill. Spanish gold had its attractions, as had been proven, and there was confidential talk of marrying Prince Charles, fourteen, to the Spanish Infanta. Carr began to follow the pro-Spanish line of the Howards. He quarreled with his former patron, Lord Hay, who favored a French match for Charles. The Earl of Somerset thought himself long past needing Hay, little dreaming there would ever come a time again when Hay could do him a favor. The useful maxim had not yet been uttered: "Better be nice to the people you meet on the way up, for they are the same people you meet on the way down." Carr was reveling in power, even though he did not know how to handle it and his schemes fell through both at home and abroad. Judging by the State Papers Domestic, that brief Parliament itself came and went only by the arrangement and consent of this virtual Prime Minister.

Northampton's intrigues that did much to separate King and Parliament were his last. Within a week of Parliament's end he was dead and Carr without a rudder. The old fox took the chance of having an operation for an abscess on his leg. Gangrene set in. This proved, it was said, that he was rotten to the core. "It should seem the matter was very venomous, when it so poisoned Felton, the surgeon that lanced it, that he hath ever since lain at death's door and the bell hath tolled for him twice or thrice: and it was very noisome all the room over for a day or two before he died." His last letter, conscious of his end, was singularly free of any religious reference. The only Lord mentioned was the favorite to whom he was writing about the disposition of various offices, with a view to keeping them within the family. He concluded:

Dear Lord, my spirits spend, and my strength decays and all that remains is, with my dying hand to witness, what my living heart did vow when it gave itself to your Lordship, as to the choice friend whom I did love for his virtues, and not court for his fortune. Farewell, noble Lord; and the last farewell in the last letter I look to write to any man. I presume confidently of your favor in these poor suits, and will be, both living and dying, your affectionate friend and servant,

H. NORTHAMPTON.

Against the grain of the usual practice, God's blessing was invoked neither for the writer nor for Carr. This seems deliberate and leathery worldliness rather than Macbeth's guilty and oversensitive inhibition: "But wherefore could I not pro-

nounce 'Amen'?/I had most need of blessing, and 'Amen'/
Stuck in my throat." The Howards had oily and capacious
throats.

In taking on the Howards, Carr also acquired their enemies. Sir Ralph Winwood, appointed Principal Secretary
after his donation of steeds for the wedding coach, proved uncooperative. He was Puritanically opposed to any dealings
with Spain. A coalition led by Archbishop Abbot and the
Herberts met to plot a course. The old idea of finding a new
Ganymede to replace the reigning one prevailed. In Abbot's
words, "We could have no way so good to effectuate that
which was the common desire as to bring in another in his
room, one nail (as the proverb is) being to be driven out by
another." Carr was past his bloom, within three years of
thirty, and moreover had been somewhat neglectful of the
King since his marriage—just as Overbury had predicted he
would be—and a growing petulance was noted. This was so
despite his July appointment to be Lord Chamberlain, suc-
ceeding his father-in-law, who became Lord Treasurer. The
Chamberlainship involved, the King pointed out, being close
to the royal person, and accordingly the choice fell on one
"whom, of all men living, he most cherished." The staff of
office was tendered in openly affectionate terms: "Lo! here,
friend Somerset." Eyes could not have been dry.

But dirt was flung in the painted eyes of the favorite. It
happened when members of the opposing faction were on
their way to a conclave. In Fleet Street, they passed a painter's
stall where Somerset's portrait was set out. The sallow features, the watery blue eyes, the sandy mustachio and goatee:
the Protestant lords found them resistible, and one of them
instructed his servant to scoop up mud and let the public
know who merited what.

They were priming for their monarch someone five years

younger, and not Scotch, tall and graceful and slim-calved, with sparkling dark eyes and hair: a change, but not too rugged a one; the King could not stand such hard burly types as Sir Walter Ralegh, who was depressingly aggressive. George Villiers had hands and feet "specially effeminate and curious [well made]." The second son of a Leicestershire knight, deceased, and a mother as pushing as the Countess of Suffolk, he was seen in threadbare clothes at a horse race. Connoisseurs sensed his potential instantly. Properly polished, here was the supremely magnetic new nail to drive out the rusty one.

While the King was on progress an introduction was arranged, in August, that had consequences even far into the reign of Charles I. Court astronomers bent their quills to trace the rising star. Fenton wrote in September that although a youth named Villiers "begins to be in favor with His Majesty, yet all things are absolutely done by one man and he more absolute than ever he was. Neither his father-in-law, with whom he keeps good quarter, nor any man else dare touch him." By November, Chamberlain was referring to "the new favorite," even while saying that his "fortune . . . seems to be at a stand." But the twenty-two-year-old aspirant, his "old black suit, broken out in places," discarded for finery bought by such sponsors as William Herbert, the third Earl of Pembroke, had been procured the "appropriate" office of Cupbearer to His Majesty. Carr blocked his becoming Gentleman of the Bedchamber, thrusting a bastard kinsman into a vacancy. Carr smelt danger, a plot against him. In the words of Sir Henry Wotton, "This was quickly discovered by him who was still as yet in some possession of the King's heart. For there is nothing more vigilant, nothing more jealous, than a favorite, especially towards the waning time."

John Donne, who had so catered to Carr in prose and

verse, was wondering whether the Archbishop was aware of a sycophancy he now saw as unfortunate. In December "Mr. Villiers" begins to figure in Donne's letters. "They are preparing for a masque of gentlemen, in which Mr. Villiers is." As to "whether Mr. Villiers have received from the King any additions of honor or profit: without doubt he hath yet none." "I have something else to say of Mr. Villiers, but because I hope to see you here shortly, and because new additions to the truths or rumors which concern him are likely to be made by occasion of this masque, I forbear." Jonson was the poet of the masque in which the suave young man (whose education included Paris and a disappointing love affair) demonstrated he could outdance Carr. George was nimble, George was quick, and dangerously endowed with a mind as well as a body.

The fresh young cupbearer, as he went about his pleasant duties, seemed to have a veritable halo. His master took to calling him "Steenie," from a fancied resemblance to a picture of St. Stephen, the first martyr. As a benedict, it was unreasonable of Carr to be jealous. By sulking or making scenes he invited the loss of all he had, which he might otherwise have retained. He should have striven to continue to earn the monarch's favor—or should have withdrawn with good grace and therefore in good graces. James never dropped any responsive friend abruptly. He protested there had been no diminution in his affection for Robin.

Used to power, fancying he had only to complain to be heeded, Carr made things difficult, for rival, for master and for himself. What influence had Fanny on the situation in the winter of 1614–15? Was her husband irritable because he loved her, and wanted to go on riding the crest so that she might shine beside him, queen of courtiers? Or had he sunk into disillusion or even knowledge of crime? Did the head reel before abysses that the runner had been made aware of but to which the smirking Court observers as yet lacked a proper clue? It was mostly the common folk, always ready to suspect their betters, who continued to entertain doubts about Overbury's death. The knight's ghost, in the form of four reprintings of his works, traversed the land. Mrs. Turner had a long and worried meeting with Weston in a tavern. Carr retrieved through Sir Robert Cotton (an antiquary with a taste for politicking) his letters to Northampton. A servant of Overbury's also yielded up some letters.

Unrestrained by any wise head, Carr lashed out, feuding like a Highlander. Since his portrait had been soiled, he would retaliate on the white suit of the cupbearer: one of his retainers "accidentally" dropped a bowl of soup on it. Villiers jumped up and struck the server. The Earl of Somerset grimly demanded the exaction of the penalty for brawling in the King's presence. According to a law dating from Henry VIII, Villiers's blow made him subject to the loss of his right hand. It would be the Lord Chamberlain's agreeable function "to be ready at the place and time of execution, as shall be appointed, as is aforesaid, to sear the stump when the hand is stricken off." He really expected the King to give this order. When the King merely laughed, Carr tried to arrange to have his rival ambushed. But this move was no more successful than Fanny's first move against Overbury.

"Strange streams of unquietness, passion, fury," "licentious freedom," "dogged sullen behavior," "mad fits"—the Earl of Essex and other observers would have thought such phrases no more than a just description of Fanny. They in fact come from a letter James wrote to Carr in January 1615. The King could sound like a neglected lover, too. "I leave out of this reckoning your long creeping back and withdrawing yourself from lying in my chamber, notwithstanding my many hundred times earnest soliciting you to the contrary." What Carr did now in that chamber was to burst in "at unseasonable hours" with furious demands and complaints, "bereaving" the monarch of his rest. James could see no reason for this paranoia, and so stated in his preamble. "First, I take God, the searcher of all hearts, to record that in all the time past of idle talk, I never knew nor could, out of any observation of mine, find any appearance of any such Court faction as you have apprehended, and so far was I ever from overseeing or indirectly feeling of it (if I had apprehended it) as, I protest to God, I would have run upon it with my feet, as upon fire, to have extinguished it, if I could have seen any sparkle of it." This hyperbolic assurance was inaccurate, but James must be given credit for patience, a patience that included sitting down and inditing more than two thousand heartfelt words in an effort to straighten out his still dear servant. And this was neither his first such letter nor his last.

The favorite had objected that a previous epistle was not couched in sufficiently affectionate terms. The King mildly pointed out that it was for Majesty "to follow my own style, which I thought the comeliest." He had sought to still "idle talk" by such shows of favor as installing one of Carr's kinsmen in the royal bedchamber ("the fashion thereof being done in a needless bravery of the Queen"), another in Charles's chamber. "Do not all courtesies and places come through your office as chamberlain, and rewards through your father-in-law as treasurer? Do not you two (as it were) hedge in all the Court with a manner of necessity to depend upon you?" But all the King got of late was railing, "yea even to rebuke me more sharply and bitterly than even my masters durst do." It would certainly be unfortunate for this bullying Scot to raise memories of another, the dour dominie George Buchanan, who had had no scruples about applying his ferule to the boy King whenever he faltered in Latin or conduct and who, on one occasion, when asked by Lady Mar, "How dare you lay hands on the Lord's Anointed?" answered shortly, "Madam, I have whipped his arse: you can kiss it if you like." Let there be no gross reversal of roles, no threat "that you mean not so much to hold me by love as by awe, and that you have me so far in your reverence as that I dare not offend you or resist your appetites." Carr could yet be forgiven, his recent transgressions sponged, but the King would never forgive himself "for raising a man so high, as might make him presume to pierce my ears with such speeches." One hears the raised voice in scene after scene, scarcely distinguishable from a shrew's. Danish Anne was less trouble. The attendants could not help but know, and this was not the least of James's humiliations, "their observation of my sadness after your parting, and want of rest."

So another beautiful friendship slowly died. Carr continued to be intolerable, whether from security or from insecurity. In March, the King sought diversion at Cambridge, where some English and Latin comedies were presented. The occasion was very much a Howard occasion, Suffolk being now Chancellor of the University in succession to Northampton. The Lord Treasurer invited no ladies except Howards—the Lady Frances and her sister and her mother. It seemed a calculated insult to the Queen. The opposition decided it was time to enlist Anne on their side. Carr and Cotton were negotiating a Spanish match for Charles, a revolting thought to any true-blue Englishman.

Archbishop Abbot had noticed that "the King made it a practice never to admit any to nearness about himself but such an one as the Queen should commend to him; that if the Queen afterwards being ill-treated, should complain of this dear one, he might make his answer, 'It is along of your-

self, for you were the party that commended him unto me.' "
Anne had been regretting Carr for about eight years, but that
did not mean she looked forward to Villiers. "My Lord," she
warned the Archbishop, "you and the rest of your friends
know not what you do. I know your master better than you
all; for if this young man be once brought in, the first persons
that he will plague must be you that labor for him; yea, I
shall have my part also. The King will teach him to despise
and hardly entreat us all, that he may seem to be beholden to
none but himself." Telling the story years later, Archbishop
Abbot here interjected, "Noble Queen! how like a prophetess
or oracle did you speak!"

However, the Queen was persuaded to go along with a
carefully staged advancement for George on St. George's Day,
April 23, 1615. On waking up that morning the King was appalled to see his wife advancing upon him with a naked
sword. Before he could cry out she knelt to urge that this was
the ideal moment to dub handsome George, who was waiting
outside, Sir George—and make him a Gentleman of the Bedchamber. Carr, also hovering at the door and glaring at his
clever enemies—the cupbearer, Abbot, Pembroke—sent in
word that Villiers should be made a Groom only. Abbot
promptly countermanded with a plea for the higher position.
Delighted at the echo of his own wishes, James bestowed the
honors the rival faction requested. Sir George Villiers now
had the right, nay the duty, of access to the King, and his
pension was set at £1000 per year.

James could have quoted the first line of a recently published sonnet: "Two loves I have, of comfort and despair."
George—with his remarkable delicacy of mind and body—
was turned to more and more for comfort. He, in turn, was
grateful for that which he received. Robin meant despair, and
showed it. If it had been true that the more the Earl had the

more he wanted, he was far from simmering down in defeat. As if the spirit of Overbury had entered him, as if he had assumed his dead friend's self-destructive *hybris,* he went on to badger the King unremittingly over two offices that Northampton had held. He demanded that he be confirmed as Warden of the Cinque Ports, and that Bishop Bilson, who had been so pliable in the annulment case, be appointed Lord Privy Seal. In July the former office went to Lord Zouche, and Bilson was sent packing, James saying "that he thought well of him, and perhaps meant to bestow the place upon him; but he would take his own time, and not do it at other men's instance, so that he should do well to go home, and when there were use of him, he would send for him." (A neat seventeenth-century example of "Don't call me—I'll call you"!) The old sycophant lived long enough to see "the place" go to another man.

"Other men's instance"—this was the unkindest cut, but Carr had done nothing lately to deserve anything else. When his King went on summer progress, he was not by his side. Nothing came from him but frantic, importunate letters. In July, James put him in his place much more coolly—and briefly—than he had in January. "I have been needlessly troubled this day with your desperate letters. You may take the right way, if you list, and neither grieve me nor yourself. No man's nor woman's credit is able to cross you at my hands, if you pay me a part of that you owe me. But how you can give over that inward affection and yet be a dutiful servant, I cannot understand that distinction. Heaven and earth shall bear me witness that, if you do but the half your duty unto me, you may be with me in the old manner, only by expressing that love to my person and respect to your master that God and man crave of you, with a hearty and feeling penitence of your bypast errors."

Tactless the Earl's methods, tactless his not accompanying the King, but there was a new reason for that. Lady Frances became pregnant in March. The couple summered at Rotherfield Greys, the home of her brother-in-law, Lord Knollys, the one who had married her older sister Elizabeth. Thus the Howard clannishness was manifest once again. Greys, near Henley-on-Thames with its swans, was a pleasant place for those who brought a peaceful spirit to it. "The world," according to that invaluable barometer, Chamberlain, was skeptical that the former Countess of Essex was really on the way to motherhood. It was harsh, and not very consistent, but in a way just, that, having doubted her virginity, they now had no faith in her maternity. The classification of women as either courtesans or mothers is as old as Lilith and Eve. Either courtesans know more about birth control, or God denies them increase. It is a fact that none of Shakespeare's villains have children. How could *she*?

By now her husband felt enough anxiety to have a form drawn up that protected him with the King's pardon for any crimes with which he might be charged, including that of being accessory before the fact to murder. Statesmen going back to Wolsey had used this device of a general pardon against the time when, on their relinquishing office or falling out of favor, their enemies might bark and bite. James was perfectly willing that this be given the Great Seal, but his Solicitor-General and his Lord Chancellor objected. The latter, stout old Baron Ellesmere, declared that no man should be put beyond the reach of the law in this sweeping way. He infuriated James with repeated refusal to affix the seal, saying he would himself have to be pardoned for participating in such an outrage. The King stalked out of the Council chamber. The pardon remained unsealed. Carr had only aroused speculation as to his motive and given proof of how insecurely he walked on those legs (no longer the comeliest) that had tried to go independently of Overbury. Chamberlain, who belonged to Winwood's party, offered his usual keen comment: "some grow downward every day, their own courses indeed doing them more harm than all their enemies could do, and it is sign they fear themselves when they procure such kind of·pardons. . . ."

On August 15 he was given one last chance for reconciliation. He was briefly with the King at Lulworth Castle in the South Downs of Dorset: at the monarch's bidding Sir Humphrey May propositioned Carr: "My Lord, Sir George Villiers will come to you to offer his service and desire to be your creature; and therefore refuse him not—embrace him—and your Lordship shall still stand a great man, though not the sole favorite." James was still the peacemaker. He spared no pains to avoid scenes, whether with wife or friends. There had been enough sulking. All should live in happy harmony. But May had something of a reputation as a hypocrite, and it was not a point in his favor in the Earl's eyes that he had taken into his employ a servant of the late Sir Thomas's that the "great man," no mean hand at hypocrisy himself, had turned away. Carr remained stonily unresponsive. He was beyond dissimulation now. His demeanor was not difficult to decipher when the new favorite entered a half hour later and went through with his set speech. "My Lord, I desire to be your servant and your creature and I shall desire you to take my Court preferment under your favor, and your Lordship shall find me as faithful a servant unto you as ever did serve you." Was he mocking? Was that a sneer on the impertinent boyish face? Carr could not control himself, or did not want to. He had once snapped at Overbury, "I will be even with you for this"—and he had been, rather more so than was meant at the time. Now, "My Lord returned this quick and short answer: 'I will none of your service, and you shall none of my favor. I will, if I can, break your neck, and of that be confident.' " This was literal, as one or two moves against the upstart had fully proved.

But with this final show of obstinacy the neck that he needed to watch out for was his own—and that of his dear wife. The axe was rising to fall, just as it had fallen, for one of numerous historical instances, on that Howard, Anne Boleyn, who actually measured her neck with her slender fingers and pretended to rejoice that, as it was but "little," the executioner could not possibly bungle his job, as, alas, some executioners did, having to strike more than once. (It was, finally, her honor to be beheaded by a sword.) Mary Queen of Scots required three blows, though no man had ever called her thick-necked. James had taken no action to save his mother. What would he do for convicted murderers who were out of favor?

Now that everyone could see which way the wind was blowing, rumors about Overbury's death could afford to increase and multiply. They had become more persistent all summer. As mentioned, by July Mrs. Turner was scared enough to meet with Weston, the ex-underkeeper and purveyor of poisons, in order to get their stories straight in case of examination. The waning favorite decided he would have to be friendly, after all, with Lawrence Davies, the Overbury servant whom he had refused to do anything for. He asked for letters and copies of letters that had passed between him and the late knight. He received about thirty. Was that all there were? In October, he made a payment of thirty pounds to find out. "I have heretofore been moved to retain thee, but out of sight, out of mind, and so I forgot thee; but now I will remember thee. Hast thou any more writings?" This was crude, and Davies would have had to be exceedingly stupid not to realize that holding back some material could lead to still more money for him. Not that thirty pounds was not a substantial sum (twice what Milton was to receive for *Paradise Lost,* for instance)—it was precisely that, the sudden generosity, that gave to think.

William Reeve, the apothecary's boy who had administered to Overbury that last deadly clyster of mercury sublimate and then fled abroad, took ill in Flushing and felt himself to be on his deathbed. The fate of his soul depended on his unburdening himself of his crime, which he did to a representative of the English envoy at Brussels. The ambassador sailed the Channel on business which included the conveying of this information to Winwood. Reeve recovered and failed to carry repentance so far as to put himself within the rough grasp of British law. But Elwes was still Lieutenant of the Tower and hoping for further advancement. Winwood saw a cunning way of getting him to talk. He dropped a remark to a mutual friend, Lord Shrewsbury, "There lies a kind of heavy imputation on him about Overbury's death. I could wish he would clear himself and give some satisfaction in that point." That was the bait: "clear himself." Thereafter Sir Jervis, the perfect headwaiter, ready to do anything to please his betters, could climb the ladder. It appears that the Lieutenant and the dour black-suited Secretary did not have in mind the same ladder.

Shrewsbury and Winwood gave a little party for Elwes. He drank and he flowed with answers to questions, while protesting that he really knew very little. When Winwood had pumped him enough and they were saying a cordial good-bye, the Secretary asked for a brief account in writing. It would all be in a good cause. Elwes obliged. Winwood took the interesting composition to the King.

With a due regard for appearances, public and official appearances, James knew what he had to do. An investigation would have to be conducted. The King's justice must be maintained. He demanded of Elwes a more thorough account. This the Lieutenant delivered in writing on September 10.

"May it please Your Majesty," he began, and declared he welcomed the opportunity of "the clearing of my own poor credit in the world." He told of Weston's poisoned phial and of "my Lord of Somerset's tenderness towards Sir Thomas Overbury, who sent him tarts and pots of jelly." Lest this sound sarcastic, he added that the underkeeper had not named "any as an actor in this business but Mrs. Turner." Elwes ended with Weston's admission about the poisoned clyster. "I have herein obeyed your Majesty's command and have eased myself of a heavy burthen; for malice have I none, nor other respect in the world. I have set down the truth, peradventure not the whole truth; but I have set down whatsoever is fundamental, and will be ready faithfully to answer whatsoever shall be demanded of me." "Not the whole truth"? The royal eyebrows went up. Lady Frances was not mentioned, but there was enough here to hang Weston and Mrs. Turner, for a start. Elwes had also, naïvely, incriminated himself as an accessory after—and very likely before—the fact.

Bulldog Coke was set to work, Lord Chief Justice Sir Edward Coke. The King still exhibited an open mind, but that included not separating husband and wife in this affair, since the Lady's reasons for wanting to get rid of Overbury were as strong as anyone's. "There be two things in this cause to be tried and the verity can be in but one of them. First: whether My Lord of Somerset and My Lady were the procurers of Overbury's death; or, that this imputation hath been by some practised to cast an aspersion on them. I would first have you diligently inquire of the first: and if you find them clear, then I would have you as carefully look after the other, to the intent such practices may be discovered and not pass with impunity." Coke diligently inquired to the extent of more than 300 examinations taken down in his own hand.

Carr, having no one better to advise him than Cotton, the antiquary, behaved foolishly. He pressed again for a general pardon. He may well by now have been let in on the truth by his terrified wife (assuming he was not a partner in her crime). There could be some gallantry in his attempts to destroy evidence, such as suspicious-sounding letters, and shore up his legal position, his and hers. But the carelessness of all the parties had been massive. They obviously expected what was buried, however lightly, to pass into oblivion: who would dare to paw at the dirt? It was outrageous that a man two years in his grave did not stay there. The suspects, whether high or low, ignominiously failed to be clever when, now, they most needed to be: no grace, no wits under pressure. Coke gathered all too much too fast.

On the night of September 27, at an hour when good people were in bed, one of Mrs. Turner's maids escorted Franklin into Somerset's chambers in London by the Cockpit. Lady Somerset and Mrs. Turner were there, and the candlelight etched the panic in their faces.

"Weston hath been sent for by a pursuivant," the Countess blurted, "and he hath confessed all, and we shall all be hanged. But on your life," she warned, "do not you confess that you brought any poison to me, or to Mrs. Turner. For if you do, you shall be hanged, for I will not hang for you."

Mrs. Turner cut in, "I will not hang for you both."

Fanny disappeared into a bedroom, as if to consult with her husband. On her return she remarked that in all likelihood the examining lord would cunningly dangle a pardon before Franklin in exchange for his confession.

"But believe him not, for they will hang thee when all is done."

Franklin had been through all this sort of talk years before in response to rumors that he had poisoned his wife. All hoped—the now "factious crew"—by mentioning the unmentionable to fend it off.

Imagine a *lady*, an Earl's daughter, in such company! What had she descended to? They were all threatened by a rope. It should have bound them together. In a way it did: thus, their meeting. In another way they were spluttering their independence of each other, as they prepared to scamper to different holes. She would not hang for them. They would not hang for her. They had reached the limits of class obligations and class differences. What they had in common was a well-justified fear for their lives. And that was what was scattering them, as each clutched his still intact neck—not for one moment to be confounded with anyone else's neck—and ran.

As a consequence of Weston's successive revelations under intensive interrogation, Ann Turner was placed under arrest on October 1 in the home of Alderman Jones. Frances, in Blackfriars, could not go to her, but she sent her steward every day with presents and exhortations. Mrs. Turner was denying everything, but the two women had no means of learning what progress Coke was making elsewhere. They could only cower, and tremble, and wait. Finally, the Alderman found out about these daily communications, and not even the attempted bribe of a piece of plate could lead him to countenance them. On the contrary, he told all to the King—information which, of course, did nothing to make the Somersets look innocent.

On the unlucky day of Friday, October 13, Carr encountered Coke on the road between Royston—where the King was hunting as usual—and London. The erstwhile favorite was symbolically leaving his master's side again, in order to learn the worst and subvert evidence if he could, and the judge had by now uncovered so much that he felt the need of asking the King for a Commission to be set up to strengthen his legal hand, since the high and mighty were being implicated. With grim satisfaction, Coke told what *his* errand was, and listened unmoved to Carr's arguments that he should turn back. Next day they met going in opposite directions on the same road, but this time gave "nothing more than a mutual salute." Coke had obtained his Commission, and left word that the Lord Chamberlain would have to make himself available for examination. Carr flatly protested he would not go and asked James to back him.

"Nay, man," the King told him, "if Coke sends for me, I must go."

Their parting was, on the surface, touching. Said James, "For God's sake, when shall I see thee again? On my soul, I shall neither eat nor sleep until you come again." Carr swore he would return the next day, despite everything. They hugged on the stairs, the King at last saying, "For God's sake, give thy lady this kiss for me."

But it was the kiss of Judas, for when Carr had driven away, the King muttered, "Now the de'il go with thee, for I shall never see thy face more!" At least he said, by three accounts, the second part of this sentence. It is Roger Coke, Sir Edward Coke's grandson, who luridly brings in the Devil (and Wilson has the King secretly smiling). Whatever our distaste for slobbering and crafty James, these last embraces may have been sincere, or sentimental, a regretful, memory-filled farewell to a now impossible friend.

On October 16 the Earl, abusing his authority under the Privy Seal, sent a pursuivant, a constable and a smith after some papers that had long been locked in a trunk in the house of the master of Richard Weston's son. The bundles were brought to Carr in his chambers by the Cockpit, but the constable became suspicious and notified Coke.

The next day the Commission ordered the Somersets to be confined in separate houses in London. That night the Earl at last committed to the flames his letters to Northampton. Some other damaging writings that he had entrusted to Cotton were not as safely laid away as they both hoped.

On Trial

8

One by one, her accomplices were pronounced guilty and hanged. Trial procedure at that period was heavily weighted in favor of the prosecution. What was the use of putting someone on trial if he—or she—was not guilty? Preliminary examination had already determined the guilt, and all that Coke now expected of the deferential juries was formal acquiescence in the conclusions he had already drawn, public approbation of his zeal in behalf of the Crown. This champion of the common law and future upholder of the privileges of Parliament showed a minimum of regard for the rights of such as Weston, Franklin, Elwes, Anne Turner. As they stood before the bar they had no defense counsel—standard, that. Standard, too, was not knowing exactly what the indictment was until it was too late to work out an answer to it. But—even beyond the ordinary—Coke bullied them, threatened them with torture, and left them to languish in confinement until they gave the "right" answers. Hearsay evidence was used against them, and sometimes it was hearsay of hearsay (as the legal writer Andrew Amos pointed out in his critique of 1846, *The Great Oyer of Poisoning*—which was what Coke called the case, an "oyer" referring to a criminal trial and having some echo of the Sergeant Crier's call at the beginning of sessions, *Oyez, Oyez,* "Hear ye, hear ye"). Innocence would have proved slight shield for a prisoner as uneducated, scared and reduced to stammering incoherence as Weston, or as blandly unaware of the trapdoor as Elwes. No wonder that a recent popular and on the whole admiring biography of Coke passes over this episode in his career fast. Even at the time, a legate from Florence was appalled at the English methods. "This seems a very strange kind of justice," he wrote back home, "that the accused is not permitted to have a lawyer to defend him, nor even to be able to produce documents or testimonies in his favor, but has to depend on himself to speak for himself against the charges of the more expert advocates of the court, who *are* able to use against him testimonies and writings." But Coke repaid, even though he was unaware of, such foreign criticism by emphasizing repeatedly that "this damned crime of poisoning" was most un-English—in fact, to make no bones about it, it was a peculiarly popish and Italian trick.

Was Coke being Prosecutor or Judge when he gave the charge, in the first of the trials, Weston's, at the Guildhall October 19. The Lord Chief Justice took some whacks at well-born culprits. The truth must be brought out, "notwithstanding the greatness of any that upon their evidence should appear guilty." Adultery, Coke noted, was "most often the begetter of" murder. He did not hesitate to mention the dereliction of one of the Lord's anointed, David's disposing of Uriah, the husband who stood in the way of his acquiring the wife he had already gotten with child. The analogy was imperfect, like all historical analogies, but it did serve as a reminder of how old sin was, even in the best of families. As another official assailant, naming names, was to pronounce later in the day, that particular Howard daughter was "a dead and rotten branch, which being lopt off, the noble tree, meaning that noble family, would prosper the better." *That* analogy was all too vivid; some in the crowded hall gasped at its boldness.

She was not there to turn pale. The day before Fanny had been moved from one house to another, to stricter custody. Unrestrained her whole life, she kept trying to elude the legal watchdogs, not by gross bodily escape—she herself was big with child—but by messengers and forbidden communications. She was not supposed to be in touch with her husband, but she was. They despatched someone to find out what was the latest that Mrs. Turner was saying, but the sheriff turned the man away and tattled to the Commissioners. That prompted the tougher confinement for both, especially as Somerset had succeeded in burning some letters and tampering with—as by changing the dates of—others. As McElwee chides, the two "behaved throughout like spoilt children, incapable of grasping that rules and orders which governed ordinary people could ever be strictly applied to themselves." The new quarters for the Countess were found to suffer from "too many doors and too few keys." A third change was in the offing. Being a lady, she had to have six women and several man servants, although she was not in possession of money for their wages. Her reluctant jailer, Sir William Smith, came to feel like a hotelkeeper whose mounting bills would forever go superciliously unpaid. Carr was now being "kept"—no bad word—by that Dean of Westminster who had hymned the praises of all the Howards at the wedding. That clan still did some sticking together. Although her parents lapsed into embarrassed silence, her brother Henry persisted in attempts to see her. One servant was confident he could approach the father or the sister, Lady Knollys, for money for firewood.

In the midst of much funking someone apparently got in

a word of legal advice to Richard Weston. "Indictment being read, he was demanded if he were guilty of the felony, murdering, and poisoning, as aforesaid, Yea or No. To which he answered, doubling his speech, 'Lord have mercy upon me! Lord have mercy upon me!' But being again demanded, he answered, 'Not Guilty.' " This contradicted confessions that had been wrung from him in six interrogations between September 27 and October 6, but was not surprising. However, he handled the next question with the cunning of the cornered. In those days the accused had to be asked how he would be tried, and was supposed to answer, "By God and my country." The "my country" part acknowledged the right of the court to try him. But Weston would answer only, "By God," refusing to complete the formula.

God was not available. The judges remonstrated with the prisoner for an hour. A crowd had gone to considerable trouble to find or purchase seats or standing room for a trial, and there could be no trial if this stubbornness persisted. Such an evasion, a frustration of justice and particularly Chief Justice Coke, would be a disgrace to everybody, from the King down. Moreover it would be a form of suicide on Weston's part. For the penalty for refusing to plead was pressing to death—*peine forte et dure*. It was spelled out to Weston exactly what would happen to him. First he was to be pressed, weights laid upon him "which were by little and little to be increased." If he somehow survived this torture, he was next to be left exposed naked to the cold. Lastly, "he was to be preserved with the coarsest bread that could be got, and water out of the next sink or puddle to the place of execution, and that day he had water he should have no bread, and that day he had bread he should have no water; and in this torment he was to linger as long as nature could linger out, so that oftentimes men lived in that extremity eight or nine days." The eternal judgment, the confident interpreters explained, would deem that the mortal sin of suicide. Some chose this end to preserve for their heirs their estates, which, if they were convicted in a regular trial, were confiscated. But what property had this servant?

He may have had in mind his son William. The boy was implicated because he had borne from Fanny to his father in the Tower the sinister phial that Elwes had thrown out. If Richard Weston was not convicted of the principal act of poisoning, none of the accessories could even be tried. Coke saw the Somersets and all intermediate culprits slipping through the fingers that had groped so zestfully, with such meticulous labor and zeal, for their throats. He was outraged at "a Machiavellian trick to save certain accessories" (that is, the Somersets, by whose fall he expected to rise; in fact, he was going to coerce his stepdaughter into marrying Villiers's feeble-minded brother).

But all Weston would say was, "Welcome by the grace of God!" It was as if he were experiencing another religious fit, like the one Elwes induced on the evening of the phial.

Chief Justice Coke proceeded to have the evidence read notwithstanding. This was illegal, as no one for the moment was on trial. It was no better than libel. Writing to the King that night, the Chief Justice gave two reasons for a flagrant breach that some were quick to interpret as mere court intrigue—in all senses of "court"—on the side of Villiers. The evidence had to be set out, "as well to inform our consciences, as to satisfy the multitude." Bread and circuses. That avid crowd—who could dare to offer them nothing? When their hungry ears had been filled, there was an adjournment from Thursday to the following Monday. Meanwhile, Weston, his hands and feet manacled, would be worked on.

During the weekend he was subjected to the lengthy per-

suasions of an alderman, a sheriff, and two bishops. It was all
"for the saving of his soul." He was even offered, most ir-
regularly, a Roman Catholic confessor, any that the jails held,
but replied, "If the Bishop of London and the Bishop of Ely
cannot persuade me, neither Jesuit nor priest shall do it." It
was flattering, all this attention, and he was worth every iota
of it, since if he did not save his soul as admonished, all would
escape, never forgetting that the only other possible principal,
the apothecary's assistant, William Reeve, who had administered the last poison "into the guts of said Sir Thomas," was
in hiding abroad. Lady Somerset, for example, could not be
convicted as a principal, since she had not personally administered the poison. She could only be convicted as an accessory (though the capital punishment was the same), following
the conviction of a principal. The two bishops had been on
opposite sides in the annulment case, but, famous preachers,
each unstintingly gave two hours of private eloquence to preserve this sinner for the hangman.

The Church prevailed. Back before "the jury of life and
death" on Monday, Weston answered the obligatory question with "By God and my country." Either the fear of God
was in him or he had certain worldly hopes. Poisoning was
very difficult to prove, and he was now admitting nothing. If
he himself did not *know* he had poisoned Overbury, how
could anyone else know? Simple man, he imagined suspicion
was not enough. But the Lord Chief Justice had a surprise
for him. In his exhortation to the jury, after the charges had
been read again, Coke explained they "were not to expect
precise proof . . . showing how impossible it were to convict a poisoner who useth not to take any witnesses to the
composing of his sibber sauces." So the evidence was circum-
stantial, or based on hearsay. Then "Weston was demanded
what he could say for himself? Who, although he had before

confessed all his examinations to be true [so says the official account], yet he seemed to excuse himself in a kind of ignorance or unawares." By modern ideas of justice the burden of proof was on the other side. The question should have been, Had the State proved him guilty? rather than, Had he proved himself innocent? It was immaterial how much the prisoner stammered. But the jury quickly found for the prosecution.

Before condescending to sentence the prisoner, Coke made a speech to satisfy "the auditory." It is interesting that he should have felt this necessary. He granted the existence of skeptics who "went about so untruly and wickedly to slander the course of justice." In his speech the Chief Justice alternately flattered and bullied. He praised God and flattered the people, giving unctuous expression to the *vox populi vox Dei* equation: "he observed the finger of God in the manifestation and bringing to light of this matter, having slept two years, being shadowed with greatness [the Somersets], which cannot overcome the cry of the people." But he thundered against the evidently tempting notion that the charges were trumped up and political, a conspiracy of one Court faction against another.

Weston had been quoted as having told the sheriff, "He hoped he would not make a net to catch little birds, and let the great ones go." Coke, shifting species, in effect thanked the prisoner for being the self-obliterating instrument by which "the great flies shall not escape, but receive their punishment." Maybe what Coke really said was "great fliers."

Two days later Weston was carried to Tyburn, the place of execution in the center of London now marked by a plaque near the Marble Arch. The last scene was marred by the intrusion of a group of horsemen who pressed their way to the scaffold and insisted on asking the condemned whether or not he had poisoned Overbury. These knights were mostly of the Howard faction, but Sir John Lidcote, Overbury's brother-in-law, was there too, expecting a definitive confession of guilt as the others looked for a denial. Overbury's former underkeeper, the rope around his neck as he stood in the cart, turned to the sheriff, appropriately named Goare, and reproached him: "You promised me I should not be troubled at this time." Shouts went up. The crucial question was repeated. But Weston gave no clear satisfaction. His last words were: "I die not unworthily. My Lord Chief Justice hath my mind under my hand [that is, sworn statements], and he is an honorable and just judge." These must rank among the most remarkable last respects on record, a triumph of repentance—or the class system (thirty years before the Battle of Naseby). For this ragged and illiterate servant, who could identify shops and taverns only by the pictures on their signs, the felt gap between him and the Lord Chief Justice, that awesome embodiment of the dignity and the power of the Crown, was such that my Lord Coke *must be* right, even if he was wrong. But within a generation came the first of the modern revolutions that narrowed the distance between the King and the commonest of his commoners to—shall we say —a pike. Did Richard Weston's son, William, like the Earl of Essex, find satisfaction by taking up arms against Charles Stuart?

Those prerevolutionaries, the intruding skeptics, the factionists on horseback, were severely dealt with in Star Chamber. Three were fined and sent to the Tower for a year as a lesson to all who might be inclined to cast doubt on the King's justice.

Two days after the sixty-year-old body of Weston was left dangling, the Lady Frances was moved to a third house. Her pregnancy insured a postponement of her trial, but there was small comfort in that. Any aplomb she may have had vanished with the first execution. The law really was taking Overbury's death seriously. She was by contemporary report "very pensive, silent, and much grieved." She was resolved to cheat the hangman, one way or another. The King ordered a special watch to be kept lest she miscarry, "either by her own wilfulness, or by the malice of any other." "Laying her hand on her belly," she told Smith her jailor, "If I were rid of this burden, it is my death that is looked for, and my death they shall have." The moment the baby was born she would swathe herself in a cold wet towel and that would be the end.

Her husband was shut up in the Tower on November 2nd. The same day Coke examined a waterman who admitted he had delivered letters to Fanny in one of her present desperate flings at information. He was yet to be paid, unlike a messenger who had been caught five days earlier nosing for news of Mrs. Turner's revelations.

Anne Turner, the next to go on trial, was terribly easy to identify with. The two women had been companions in everything from fashions and assignations to love potions and mommets and peculiar-tasting desserts. For a while they had been united in fear, but the pretty widow, less informed than her betters, ignorant of the latest developments, and stout in denials, had got up the nerve to ask for her release, considering that "your Petitioner hath been by your Lordship three or four times strictly examined of matters whereof your Petitioner hopes your Lordship is fully satisfied that she is most clear and innocent." At the least, "Your Petitioner humbly prays that in tender consideration of the premises, as also in regard of many poor fatherless children which in time of your Petitioner's close restraint endure much grief and distress for lack of such comfort as by your Petitioner's liberty they are wont to receive, your Lordship would be pleased to do her that justice, which she hopes cannot be denied to the meanest of His Majesty's subjects, that if in your Lordship's judgment she be found guilty of that whereof she has been most falsely and injuriously accused, she may come to her speedy and ordinary trial in due course of law."

Where was Sir Arthur Mainwaring, who should have been taking care of the allegedly "fatherless" children? Coke smiled his grim smile and arranged the "speedy trial." Uppity, that one was. Keeping humbly still might have enabled her to live a little longer. But she had received assurances and even jewelry from the great ones. Everything was being straightened out, and all that was left was a formality.

The Athenian courtesan Phryne, charged with profaning the Eleusinian mysteries, won an overwhelming acquittal by exposing her naked charms to the judges. Little Mrs. Turner came in all good cheer before the King's Bench bar dressed in her most alluring best, including hat and the yellow ruffs she had made fashionable. The Lord Chief Justice testily put her on notice that "women must be covered in the church, but not when they are arraigned." She had to expose her hair, which was not as bright as it used to be, substituting a kerchief for the hat. It was a meaningful setback. This was not going to be any kind of Sunday outing, and the grim men facing her were as seducible as a row of tombstones.

The trial was not lacking in erotic elements, in the form of references to love affairs and to the activities of Dr. Forman, and memorabilia from his study were produced in evidence. Yes, there were copulating figures in lead, and the brass mould in which they had been cast. There was shown a black scarf full of white crosses, declared to have been part of Mrs. Turner's wardrobe. These and other forbidden objects made the audience lean forward for a better view. All at once "there was heard a crack from the scaffolds, which caused great fear, tumult, and confusion among the spectators, and throughout the hall, everyone fearing hurt, as if the devil had been present, and grown angry to have his workmanship showed by such as were not his own scholars."

Dr. Forman's widow had her revenge by appearing in person to testify that "Mrs. Turner came to her house immediately after her husband's death, and did demand certain pictures which were in her husband's study: namely, one picture in wax, very sumptuously apparelled in silks and satins, as also one other sitting in form of a naked woman, spreading and laying forth her hair in a looking-glass, which Mrs. Turner did confidently affirm to be in a box, and that she knew in what part or room of the study they were"; further, "that Mrs. Turner and her husband would be sometimes three or four hours locked up in his study together." Mrs. Forman clearly did not go along with the proverb that nothing but good should be said of the dead, especially if there were living persons who deserved a nudge in the same direction. She raised eyebrows higher with the assertion "that her husband had a ring [that] would open like a watch." The implication was that it held poison. One rumor had long whispered that the harassed man committed suicide in order to render his death prophecy true.

The titillating revelations came to an abrupt halt when Coke refused to read out loud a parchment in Dr. Forman's handwriting listing the names of "what ladies loved what lords in the court." Was it really true, as the town talk had it by nightfall, that the first name to greet the Chief Justice's eye was his own wife's?

Her head whirling from so much digression and irrelevance, Anne Turner did at last gather that Weston had been convicted and executed. This "so much dejected her that in a manner she spake nothing for herself." Coke was eloquent enough for two, telling her, before the jury filed out for its so-called deliberations, that "she had the seven deadly sins: viz. a whore, a bawd, a sorcerer, a witch, a papist, a felon, and a murderer, the daughter of the devil Forman." Calling her a papist was a bit unfair, since, according to the lady herself, she had had doubts about Roman Catholicism ever since the Gunpowder Plot. Of course, Coke wanted to say the same things of the Howard daughter.

"She desired the Lord Chief Justice to be good unto her, saying, she was ever brought up with the Countess of Somerset, and had been of a long time her servant, and knew not that there was poison in any of those things sent to Sir T. Overbury."

"Then the jury went forth, and not long after returned, finding her Guilty. Who, being asked what she had to say for herself why judgment should not be pronounced against her, she only desired favor, but could not speak anything for weeping."

She was turned off in yellow ruffs, by Coke's order, to put an end to them as well as her. Anyone needing an example of gallows humor has it in the circumstance that the hangman wore yellow ruffs, too. The final scene is known to have provided inspiration for *The Scarlet Letter*. Each sees what he is prone to see. A contemporary poet praised "Her crystal eye, beneath an ivory brow." Overbury's father, there to see justice done, found that, like Hester Prynne, she was not what she had been. "She had been handsome once; but when she went to execution she was lean and long-visaged." The carvings of time? sin? prison? fear?

She died without directly implicating Lady Somerset, who, she told the minister, was "as dear unto her as her own soul." The worst she would say was, "Oh, my Lady Somerset, woe worth that I ever knew her. My love to them and their great-ness have brought me to a dog's death."

What was happening to the fabulous beauty of the recip-ient of this last sobbing loyalty, as she awaited the birth of her child, the beginning that was to signal her end? Though only twenty-two, she had long borne the lines of petulance around her mouth.

Her ex-husband, the one who was not the father of any child, cuts a poorer figure than the poor. It sounds self-de-fensive, to say the least, that he volunteered to Coke that he had heard Franklin had received £100 to bring about, by one means or another, Frances's second marriage. Always drugs as the answer to everything—how modern!

We must be wary of generalizations about high and low, however, for James Franklin accused everybody. He was the undoing of Sir Jervis Elwes. The former Lieutenant of the Tower, who had studied law at the Middle Temple at the same time as Sir Nicholas Overbury, made a stout and mov-ing defense—for a while. With dignity he protested the Chief Justice's bloodthirsty twisting of evidence. "My Lord," he said, "before I answer to the matter of charge against me, let me remember your Lordship of one speech which I learned from your mouth. I have heard you speak it at the Council table, and you have delivered it at the assizes in the country. That when a prisoner stands at the bar for his life, comfort-less, allowed no counsel, but strong counsel against him, per-chance affrighted with the fear of death, his wife and children to be cast forth out of doors and made to seek their bread: you have always pitied the cause of such a one. You have pro-tested you had rather hang in hell for mercy to such a one than for judgment. My Lord, you have not observed your own rule in my cause. You have paraphrased upon every examination, you have aggravated every evidence and applied it to me, so that I stand clearly condemned before I be found guilty."

There was nothing to convict Elwes of a capital crime. He was derelict merely in his duty to report the attempted poisoning as soon as he became aware of it. There was no proof he was accessory before the fact; and if he himself had felt guilty it would be hard to explain why he had so cheerfully cooperated with the authorities as soon as he was asked.

But he was struck by a thunderbolt. Coke produced from the area of his sleeve a "confession" volunteered by Franklin at five that morning. Upon the quotation of this, Elwes muttered to himself, "Lord have mercy on me!" (like an ineffectual Weston). He stood silent, and was doomed like the others. The only concession to his better class was that he was allowed to be hanged outside the Tower that he had so poorly guarded, instead of at Tyburn Hill.

Flanked by two clergymen he proceeded to the foot of the gibbet, at the lofty top of which the executioner sat, dangling-legged, looking down at him. Elwes clambered up four or five steps, then stopped. The ladder was steep and shaky. Descending, he asked that the angle be changed and the foot planted in the ground. He was, so to speak, not going to risk his life by a fall. A similar tragicomic situation was taken advantage of by William Palmer, the nineteenth-century poisoner, who, as he was told to step on the trapdoor of the scaffold, quipped, "Are you sure it's safe?"

The condemned owe it to their public to die well. Sir Jervis Elwes died at length, letting loose the floodgates of repentance to most edifying effect. All these submissive ends are understandable for believing Christians concerned with the fate of their immortal souls and realizing that if they were not guilty exactly as charged by Coke they were guilty enough

—guilty of a lifetime of sinning. Professional help was at their side to increase—not, like the modern analyst, to decrease—this consciousness. Sir Jervis recalled how he had thrown away money that would better have gone to his wife and eight children. "I confess I have been a great gamester, and . . . have wasted and played many sums of money, which exhausted a great part of my means, which I perceiving, vowed seriously (not slightly or unadvisedly) to the Lord in my vows and prayers, 'Lord, let me be hanged if ever I play any more!' Which not long after is most justly come upon me, whereof you are all eye-witnesses, because a thousand times since I brake this my vow."

Then he singled out a friend who had come on horseback to see him die. "You know, Sir Maximilian, what gaming we have had, and how we have turned days into nights and nights into days. I pray you in time to leave it off, and dishonor God no more by breaking his sabbaths, for He hath always enough to punish, as you now see me, who little thought to die thus."

Such last advice seared the soul, and might save all it reached. Sir Maximilian answered, "Sir Jervis, I am much grieved for you, and I shall never forget what you have here said."

"Look to it, do then," admonished Sir Jervis.

It was an old and ever renewed tradition. The last admonishment of Charles I would be (turning to Bishop Juxon who stood beside him on the scaffold), "Remember!"

After speaking some 2500 words of confessional, Elwes was, on signal, "turned . . . off the ladder; and being off, the executioner's man caught hold of one of his feet, his own man on the other foot, whereby they suddenly weighed his life; where hanging a small distance of time, his body not once stirred, only his hands a little stirred and moved, being tied with a little black ribbon which a little before he had reached to the executioner, putting up his hands to him for that purpose." Mrs. Turner's hands had been tied with a black ribbon, too.

Elwes's estate was turned over to William Herbert, the Earl of Pembroke. But the Earl, revealing the true nobility that the poets had often praised, gave it back to the widow and children. By one theory Pembroke, whose mother was Sir Philip Sidney's sister, is the "Mr. W. H.," "the onlie begetter" of Shakespeare's sonnets.

After this third execution Coke went 'round to examine Lady Somerset. Fanny mocked him when he was announced and he stood there at the door with his papers.

We have their dialogue only as reported in Italian by the Florentine envoy.

"O this Cook!" she punned, for so his name was pronounced, "wouldn't he like to put everybody into his broth!"

And she went up to him. "What do you want of me?"

"I want to question you," said the Judge.

"You have dishonored me in public, and then you come to question me?"

"No, Madame," he rejoined. "You dishonored yourself when you repudiated your first husband."

"Away with you!" she flared. "Don't think with your shyster's tricks-and-turns that you can do with me as you did with those poor simple folk that you made die. Get on your way, for my life is at any hour at the disposal of the King. You can go do your worst."

She closed the door on him, and that was the end of the attempted examination. He would have to come back another day, with allies.

What stands out is her aristocratic disdain and sense of privilege. Just as Coke looked down from a vast distance at

Weston, so the Countess, her proud Howard blood coursing a rich blue, made no effort to disguise her contempt for a mere knight and busybody judge, one, moreover, who had dared to say even worse things of her than Overbury had said. She acknowledged only the right of the King to deal with her. Or at least, let them send her peers.

Whether in this ingrained attitude is also individual callousness toward the poor victims, *her* poor victims (which she called *his*), those *"poveri semplici,"* is hard to say. Her mind was principally on the fact that she had been insulted in public, and, as with Overbury's remarks, whether what was said was true or not was beside the point. How could such a low person *dare*!

She was not always so defiant, but that was her mood of the day. It is known that women in the later stages of pregnancy are provided by Nature with a certain protective insulation or euphoria.

Coke had been correct in his original feeling that he needed a Commission to deal with the Somersets, a Commission with some lords on it. In fact, the five-man body even had a duke on it—albeit a Scotch one, the Duke of Lennox. There were no English dukes again until George Villiers was made Duke of Buckingham.

Now came the turn—for Coke's broth—of the literally poxy apothecary, Franklin, who, having helped to hang others, co-operated remarkably well in hanging himself. His only defense was, "That at the entreaty of the Countess and Mrs. Turner, he did buy these poisons, but protested his ignorance what they meant to do with them." Were they possibly for some pest such as a rat? Admittedly, *aqua fortis* had been tried on a feline. Coke's investigations did not stop at inquiring where Mrs. Turner obtained a cat, and he checked with her toothless maid, Margaret. He even wrote a memorandum to ask Franklin what happened to Fanny's first wedding ring. Such relics were not trivial to magicians. Besides, it might have held poison. That token from Essex was one of the most unwanted wedding rings on record. Frances gave the despised object to one of her maids, and the maid passed it on to her sister, who needed it or deserved it, being married to an Italian. There was no end to the contempt being handed around, for the maid now was speaking as ill as she could of the Somersets, letting it be known that Carr had re-joiced at Overbury's death.

A promising line for Franklin to take would have been that what he supplied the two women was not really poison, or so he judged. This would have made a tremendous dent in the Crown's case. But these victims seldom ceased to be docile. By multiplying accusations and hinting at more, Franklin hoped for a pardon. "I could make one discovery that should deserve my life," he said beguilingly. But the authorities had heard enough.

He ended with the customary good will. "God bless the Chief Justice, for he is an honorable and worthy judge as ever was in that place." He shook hands with—and tipped—the hangman. "When time shall come, do me a kindness, hang me finely and handsomely. Art thou the man that shall hang me? Thou lookest like a man to do better service, and I hope thou shalt do a greater service shortly among some great or noble ones that shall follow after." So there was a double echo of Weston (the pacesetter), the laudation of Coke and the wish that the big ones not get away.

The day, December 9th, this fourth neck was snapped, Fanny gave birth to a girl. In this crisis there was no hesita-tion as to what to name the infant. She would be called Anne, after the Queen (no thought of Mrs. Turner?). Others were unctuous when it was too late, after they had been condemned to death. Maybe this compliment would prove timely. But no christening gifts came to Blackfriars, the place of double confinement. The infant was borne to the font of the church of St. Martin in Ludgate. Prevented from doing anything desperate, the mother lived on but marginally, her health drained away. What incentive had she for being well? To be found fit was to face trial for her life. Her husband tried to get a letter through to her but had to burn it instead—and then be quizzed for it.

Would the great ones escape after all? Christmas came and went, and as far as the public knew she was more comfortable with her baby than she deserved to be, and no date was set for trial. Her husband, in the Tower, rejected all pressures to confess.

Coke overreached himself and had to be replaced. He was prevented, by the King and rightly, from pushing through a guilty verdict on Sir Thomas Monson, Keeper of the Armory at the Tower, who had had something to do with the appointment of Elwes. At the abortive trial Coke showed he had listened to too many wild tales and sinister rumors. He began to sound like Franklin. "God knows," he exclaimed to the assembly, "what became of that sweet babe Prince Henry, but I know somewhat." The Lord Chief Justice was convinced there had been a widespread "powder-poison plot" involving Catholic interests and threatening the whole royal family. Prince Henry had died of something he had eaten, that was sure. Mrs. Turner gave out that the Prince had been poisoned by a bunch of dried grapes. Henry's master cook had once made jellies for Somerset. Jellies! Everyone knew no love had been lost between the late prince and the favorite. But no love had been lost between Henry and James either, and the circumstances surrounding the death of his non-favorite son constituted a forbidden subject that the

King was not going to allow Coke or anyone else to bandy about. Rumors about that were as bad as the rumors that James was not really Henry's father. (Goodness knows, they had been painfully different, even differing, persons, and it was just as well that Charles would be Prince of Wales, but was Anne capable of being culpable?)

Coke shot his last bolt in the new year with another shift of species, now, in a long letter to the King, quoting Weston as having been concerned "lest . . . the net should be spread for the small fishes and not for the great." Carelessness of quotation was Coke's forte as a hanging judge. But safely entangling the great birds, or flies, or fishes called for great sophistication. As the man who took Coke's place pointed out, "Your Majesty knoweth it is one thing to deal with a jury of Middlesex and Londoners and another to deal with the peers." Handling an earl who would not confess (and who was threatening certain counterrevelations) required far more delicacy and tact than this blunderbuss of a prosecutor had lately been displaying. The Lord Chief Justice was supplanted by Attorney General Sir Francis Bacon, who had been waiting in the wings with at least one glittering calculating eye on the Lord Chancellorship. Coke and Bacon had once been rivals for the same rich widow, Lady Hatton. Coke had won, to his unending sorrow. She was a virago. Their quarrels were famous. Now it was Bacon's turn to ease him out with faint praise, "whose great travails as I much commend," he told the King, "yet that same plerophoria, or over-confidence, doth always subject things to a great deal of chance."

The Somersets were indicted in January 1616. Parliament not being in session, they were to go before a jury of their peers, impaneled from the House of Lords. Would the Earl of Essex be ruled out as prejudiced?

Fanny collapsed into truth-telling. On January 8th she was confronted with her letter to Lieutenant Elwes about tarts and jellies and what the Lieutenant's wife must not touch. There, in her undeniable hand, was the tangled sentence: "This much more I was bid to tell you, that if he should send this tart and jelly to your wife, then you must take the tart from her, and the jelly, but the wine she may drink it if she will, for in that there are no letters I know, but in the tart and jelly I know there is, as you shall know, and from whom when we get the answer as that we shall too." Did not the tart and jelly contain poison? She made no denial, while still not clearing up who bade her and who "he" was. The examiners wanted her to say that "he" was Somerset.

She did not care for these lawyers. If they sent her her equals, to whom she could talk woman to man, she might reveal more. Accordingly, on the 12th, she was visited by Lord Fenton and the Earl of Montgomery. Fenton was a Scot, like her husband, but old enough to be her father and therefore her father confessor. He was an intimate of—and the same age as—the King, whose life he had saved in the Gowrie conspiracy of 1600. But for Fenton to be accompanied by Philip Herbert, the first Earl of Montgomery, was strange. Or was it appropriate? The Herberts were actively anti-Howard and anti-Carr. Philip Herbert's brother had just succeeded Carr as Lord Chamberlain. Perhaps the Commissioners thought the pairing of Fenton and Montgomery a good balance. She would have remembered that two years before both Herberts had been acquiescent enough to dance at her wedding. Might she not hope for gallantry again? Was all her power of charming gone?

In any case she made to those two noblemen a confession full enough to convict her. At the same time she declared her husband innocent.

Both had been told that their only hope for mercy, of the eventual royal pardon, lay in freely admitting their guilt.

It was Coke's satisfaction to rush to the Tower to inform the prisoner there that his wife "had voluntarily confessed the offence." He was also able to announce that Somerset had been stripped of all his offices at court. "Which when he had heard, we leaving, he never (we well observing him) changed countenance or seemed to us to grieve at all, only he said indeed (without passion or sign of sorrow) that he was sorry that his wife was guilty of so foul a fact." He must have known it for some time.

There were months of delay while Bacon prepared the cases. The nets were made of most fragile threads. It was important that at her trial, planned as a convincing preliminary to his, she not digress to exonerate her husband. She must be kept strictly to the point: the only word required of her was "Guilty." But women were garrulous, wives (sometimes) hysterically loyal. Could she be counted on not to breach the standard trial procedure? Bacon, as homosexual as any of the principals, took a dim view. The essays that he kept composing and polishing portrayed women as the handicaps of men, impediments to men's rise to fortune and power. It would be too ironical if she put a spoke in Bacon's career. Like Coke, he was turning to the rising sun, Villiers, with whom he was in confidential correspondence about the trials. Setting aside as a dead loss all he had expended at her wedding, that two-thousand-pound Masque of Flowers, the "Flowers of affection, flowers of duty," all he asked of the Lady Frances was that she dispose of herself smoothly and fast, when the public time came.

Sir George became Master of the Horse in January, Knight of the Garter in April. Robert Carr was allowed to retain his insignia in that highest of orders, to the scandal of some. On the other hand, there were too many who suspected that the charges against him were made out of whole cloth to make room for the new favorite. James was in the predicament of having his honor and his justice questioned no matter what he did. Carr was muttering dark threats that if brought to trial he would make revelations that the King would be sorry for. What could he tell? Like any cast-off lover he knew all too much. There was the horrendous vulnerability that James stood self-convicted of disliking Overbury and wanting to get him out of the way. Would it dared be said that *he* was implicated in that final disposal? Coke, whose indiscretion apparently knew no bounds, had let it transpire that "Northampton had told the Lieutenant that the King would not be displeased if Overbury were to die."

It was a most peculiar working of justice that four persons who had had no grudge whatsoever against Overbury had been hanged for his death, while his active enemies were as comfortable as their consciences allowed them to be. How long would the Countess, a confessed poisoner, be permitted to remain in a private residence with her baby? First she had been able to "plead her belly"—like Moll Cutpurse and many another criminal. Pregnant women were not executed, a charming nook and cranny in the law that caused many a captive to entice or bribe her gaoler to carnal acts. Afterward, if the baby were to live, it had to be nursed: and who more fit than the mother? It is not on record that Fanny gave milk from breasts that had for years seemed overflowing (wet-nurses were available), but this would be a plausible explanation for her not being separated from her child until nearly four months had passed from Anne's birth. Justice had long called for her to be imprisoned in the Tower, like her husband, but this did not happen until March 27th—"upon so short warning [Chamberlain heard] that she had scant leisure to shed a few tears over her little daughter at the parting."

The warrant to the Lieutenant read: "After our very hearty commendations, forasmuch as it is His Majesty's pleasure that the Countess of Somerset be removed from the Blackfriars, where she is restrained, to the Tower of London, This shall be to will and require you to repair to the place of her restraint, and there to receive from the hands of Sir William Smith, Knight, the person of the said Countess of Somerset, and to carry her to the Tower, there to remain close prisoner under your charge, admitting such persons to attend her as are now with her at the Blackfriars, to be shut up close with her, as is usual in such cases, together with such honorable usage as is convenient and fitting a prisoner of her quality."

That evening she went completely to pieces on being informed by the Lieutenant, Sir George More, father-in-law of the poet Donne, who had so splendidly celebrated her wedding, that she was to occupy Overbury's cell. Her husband had been put there on *his* first night. This was poetic justice with a vengeance. She screamed and wept. Death was there, in that corner, at that dark window; she would smell it, she would see it: a white ghost, a putrescent body. Months before, when she had been young, beautiful, healthy, and revengeful, death had not been a reality. She had never truly imagined it. It was just a way of winning peace from a man who was dangerous. It was remote from her. The young and thriving do not feel that they will ever die. Now she could sense it at her throat, whispering, the last, ineludible, enemy.

They really had not prepared any other lodgings. Why was she being so delicate? At her second wedding it had not bothered her to be married by the same minister who gave her

Essex, and before the same witnesses. Life repeated itself: why should not death? The wheel of fortune was deceptive in its lurchings up and down. For instance, the week before, Sir Walter Ralegh had been released from the Tower to go on his last voyage in quest of the gold of El Dorado. This looked promising for him, but when he came back in failure, without gold, he was executed. If she insisted on being so hysterical, she could have his apartment, but it had to be fixed up first. The Lieutenant, meanwhile, "was fain to remove himself out of his own chamber for two or three nights." All for a woman who was guilty of murder, but the King was handling these Somersets with velvet gloves for reasons best known to himself. Sir George More had a reputation for irascibility, and had only gradually become reconciled with his son-in-law, whom he had first thrown in jail for eloping with his daughter, but, a new appointee anxious to make good at a coveted post (the next January he sold it for £2400—the price had risen since Elwes's unlucky day), he bowed to the prevailing winds, which included a silly and wicked woman's sighs.

Her particular tower, among the towers within the Tower, was the one by the Traitors' Gate that came to be known as the "Bloody Tower." There the little Princes had been murdered. Against this and the death of one bachelor was the circumstance that for years Ralegh had been allowed to have his wife Bess Throckmorton there, and there their son Carew was born. That too put Fanny in mind of all she had lost.

Sir George More was given orders in April for further pampering. "Whereas humble suit hath been made unto us by the Countess of Somerset that her cook and bottleman may be admitted to attend her in the Tower, This shall be to will and require you to suffer the said cook and bottleman to attend upon the Countess of Somerset, in such manner as the Earl of Somerset's cook and bottleman do now attend him.

You may likewise suffer your Lady to accompany the Countess at all times as shall be requisite." It was the old hotel attitude (as if in remembrance of the Tower as a royal residence), with the important exception that husband and lady did not share a suite nor have any means of communication through walls thirteen feet thick. So near and yet so far: first at the same bed and board with one man, now in the same prison with another. How well she remembered the second Robert's beds, which had lately, under Coke's instructions, been inventoried along with the ample rest of his property: "A bedstead with gilt pillars, the furniture purple velvet, lined with yellow damask, trimmed with lace, fringes, and caul-work of gold; another furnished with white velvet, lined with carnation velvet, trimmed with silver; another bed of green velvet; another of crimson damask, trimmed with gold. . . ." Then there was that "pavilion [tent] of cobweb lawn, embroidered with silk flowers." Would either of them see another summer?

Toward the end of April, Bacon had Fanny reexamined about the vague antecedents of her letter to Elwes: "This much more I was bid to tell you, that if he should send this tart and jelly to your wife. . . ." A life hung on a woman's grammar. Surely she "was bid" by her lover and future husband. From whom else would she have taken orders? And "he" would be Somerset also, making him an active poisoner. Let her concede this, and she would instantly become the lesser culprit: scarcely more, indeed, than a docile wife, a passive partner in her husband's crime, guaranteed mercy. This was how Coke read the letter and how Bacon wanted to read it, but the King had his doubts.

And the King was right, as kings should be, as Bacon regretfully acknowledged to Villiers, who was following the

case with contemptible eagerness. "My lady Somerset hath
been re-examined, and His Majesty is found both a true
prophet and a most just king in that scruple he made; for
now she expoundeth that word He, that should send the tarts
to Elwes's wife, to be of Overbury, and not of Somerset; but
for the person that should bid her, she said it was Northampton or Weston, not pitching upon certainty, which giveth
some advantage to the evidence."

Bacon assured the King he would not use the letter.

If they were putting pressure on her they were also using
psychological *peine forte et dure* on him. If he cooperated the
way he ought, Bacon strongly held out "some hopes that His
Majesty will be good to his lady and child; and that time,
when justice and His Majesty's honor is once saved and satisfied, may produce further fruit of His Majesty's compassion."

She would go on trial in the latter part of May. Like others
facing their final days she began to pay some heed to religion.
We do not know whether this was powerfully suggested to
her or was her own spontaneous idea. As a petitioner for
mercy it certainly would not do her any harm to look penitent, though it was a little late for her to pass as pious. On
May 7th the request went out for a divine, along with permission "to walk in the garden adjoining to her lodging, for
her health." On the latter occasions she was always to be accompanied by the Lieutenant. No husbandly notes to be
dropped from cell windows, no signals, no cunning messengers. In fact the Lieutenant was to supervise the visits of the
preacher, too, who, it did not go without saying, was to be
"some discreet and sufficient person" of More's choice. Did
More give any consideration to summoning John Donne, ordained the year before in the Church of England, though
once a Romanist and a rake? Donne was busy making his

peace with the Archbishop of Canterbury and hoping for oblivion regarding his relationship with the Somersets.

Whoever it was who came to her, Fanny did not find all the comfort she needed. When, on Saturday, May 11, she was told to get ready for her trial the following Wednesday, she began vomiting. She was sick all that night and into the next day. The letter writer Chamberlain was uncertain "whether it were the apprehension wrought so violently with her or that she had taken a dram." On Tuesday a week's postponement was announced. Those preparing the Earl's trial, which would follow hers by one day, could use the extra time. Somerset not only remained unyielding, he continued to threaten the disclosure of deadly secrets, like another Overbury. (How cyclical life was!)

Came the day that would not be postponed, Friday, May 24th. Early in the morning—for our ancestors made the most of daylight—she stepped into a boat at the Traitors' Gate and was carried to Westminster Hall to face the High Steward's Court of twenty-two select peers. The scramble among the public for seats reached a new high. Chamberlain knew "a lawyer that had agreed to give ten pound for himself and his wife for the two days, and fifty pound was given for a corner that could hardly contain a dozen." He himself had found it necessary to be there at 6 A.M. to claim his ten-shilling place. Then he found it hot and stifling. Bacon wrote, with a mixture of pride and scorn: "The [law] term hath been almost turned into a justitium or vacancy; the people themselves being more willing to be lookers on in this business than to follow their own." But the Countess's parents, many days before, had discreetly left town for Audley End.

It was a sight to strike awe in beholders, the court of justice in full panoply. At the upper end of the Hall sat Lord

Chancellor Ellesmere presiding as Lord High Steward, under a "cloth of estate." By him stood an usher bearing a white rod, the insignia of his office. The Garter King of Arms and the Great Seal-Bearer were on his right hand; on his left the Bearer of the Black Rod. Sergeants-at-arms with their maces lined each side, with more behind. The twenty-two peers faced each other on benches somewhat lower than the raised dais of the High Steward, and still lower was the row of judges in their scarlet robes—eight of them. There were ten counsel, headed by Attorney General Bacon: ten for the Crown, none for the defendant. (Somerset, as his case was more difficult, would face twelve.)

After the Sergeant Crier's Oyers and the certification of the indictment, the accused was led before the bar that separated her from the lawyers. As a peeress she was entitled to have a Gentleman Porter stand before her holding an axe with its edge turned away from her; on sentence of death it would be reversed.

She made three reverences to the High Steward and the peers. This cynosure of all eyes was dressed for contrasting effects, in black stammel, a coarse cloth, usually—Heaven for-fend!—scarlet, on her head "a cypress chaperon," with "cob-web lawn ruff and cuffs." Black for penitence, touches of white for remnants of innocence? A visual plea of extenuating circumstances? The chaperon or hood was not too different from that worn by a Knight of the Garter, which her husband still was. The ruff and cuffs went well with her fairness. At least to those far enough away, she was still breathtakingly beautiful.

From the throne of judgment reverberated the voice of the Lord High Steward, who was old enough to look like God. (Bacon had long been expecting his place and was openly solicitous of his health.) "My Lords, the reason why you be called hither this day is to sit as peers of Frances, Countess of Somerset."

The Clerk of the Crown addressed her. "Frances, Countess of Somerset, hold up thy hand."

She did so, and continued holding it up until the Lieutenant told her she could put it down. Meanwhile, the pertinent charges were read. She "stood, looking pale, trembled, and shed some few tears; and at the first naming of Weston in the indictment, put her fan before her face, and there held it half covered till the indictment was read."

In the crowd of spectators was the Earl of Essex, but he made no effort to be conspicuous.

After the reading the Clerk asked her, "Frances, Countess of Somerset, what sayest thou? Art thou guilty of this felony and murder, or not guilty?"

She, "making an obeisance to the Lord High Steward, answered 'Guilty,' with a low voice, but wonderful fearful."

Sentence should thereupon have followed, but Bacon had a speech to make. The audience was entitled to something more than such brief formalities. The Attorney General had some time before leveled one of his aphorisms at her that was perhaps more deadly than Overbury's insults: "There is no pomegranate so fair or sound, but may have a perished kernel." But now he was satisfied: she had not been garrulous, and he paved the way for the King's mercy, while speaking of the King's justice. "I am glad to hear this lady's so free acknowledgment, for confession is noble." She was in contrast to the four deniers, who had been executed. "No noble blood," he purred, "hath yet been spilt since His Majesty's reign."

So the double standard, the double standard that Weston had foreseen, was planted on the tidy (and rather Christian) ground that the Countess alone had pleaded Guilty, although Bacon acknowledged that the previous four "were actors in this tragedy, without malice, but no authors." Of course the Attorney General was getting ready to present Somerset ("This day and tomorrow is to crown justice") as the big author, despite the wife's denial—luckily not in open court—of his complicity.

Bacon had prepared for every contingency. In the event of a typically female outburst, an embarrassing digression, "my Lord Chancellor and I have devised that upon the entrance into that declaration she shall, in respect of her weakness, and not to add further affliction, be withdrawn." In the event of her pleading Not Guilty, this incomparably efficient prosecutor had written out a 2500-word charge that is printed in his Works and in the State Trials. He had Coke's diligence, but was more wary. If she had proved stubborn, he was ready to proceed apologetically but surgically: "Now for the evidence against this lady, I am sorry I must rip it up." This rather womblike expression had shortly been preceded (in the speech that never had to be delivered) by an explanation that the original delay was "in respect of her great belly."

Now he could say instead: "She meets justice in the way, by confession, which is the cornerstone either of mercy or judgment; yet it is said that mercy and truth be met together. Truth you have in her confession, and that may be a degree to mercy, which we must leave to him in whose power it resides. In the meantime this day must be reserved for judgment."

Coke was put on the defensive by Bacon's emphasizing that the others had not confessed. He butted in to declare that "whatsoever whisperings there be abroad of the death of Weston, they all (some before the hour of their death) confessed the fact, and died penitent; and if need should require,

I have brought their confessor along (namely, Dr. Whiting)."

The Lord High Steward ignored him. "My Lords, you see and have heard those directions under the King's hand. Give the glory to God and honor to the King."

She was instructed by the clerk to raise her hand again. "Whereas thou hast been indicted, arraigned, and pleaded Guilty, as accessory before the fact, of the wilful poisoning and murder of Sir Thomas Overbury, what canst thou now say for thyself, why judgment of death should not be pronounced against thee?"

All strained to hear as she spoke "humbly, fearfully, and . . . low": "I can much aggravate, but nothing extenuate my fault. I desire mercy, and that the Lords will intercede for me to the King."

As the Lord High Steward had not been able to make out her words, Bacon intervened to interpret. "The lady is so touched with remorse and sense of her fault that grief surprises her from expressing of herself. But that which she hath confusedly said is to this effect, That she cannot excuse herself, but desires mercy."

Then the voice from the judgment seat struck: "Frances, Countess of Somerset, whereas thou hast been indicted, arraigned, pleaded Guilty, and that thou hast nothing to say for thyself, it is now my part to pronounce judgment. Only this much before, since my Lords have heard with what humility and grief you have confessed the fact, I do not doubt they will signify so much to the King, and mediate for his grace towards you. But in the meantime, according to the law, the sentence must be this: That thou shalt be carried from hence to the Tower of London, and from thence to the place of execution, where you are to be hanged by the neck till you be dead. And the Lord have mercy upon your soul."

She was led out, the axe turned toward her.

Condemned

9

Fanny's last public appearance stirred different reactions. All that was agreed was that she had exhibited a measure of self-control. Some thought it a mere performance, as when she had danced in masques. That inveterate bachelor, Chamberlain, refused to be impressed. "She won pity by her sober demeanor, which in my opinion was more curious [artful] and confident than was fit for a lady in such distress, yet she shed or made show of some few tears divers times." Others were fully persuaded of the genuineness of her penitence. In what other spirit would she have clad herself in homely linsey-woolsey, the traditional garb of penitents, like that German emperor who stood barefoot three days in the snow at Canossa seeking the pope's absolution? (By the way, was she a papist, like some of her fell associates? Those Howards were always suspect.) One correspondent found her bearing nothing short of "noble, graceful, and modest." But allowance has to be made for the fact that he was an Italian. A countryman of his—to give an idea of how susceptible the race was—just could not imagine the sentence would be carried out, since the lady was so young and so beautiful!

Her ordeal lasted less than two hours (not counting the procession forth and back), was lightened by an extraordinarily deferential treatment that included half-promises. In addition to any private messages that had been brought her during the past months by the King's representatives, the prospect of mercy was now a matter of public record. Bacon had told the Hall there was such hope, and the Judge, before he pronounced the awful words, "hanged by the neck till you be dead," had said he was sure the lords would "mediate for" the royal "grace towards you." The King was above the law in this respect; he had complete power to pardon. Even now, as she was entering the barge that would take her back to the Tower, my Lord Hay, Carr's original patron and still close to the King, came and murmured in her ear some words of comfort. She needed them, for though the ordeal could have been longer and harsher and totally without hope, she had been humiliated for all to see—we know how sensitive she was about that—and still had much to worry about. For whatever days remained to her she had the cud to chew that what she had done was—to borrow the French epigram —"worse than a crime: it was a blunder."

With Lady Frances now officially disposed of, what would be the outcome of her husband's trial? Bacon hoped for the maximum of prejudice against him. If the one was guilty, surely the other was, in that most unholy of matrimonial unions. The Attorney General considered letting a day elapse between the trials, "to see if, after condemnation, the lady will confess of this lord; which done, there is no doubt but he will confess of himself." But this was given up as being, from the looks of things, both a false premise and a false conclusion. Those with any small acquaintance with Bacon and the situation he was trying to wrest to a successful outcome for his masters knew that whenever he said "there is no doubt" there was plenty of doubt, which sometimes seeped through his memoranda to James.

The King was on tenterhooks. He had been, he felt, generous, asking only that Carr "leave some place for my mercy to work upon." During May he sent four highly secret missives to the Lieutenant of the Tower revealing his mounting anxiety and his willingness to resort to almost any skulduggery that might get results from the uncooperative prisoner. For instance, "Good Sir George" was to try telling Carr that his wife was on the verge of accusing him. "Let none living know of this, and if it take good effect, move him to send in haste for the Commissioners to give them satisfaction, but if he remain obstinate, I desire not that you should trouble me with an answer, for it is to no end, and no news is better than evil news; and so farewell, and God bless your labours." But the monarch did not maintain this ostrich stance on the day of the trial itself. As Weldon slyly reported, "But who had seen the King's restless motion all that day, sending to every boat he sees landing at the Bridge, cursing all that came without tidings, would have easily judged all was not right and there had been some grounds for his fears of Somerset's boldness." There, at Greenwich Palace (which Cromwell took down), six miles downstream from the crowd-packed, suspenseful, and unusually protracted scene at Westminster Hall, James failed to eat his dinner, and then, at dusk, his supper.

One of the fears was that the accused would refuse to plead, would stand mute, like Weston. They could not press an *earl* to death. According to Weldon, it took a ruse to get Somerset to appear in court at all. On being told by the Lieutenant that the trial was set for the next day, he replied that they would have to carry him in his bed, "that the King had assured him he should not come to any trial, neither durst the King bring him to trial." This sent More off to Greenwich in the middle of the night, "bouncing at the back stairs as if mad," where he aroused his sovereign. James "fell into a passion of tears. 'On my soul, More, I wot not what to do; thou art a wise man, help me in this great strait, and thou shalt find thou doest it for a thankful master.' " Such an appeal would inspire the dullest of His Majesty's subjects to come up with some contrivance. The Lieutenant went back to the Earl with the speech: "To satisfy justice, you must appear, although return instantly again, without any further proceeding, only you shall know your enemies and their malice, though they shall have no power over you." If Overbury had been gullible in such a situation, why should not Somerset be?—and he was. The blindness of *hybris*. To guard against any unseemly outburst, the Lieutenant had two men stand beside his prisoner at Westminster Hall ready to muffle him with a hood, inconspicuously carried.

Addressing him, the court announced that, as a rare and useful privilege, he would be allowed to assist his memory by taking notes on the prosecution speeches.

Like his wife he was dressed in black, but of more elegant material: "a plain black satin suit, laid with two satin laces in a seam; a gown of uncut velvet lined with unshorn, all the sleeves laid with satin lace; a pair of gloves with satin tops." Below the fair curled hair hung his George defiantly: he was still K. G. and, the implication was, deservedly so. However, his beard needed trimming, and his face was pale, his eyes cavernous as he bent himself to an unfamiliar task with pen and ink. What had Overbury prophesied from that place where Carr had already languished for even more months than his secretary? In case he had forgotten, the ringing words were read that day to the jammed Hall: "I pray God that you may not repent the omission of this my counsel, in this place, whence I now write this letter."

As had happened with his wife, he kept his hand up during the reading of the indictment until told by the Lieutenant to lower it. He whispered to More three or four times, no doubt with reference to the false promise he had been given a few hours before, that he was just to put in an appearance, not be tried.

In the front row of spectators, there to stare him down, was the Earl of Essex, not skulking as on the previous day. This other Robin had been extremely chirrupy in recent months. After the divorce in 1613 he had retreated to Chartley, licking his wounds, one of which was having to give back the dowry. As long as he was losing money he thought he might as well go on spending, and he wasted his substance, having to sell property and even to borrow from his grandmother. He did not marry, convenient as another dowry would have been. In October 1615, when the Somersets were taken into custody, he came bounding back to Court, the King and Queen showing him special favor. He was even mentioned as a possibility to succeed Carr as Lord Chamberlain. In the Christmas festivities he led all the dancers.

But after his former lady confessed, it was reported that he interceded for her. However, there was supposed to be a subtle complication. Although Archbishop Abbot had heard as long ago as 1611 that it was Essex who first decided upon divorce, that Earl was now saying (according to the Florentine envoy, Quaratesi) that he regarded himself as still married to her and not free to marry anyone else as long as she was alive. This could have been a rationalization—and a public defense as to why he had not married again. Taking it seriously, there were obviously only two solutions: for him and Frances to be reconciled, her marriage to Carr being declared void or bigamous; or for her to die, leaving him genuinely single. The latter solution, now legally decreed, was, of course, at cross-purposes with his alleged plea for her life. But if the man who had taken away his wife were condemned that very day, May 25, 1616, and the sentence duly carried out, and Frankie pardoned, then? The first Robert's head swarmed as he confronted his cornered rival.

The latter, turning to the jury of peers, saw either active enemies or those who had long looked down upon him—even, or especially, when they had had to sue to him—as an impudent upstart and usurper of purely English privileges. In fact, for all his lacy, gloved airs, he betrayed his peasant origin by answering the time-honored question with "By God and the country," only after a moment correcting to, "By God and my peers." He did not even say *my* country," because Scotland was *his* country (would he had stayed there!). His proud, blue-blooded wife could never have committed such a blunder. Blood told, and the lords settled back for a tale of blood. The accused's unpopularity was of course far more universal and deeper-grounded than that ever encountered by the minor knight they were prepared to believe he had, "under color of friendship," pitilessly murdered. Only Bacon was capable of commiserating with the lords, without a smile, over their duty, their painful duty, since "you cannot cut him off from your body, but with grief." These of Bacon's were the best crocodile tears since certain ones Carr had shed in 1613.

More than once during this long day's dying, the Lord High Steward indicated to the accused that he could save a deal of trouble for all concerned by retracting his plea of Not Guilty. "Take heed lest your wilfulness cause the gates of mercy to be shut upon you." But Somerset remained unpersuaded. "My Lord, I came with a resolution to defend myself."

Bacon outlined "four heads to prove you guilty, whereof two are precedent to the impoisonment, the third is present, and the fourth is following or subsequent." On the first two

heads the Attorney General had easy going. The first was
motive: "mortal malice coupled with fear." He had plenty
of testimony on that, while characteristically declining to believe that a mere woman was the root of the trouble: rather,
"fear of discovering secrets . . . of a dangerous and high nature." Overbury opened despatches before Carr did, and the
two had code names for principal figures. The King was "Julius," the Queen "Agrippina." An unsuccessful candidate for
secretary was rapped as "Simonist," while Carr's future
father-in-law bore the disrespectful but appropriate title of
"Wolfy." Bacon hammered home the moral: "These two
made plays of all the world besides themselves; but though it
were a play then, it hath proved tragical since."

The second head of attack was that Carr had contrived to
get Overbury into the Tower. Here there were two damaging
admissions. Carr did have some knowledge of his wife's
plan to have Sir David Wood "fall out with Overbury and
offer him some affront" (though Carr did not allow that the
object was murder). The other admission was contained in a
letter the defendant had sent to the King in February: "But
if I must come to my trial, knowing the presumptions may
be strong against me in respect I consented to and endeavored the imprisonment of Sir T. Overbury (though I designed it for his reformation, not his ruin), I therefore desire
your Majesty's mercy, and that you will be pleased to give
me leave to dispose of my lands and goods to my wife and
child, and graciously to pardon her, having confessed the
fact."

So far it looked black, though Carr denied that he had introduced Weston as underkeeper or had ever even seen him.
But the essential point was the third: that the defendant procured and consented to the poisoning. Had there in fact been
a poisoning? Among the hundreds of Coke's depositions there

was carefully none from the King's two physicians who had actually attended Overbury and prescribed remedies for a "consumption." But Somerset, who had not done too badly so far as his own lawyer, pointing to some flaws and discrepancies, would not have been allowed to cast doubt on the cause of Overbury's death, even if that strategy had occurred to him. The law had already decided that there had been a poisoning, with Weston—much cited or miscited now because safely dead—as the principal "actor."

Having no real evidence on Somerset as an accessory, Bacon sat down and let one of his subordinates struggle with this central and most dubious charge. Of course there had already been offered the old preliminary that the jury was not to "expect visible proofs in the work of darkness." But now a peculiarly outrageous thing happened. Sergeant Montague twice read from Fanny's ambiguous letter about the tarts, which Bacon had promised the King not to use in view of her explanation clearing her husband. The defendant did not know what his wife may have said on examination and reexamination. Those who did know—Bacon, Coke, the Lord High Steward, who had been one of the Commissioners and who was now supposed to be presiding over a fair trial—sat silent. No one raised a voice against a trick that was reinforced by quoting the writer as having admitted "that by *letters* she meant poison." The jury was left to infer that he who sent them and he who bade her was Carr. And the "vomit" that Carr sent Overbury at his own request, "to make him a little sick" in a bid for sympathy, this was magnified into something fatal, which nonetheless the prisoner admittedly survived.

The prosecution did not have to resort to such dishonesty for its fourth head, which was Carr's suspicious behavior after the fact. He had systematically sought to recover and destroy evidence, burning letters or altering them. Moreover, he had made efforts to obtain a general pardon, wherein was mentioned, among other possible charges, the felony of murder.

The prosecution's presentations had used up the whole day. Carr had got in a few objections, and there was one screeching collapse of a scaffold to prove the Devil was still following the case. Candles had to be brought in as the prisoner's turn to answer came. Many in the muggy hall were faint from heat and hunger. Chamberlain, feeling his sixty-two years, had gone home. There was a general shuffling and restiveness. The evidence, as presented, was cogent; why was this obstinate Scot bent on detaining them with tedious equivocations and vain denials? Sergeant Crew, who had succeeded Sergeant Montague for point four, had sneered that after the overwhelming exposure, "My Lord" would be given a chance "to sew fig-leaves." Whatever the reason, he had fallen out of grace, and he should bow to the fact. The Lord High Steward made a final attempt to discourage the prisoner's making a speech in his own defense, and the Judge's words were as sharp as the headsman's axe:

Only this (before you speak for yourself) by way of advice I will say unto you, in giving you two examples: Your wife, that yesterday confessed the fact; and there is great hope of the King's mercy, if you now mar not that which she made. On the contrary, Biron, who, when the king of France used all the means he possibly could to bring him to the acknowledgment of his offence, which if he had done there was no question to be made of the King's grace. And I think there never was, nor is, a more gracious and merciful king than our master. But Biron still persisting in the denial of his fact, you know his end.

The end was that, because he had denied his guilt, Charles, Duc de Biron, cut himself off from mercy and was beheaded in the Bastille in 1602. George Chapman, Somerset's friend, had produced a ten-act tragedy on the subject.

On the first of the four heads of accusation, Somerset denied any deep-seated malice against Overbury. "Whereas the breach of friendship betwixt Overbury and me is used for an aggravation against me, it is no great wonder for friends sometimes to fall out, and least of all with him: for I think he had never a friend in his life that he would not sometimes fall out with and give offence unto."

The second count was yielded somewhat. "I consented to his imprisonment, to the end he should make no impediment in my marriage." But "I had a care of his lodgings, that they should be where he might have the best air, and windows both to the water and within the Tower, so that he might have liberty to speak with whom he would. So you see it was against my intention to have him close prisoner."

The crucial third charge he flatly answered with, "Whereas it is pretended that I should cause poisoned tarts to be sent him to the Tower, my wife in her confession saith that there were none sent but either by me or her—and some were wholesome, and some not. Then it must needs follow that the good ones were those which I sent, and the bad hers." Lord Compton showed the effect that Fanny's unexplained letter was having on the jury by remarking, "My lady, in her letter to the Lieutenant, writes, 'I was bid to bid you do this.' Who should bid her?" Sergeant Montague cut in, "The continual letters between my lord and her argues that." Again, in a matter of life and death, the gross deceit was foisted, with the mute concurrence of those honorable men—the lawyers, the judges, the King's Commissioners. Nor could the defendant produce—though it existed—Overbury's letter asking him for a powder to contrive sympathy. And the Lord High Steward had, with a straight face, enjoined, "You that be of the King's Counsel, free your discourse from all partiality, but let truth prevail and endeavor to make it appear."

On the fourth count, Somerset admitted tampering with evidence, but indicated that his wife and Sir Robert Cotton had inspired that. As for the general pardon, Cotton, the antiquary, had pointed to good and ample precedents for one in his high office to seek it. Cotton, "being held for a delinquent" himself, was not allowed to testify—although the whole case was based on the evidence of delinquents. The erstwhile favorite, fatigued and faltering, longed for him (though he had listened to him too much) as one might miss a clever executive assistant: "I could wish that he were here to clear many things that now be obscure."

These were the main points of his defense that Saturday evening, but he did not take them up in order and got lost at times in minor matters. One of the shorthand recorders found him most unprofessional: "made answer . . . very confusedly, insisting most upon those particulars that were least material." Bacon, in an effort to get him to stop, patted him publicly: "My Lord . . . hath behaved himself modestly and wittily." But Carr did not stop until he was exhausted. "More I cannot call to mind, but desire favor."

He had not, after all, spoken one word against the King.

The lords did him the honor of taking longer in their decision than preceding juries. They even sent for the two chief justices, Coke and Hobart, to help them in their deliberations. But the end was virtually foreordained, and each and every lord, polled, stood up from the jury bench, doffed his hat, and responded Guilty.

The prisoner had already taken off his George, like the doomed man he was. He would not allow to be covered with shame, he declared, that which His Majesty had given him as an honor. He stood now in unrelievedly funereal black.

Yet he thought, too late, of what he might further have said to stem the tide, and started to defend himself anew.

The presiding magistrate interrupted. "My Lord, you are not now to speak any more in your defence, but why Judgment of Death should not be pronounced."

"Then I have no more to say, but humbly beseech you my Lord High Steward and the rest of the Lords to be intercessors to the King for his mercy towards me, if it be necessary." The "if it be necessary" was the last remnant of his belief that he had a hold on the King.

Even if the Peers had been neutral (and some of them, as reported by the historian William Camden, who was present, showed more effort to be fair than the official summary indicates), their verdict was not unreasonable as the case had been presented. Three of the four "heads" were strong, and the other looked strong. Carr had undeniably been in two conspiracies—adultery and a plot to imprison Overbury. One of the lovers had admitted sending poisons, and it was too much to ask the jury to believe that the other was either ignorant or innocent of what went on for so long. Carr's denials were those of a proved liar (to Overbury), deceiver, and conspirator.

Lacking a poll, it is impossible to generalize about contemporary reaction to the verdict. Chamberlain's quick and partisan (as the friend of Winwood) view was that "by all circumstances and most pregnant (yea almost infallible) probabilities he be more faulty and foul than any of the company." On the other hand, Sir Anthony Weldon, offering many a sneer and no gratitude to the King that had knighted him, said of Carr in his 1650 book, *The Court and Character of King James*: "Many believe him guilty of Overbury's death, but the most thought him guilty only of the breach of friendship." The modern tendency is to exonerate him of at-

tempted murder, as Fanny herself did. He was guilty of much
—base betrayal, even as Elwes was guilty of cowardice and
greed—but it does not necessarily follow that he was guilty
of more. His wife had taken certain measures against her
first husband on her own, and now she embarked on another
little venture, with hired allies, without confiding in her
lover, whom she did not wish to alienate. Carr's frantic cov-
ering actions afterward can be seen as an effort to protect her
(when at last she told him or he drew the correct inferences)
and himself, since appearances were against him and he knew
what sort of trial he would get once favor was withdrawn. He
endeavored to alter appearances, jab at the links of circum-
stantial evidence. It is, after all, a questionable maxim that
everyone who flees is guilty. On the other hand, modern students of the case are prone to forget, in their enlightened
indignation over Coke's and Bacon's procedures, that those
unfairly tried are not *ipso facto* innocent (speaking histori-
cally, not juridically). Carr might well have been an accessory, at least. He might have known of his future wife's activities while they were still going on and done nothing to stop
them. The judicious Earl of Clarendon, writing a generation
later, neither swallows whole nor utterly spews out the official verdict. On an early page of his *History of the Rebellion
and Civil Wars in England* he says that Carr, "by the instigation and wickedness of his wife, . . . became, at least,
privy to a horrible murder." At least Elwes lifted a finger to
throw out a phial.

If everyone who has a motive and acts suspiciously is a
prime suspect, there are several to consider. Professor Andrew Amos, the first to sift the evidence with his 1846 book
The Great Oyer of Poisoning, pointed the finger of suspicion
at King James. This dramatic possibility was entertained by
other nineteenth-century scholars, such as Kempe and Rim-

bault, and Bisset and Ewald. James certainly became very agitated as the case drew near its finale. That, as Spedding, Bacon's nineteenth-century biographer, showed, the monarch spent the day of Carr's trial in conversation with Gondomar, the Spanish ambassador, does not rule out the stories of his nervousness, including his nervous stomach. Not only do we have such account from Weldon in 1650, when it was fashionable and safe to tread on dead Stuarts, but Sherborne wrote to Carleton at the time (letter of May 31, 1616) about how "extreme sad and distracted" the King was the day of the trial "until he had heard what answer the said Earl had made." He feared what Carr would say. Specifically, as he wrote Sir George More, he feared "he would threaten me with laying an aspersion upon me of being in some sort accessory to his crime." What did Carr know? It is not to the point to suggest, as some have, that the deadly secret was that James liked comely youths. Everybody knew that; there was not much leverage in that, even if one threatened to lower the breeches on nasty details. Getting back, was Carr in on a murder? At the very least, had he heard His Majesty give vent to a threat? As G. P. V. Akrigg has recently conjectured, "It may be that James, who had loathed Overbury, had in one of his furies spoken somewhat after the fashion of an earlier king [Henry II] who had cried for someone to rid him of a pestilent priest [Thomas à Becket]." It was, after all, the King, not Carr, who imprisoned him. How far might jealousy carry James, jealousy of Overbury's influence on and intimacy with the friend to whom *he* wished to be all in all?

James was a coward, but cowards turn, especially in devious ways. Judge Edward Abbott Parry, in his 1925 book *The Overbury Mystery,* has a chapter entitled "The Terror of the King" and leaves open the inference that Sir Theodore Mayerne, the King's physician (who was never called upon to testify), may have been under orders to see to it that that miserable nuisance in the Tower did not survive. There could have been more than one would-be poisoner, working separately, or cooperating. *If* the Somersets were secretly confident of James's pardon, such expectation could have been part of a "deal," rather than a simple faith in his charity. He could be deadly to those he disliked, as he was to Ralegh. Two years after the final disposal of Overbury, James had pitilessly allowed his own pretty cousin Arabella Stuart to die an agonizing death in the Tower because she had ventured on a marriage that he felt was a threat to his dynasty. There were the usual rumors that she had not died a natural death. As evidence that he could smile and smile and be a villain, he had once written of this very lady: "nature enforces me to love her as the creature living nearest kin to me, next to my own children." (Which raises again the question of how fond he was of Henry.)

In the best detective-story tradition, we must not overlook the seemingly least likely suspect, Queen Anne. Anne was the quiet and plump one about whom we do not know nearly enough. It was ever her fate to be ignored. It is not easy to connect her, even in imagination, with such sins of Fanny's as adultery (gossip named Lord Pembroke) or conspiracy to murder. They had masques in common, but the Queen seemed even happier playing with her ladies such children's games as "Rise, pig, and go" and "One penny, follow me." Yet it was a seventeenth-century writer who said, "Hell hath no fury like a woman scorned." Sully called this particular woman "bold and enterprising." Overbury was part of a triangle that excluded Anne. At least twice he had directly insulted her, and she had driven him into exile abroad. He was supposed to have written poems satirizing her. She resented the King's cronies and the cronies' cronies. When

Prince Henry died at eighteen, in the wildness of her grief his mother cried out that Overbury and Carr had poisoned him. There was bad blood between the Prince and Carr, and her charge seemed to her perfectly plausible. An autopsy failed to convince her to the contrary. What neater revenge than to arrange for Overbury to be poisoned and for Carr to be hanged for the crime, since both already merited capital punishment. She was not flattered that Overbury had had the nerve to assure Carr he could win *her*: in Bacon's words, "he dared to promise this Lord the unlawful love of the greatest woman in this kingdom." That piled more insult on top of unatonable injury. She was so grateful to Coke for convicting those he did that she presented him with a diamond ring.

That congenital plotter, Henry Howard, the Earl of Northampton, James's "dear Lord Harry," "my long-approved and trusty Lord Harry," Fanny's Uncle Harry, acted as if he knew very well what he was doing when he urged Elwes to speedy disposal of Overbury's body. Mrs. Turner indicated he was guilty. Bacon, concluding that Northampton's "hand was deep in this business," used Northampton's letters to Carr against him, while Carr answered that he would never, of course, have kept them if he had thought them "dangerous to me." There is a good chance that the old fox knew what his grand-niece was doing years before Carr did, if indeed Northampton (who had been her adviser in machinations against Essex) did not put her up to it. Fanny said that the person who "bid" her "was Northampton or Weston." Overbury stood in the way of Howard ascendency, to which the wily Earl had devoted his long and unscrupulous life.

Despite, then, a confession (we presume that Fanny was not the type to confess to what she did not do, but it must be kept in mind that she possibly did not do it, only tried to do it), the Overbury case has not been cleared up. Fanny was trying—so may have been her lover, her great-uncle, the King, the Queen. Even this does not exhaust the list of suspects. For example, at the time, people were asking why the Earl and Countess of Suffolk had not been jailed. Then, among those of lower rank, there is Paul de Loubell, the apothecary, brother-in-law to the King's physician Mayerne. In the last days of Overbury's stubborn survival, it was ordered that only Weston, de Loubell, and his assistant, William Reeve, be admitted to the cell. As we know, Reeve, on being admitted, administered a deadly enema, for which deed Weston was hanged. De Loubell sent Reeve abroad out of harm's way. The son of de Loubell's landlady reported to Coke that de Loubell's parents had acted very frightened when the case broke and their son's former assistant was mentioned. As William Roughead, that acute Edinburgh student of murder, asks, Why was not Paul de Loubell put on trial? On the contrary, in the indictment of others he was mentioned just vaguely, without being named, as an apothecary. Who arranged such special treatment of the brother-in-law of the King's physician?

Thus, while Fanny is in the circle, any line excluding others is most shadowy. If it is any consolation, history has a strange way of repeating itself—and its mysteries. Not everybody would associate, offhand, Overbury and Napoleon (even though the latter boasted—with considerable exaggeration— "All the women in the world would not make me lose an hour!"). But the following item from *Parade* (February 28, 1965) is evocative:

Tests carried out in two nuclear reactors at Harwell, England, on four specimens of Napoleon's hair prove conclusively that his death on St. Helena at the age of 51 in 1821 was murder by arsenic. It is believed that Napoleon was murdered by his good friend and constant island companion, Count Montholon, who was left 2 million francs in Napoleon's will. Montholon poisoned Napoleon over the years with small amounts of arsenic, a time-honored practice of poisoners in the French court. A student of the murder is Dr. Sten Forschufvud of Gothenburg, Sweden, one of three scientists who studied the neutron bombardment of Napoleon's hair at the Atomic Energy Research Establishment in Harwell. Dr. Forshufvud has written a book on the subject.

More readily, the annulment Fanny won brings to mind modern arrangements. Recently, a childless wife who had gone to Juarez for a divorce was asked why she did not seek an annulment in New York. "No, that's too tough," she told Gertrude Samuels, *The New York Times* staff writer. "You gotta prove that some deceit has been practiced, like your husband not trying to give you children, and the judge would say, 'What, you discover this after eight years of marriage?' " Well, a judge likes precedents, and it would have saved a trip to Mexico.

The rise and fall of the Somersets was the biggest scandal of a scandal-ridden reign. Their disgrace was gradual, giving the courtiers and flatterers and poets plenty of time to look elsewhere or change their tunes. If these hangers-on ran with the hounds, who could prove that this was not moral revulsion? Bacon withdrew the flowers and stepped forward with thorns, as he had done with Elizabeth's Earl of Essex, who had thought him a friend and had been his patron. But there are greater loyalties (to follow which also happened to be advantageous), and who is under obligation to stick to a traitor —or a murderer? The crowd was now running wild against the convicted pair. Several times in June Londoners rushed to Tower Hill, peering through the iron gates, on rumors that the Somersets were about to be beheaded. On July 13 the Queen had a harrowing experience as she drove into town with three others in a private coach. "There grew a whispering that it was the Lady Somerset and her mother, whereupon people flocked together and followed the coach in great numbers, railing and reviling, and abusing the footmen, and putting them all in fear. Neither would they be otherwise persuaded till they saw them enter into Whitehall."

As regards the courtiers, a less suspect time for them to have shown moral indignation was at the period of the Somersets' wedding. But, shamelessly unwholesome already, the two were riding high, and even those who secretly wished their downfall took part in the dancing and present-giving.

What of the poets who had adorned that occasion? Donne, "a grave of his own thoughts," to quote his poem—Donne, like Bacon, turned from the "Blest pair of swans" ("Epithalamion") to Villiers, the new favorite, who was made a Viscount in August as part of a faster and higher career than Carr's. But Donne was far from the center of things, and it took time for him to be considered worthy of a correspondence. Campion spent a term in prison for his part in carrying money for Elwes's appointment. Chapman remained loyal, in a way to be noticed in the next chapter.

The case of Ben Jonson is interesting. It will be recalled that he had written for both of Frances's marriages. He published *Hymenaei* separately in 1606, with justifiable pride and full pealing of what "auspicious . . . marriage-union" it celebrated. But the reader turning to the reprint of this in the 1616 Folio of Jonson's *Works* is told merely that it was for "A Marriage." This the reader could have gathered from the title, nor is the information, bare as it is, strictly correct, since it had turned out not to be a marriage. The two entertainments for the Somerset wedding were also included, with *The Irish Masque at Court* bearing internal evidence (only) "of a great brideal [a pun worthy of Joyce or *Humphrey*

Clinker—"bridal" plus "deal" plus "ordeal"] of one o' ty lords" and the daughter of "Toumaish o' Shuffolke." Oh yes, it seems the groom was "Robyne" (but unable to flit from the Tower). That stalwart defender of Jonson's character, his nineteenth-century editor, William Gifford, conjectured that the dramatist purposely and high-mindedly left the composition of the principal masque on that disgusting occasion to Campion. But why then did he stoop to contribute *A Challenge at Tilt* and *The Irish Masque*? He had slipped in general favor, had quarreled with his great coadjutor, Inigo Jones, who was abroad studying architecture, and it is all too likely that he had no choice in his subordinate role. At loose ends, he had himself but lately returned from the Continent, where he had served as tutor to Ralegh's son, Wat, who got him "dead drunk" in Paris and had him drawn through the streets on a cart, while the boy delivered mock orations over the huge prostrate form.

The dramatist could be mischievous, too. His comedy *Epicoene, or The Silent Woman* had a passage not likely to endear him to the parties concerned. Morose, who is fanatically fond of quiet, has been tricked into a noisy marriage and wants to get out of it. Otter and Cutbeard, disguised respectively as a divine and a canon lawyer, run through the twelve grounds of nullity (enumerated in Aquinas's *Summa Theologica*), ending with—and dwelling upon—*"impedimentum gravissimum: . . . manifestam frigiditatem."* "Confess yourself but a man unable, and she will sue to be divorced first." Some ladies enter, and Morose commences to apologize:

Ladies, I must crave all your pardons—
Truewit. Silence, ladies.
Morose. For a wrong I have done to your whole sex, in marrying this fair and virtuous gentlewoman—
Clerimont. Hear him, good ladies.

Morose. Being guilty of an infirmity, which, before I conferred with these learned men, I thought I might have concealed—
Truewit. But now being better informed in his conscience by them, he is to declare it, and give satisfaction, by asking your public forgiveness.
Morose. I am no man, ladies.
All. How!
Morose. Utterly unabled in nature, by reason of frigidity, to perform the duties, or any the least office of a husband.
Mistress Mavis. Now out upon him, prodigious creature!
Lady Centaure. Bridgegroom uncarnate!
Lady Haughty. And you offer it to a young gentlewoman?
Mrs. Otter. A lady of her longings?
Epicoene [the "wife"]. Tut, a device, a device, this! It smells rankly, ladies. A mere comment of his own.
Truewit. Why, if you suspect that, ladies, you may have him searched—
Daw. As the custom is, by a jury of physicians.
La-Foole. Yes, faith, 'twill be brave.
Morose. O me, must I undergo that?
Mrs. Otter. No, let women search him, madam. We can do it ourselves.

Who, reading this in the 1616 Folio, the earliest extant text, could fail to think of the jury of women that examined the supposed virgin wife of Essex? Do we have mere comic coincidence here in a play that apparently dates back to 1609? Or did the disgruntled and irrepressibly satiric playwright add something between 1613 and 1616? Oscar Wilde said that life imitated literature, and this could be a curious instance. The dedication asserts, defensively: "There is not a line or syllable in it changed from the simplicity of the first copy." There follows some dark muttering over "how much a man's innocency may be endangered by an uncertain accusation." Doth "The Silent Woman" protest too much? Hav-

ing no opportunity to compare texts, we had better keep in
mind that dedications are far from being the most reliable
depositories of truth. The same play contains a reference
(commonplace enough) to Dr. Forman's love philters. There
is also what may be a topical allusion to Overbury: "take a
little sublimate, and go out of the world like a rat." Jonson
once did an allegorical pastoral (no longer extant) about some
of these courtiers, in which Fanny's mother figured as an en-
chantress.

The divorce seems to have rankled more than the murder.
We recall that when Coke came around to question Fanny
about what she had done to Overbury, he digressed immediately to how she had disgraced herself in casting off Essex.
As one of the myriads of the unhappily married, the Chief
Justice betrayed his obsession. She had really got away with
something in being freed from her spouse, leaving others
indignant—or envious, just as the Archbishop had foreseen.
Under the date of March 1, 1618, James Howell referred to
her as the "articulate lady, called so for articulating against
the frigidity and impotence of her former lord." Michael
Drayton, in his satirical bird fable *The Owl* of 1619, introduces her as a Wren:

> They say the *Robin* roosteth in my nest.
> Gossip, 'tis true: to you it is confessed—
> My Cock's a slug and doth me little ease:
> He must be quick his female that will please.

The more decent of the allusions here is to the country
rhyme, "The Robin and the Wren are God Almighty's Cock
and Hen." Drayton makes no reference to Overbury. A poet
of lesser fame, Richard Corbett, gratuitously insists that the
Lady Haddington, whose death he mourns in 1618, had been
truly a virgin when she married:

> Nor didst thou, *two years after*, talk of force,
> Or, Lady-like, make suit for a divorce:
> Who, when their own wild lust is falsely spent,
> Cry out, *My Lord, my Lord is impotent.*
> Nor has thou in his nuptial arms enjoyed
> Barren embraces, but wert girled and boyed.

The wits shot the slings of their puns and anagrams. Not only did "Francis Howarde" become, as previously noted, "Car finds a whore," but "Thomas Overburie" was turned into "O! O! a busie murther." He was *buried over,* and he was "blasted by a Weston wind." Somerset became "Some are set" in one rhyme. In the following he is "summer . . . set":

> Our summer sun is set,
> And winter is come on.
> The Robin redbreast leaves to chirp
> Because his voice is gone.

If this postdates Carr's trial, it agrees with the opinion of the antiquarian Camden that the defense had not been a happy one, that Carr—lacking a counselor—might have fared better if "he had not answered at all." There were numerous puns on "Carr," of which the most palatable was:

> Lady, kin to Venus' dove,
> Gently guide the Car of love.
> If you delight with sweets to play,
> There's none like to your Car-away [a triple pun].

Such lines easily turned sour:

> Old Venus with her borrowed light
> Guide beasts and riders passing right.
> At length an elvish trick was shown
> That Frank and Car were overthrown.
> Then Turner plainly did espy

How coaches creep and Carrs did fly.
To four fierce ladies this Carr did trust,
Called Pride, Oppression, Murder, Lust.

Ever there was the feeling that the man was cheated in his wife. The following is not short on coarse double entendre, beginning with calling her a pink, a vessel with a narrow stern, with the sexual implication that she is to be boarded. (In a Latin poem the two appear as Carus and Carina—like Czar and Czarina—and *carina* means keel or boat.)

From Katherine's dock was launched a pink
Which sprung a leak, but did not sink.
From thence she drove to Essex shore,
Expecting rigging, yard, and store.
The like disaster to prevent,
With wind in poop, she sailed to Kent.
At Rochester she anchor cast,
Which Canterbury did distaste.
But Winchester, with Ely's help,
Did hale on shore this lion's whelp.
She was crank-sided [rolled easily] and did reel
To Somerset to mend her keel,
To stop her leak and scale her fort,
And make her fit for sea and port.

A rebus was widely popular, judging by the number of times it turns up in manuscripts:

I.C.U.R. [I see you are]
Good Monsieur Carr,
    About to fall.

U.R.A.K. [You are a k(nave)]
As most men say,
    But that's not all.

U.O.Q.P. [You occupy]
With a nullity
    That naughty pack [worthless woman],

S.X.Y.F. [Essex' wife]
Whose wicked life
    Hath broke your back.

A poem that has been conjecturally attributed to Sir Henry Wotton labels her Canidia, the Roman sorceress:

She that could reek within the sheets of lust,
And there be searched, yet pass without mistrust;
She that could surfle up the ways of sin
And make strait posterns where wide gates had been:
    Canidia now draws on.

She that could cheat the matrimonial bed
With a false-stamped, adulterate maidenhead,
And make the husband think those kisses chaste
Which were stale panders to his spouse's waste:
    Canidia now draws on.

All that James's court and country needed was to be free of her:

The stars would seem as glorious as the moon,
And she like Phoebus in his brightest noon;
Mists, clouds, vapors, all would pass away,
And the whole year be as an halcyon day:
    Oh were Canidia gone!

A ballad pretended to be "Found in Sir Nicholas Overbury's study, 1640" kicks at her as a filly spreading the French disease:

Her dock and heels have mangie and scratches,
    Come listen to me, and you shall hear.
Her tinderbox is full of French matches,
    To serve to burn some other's gear.

> Her rider, he pricked her up and down,
>   Come listen to me, and you shall hear,
> To city, suburb, and country-town,
>   And served her turn for other gear.

As Chamberlain remarked in another connection, "When men are down the very drunkards make rhymes and songs upon them." Misogyny was even quicker to uncover itself. Essex's aunt had been similarly abused. The following played on a below-the-belt meaning of "stone" that we have had before:

> Here lies Penelope, the Lady Rich,
> Or the Countess of Devonshire—choose you which.
> One stone sufficeth (lo what death can do!)
> Her that in life was not content with two.

It took more forgiving than anyone had, to get away with a second marriage—and for love!—while the first spouse was alive. Old representations of the wheel of fortune show people clinging to it as it revolves turned upside down. And women did not wear underpants until the middle of the nineteenth century. The wheel had turned exposing Fanny and inviting snide remarks about her "tinderbox." It was a fate literally like that of Mussolini's mistress, who was caught without her drawers and hanged with her lover upside down.

It took a Scot to be sympathetic. Sir Robert Aytoun composed forty-nine elegiac couplets in Latin modeled on Ovid's *Heroides*, constituting an imagined epistle from Fanny to her beloved Carr as she is under arrest and awaiting the birth of their child. "I perish in a thousand ways. Now the goddess of childbirth threatens acute pains. Soon a judge is preparing even worse things. If by any chance I survive childbirth, what is the chance that the hand of the executioner can be warded off?" She would, with Alcestis, gladly give up her life in return for her husand's. "Whatever it was I did, it was the error of a great love. Whoever has known love will readily absolve me. . . . In any case, as a happy victim I shall go down to the dark shades, and I Carina shall die faithful to my husband Carr" (with a pun on "caro," dear).

She, who had taken allegorical or mythological parts in masques, might, with certain changes, figure in a pastoral romance. So she seems to on pages 478–9 of an interminable Arcadian fiction, *The Countess of Montgomery's Urania*, 1621, by Lady Mary Wroth, niece—and would-be literary rival—of Sir Philip Sidney. This authoress—and they were rare in those days—had been herself, Jonson (who wrote poetry to her and about her) told Drummond of Hawthornden, "unworthily married on a jealous husband." Did this give her sympathy for Fanny as against Essex? In a disguised but detectable redoing of the real-life story, the Lady becomes the stock figure of the bruised heart. She was in love with a king *before* she married and remained faithful to the idea of him. "In all these unquiets, a match was offered me, I was mad and knew nothing but mine own passions; in that distemper I gave consent and was married, but still my affection was tied and wedded to this King, this King of ungratefulness and cruelty. A wife I lived, and yet a maid, my husband sometimes chafing, sometimes telling me he thought I kept that jewel for another." As a clue for the wise, a period of three years is mentioned (the triennial probation). The King confides in a gentleman friend (Overbury), which was not the right thing to do to one "who so dearly loved him as for his sake she had lived a maiden-wife, and would have ever, had she not enjoyed him." When she found she was cruelly used she "vowed revenge and plotted for it."

Another endless narrative of 1621 that contains an allusion is John Barclay's *Argenis*. This political romance attained enormous popularity, even though, in fact partly because, it was in Latin—and thus could be read on the Continent. It went through forty editions by 1683. Ben Jonson planned to offer the public a translation (not extant), and different English versions came out in 1625 and 1629. Apparently the fun of the book was figuring out who was meant, what King or princess or courtier, by the pastoral names. Barclay, a Scotsman who lived in London from 1606 to 1616, spews out that "wedded pair" on an early page (page 18 of the 1629 translation by Robert Le Grys), observing that these poisoners deserved their punishment, considering "how much they offended: he, as forgetful of his former estate and taking it in scorn that he was beloved by many women: she, not fearing hate for divorcing herself from her husband, to whom she had been first married: both of them, not having pacified with sacrifice, displeased Juno, and ignorant that the goddesses also had their own lightning." Carr "beloved by many women"? That is not what the Latin says: it says he disdained to be popular—*a multis* [sex unspecified] *amari dedignatus.* That Fanny should have feared "hate for divorcing herself," that is now a familiar point, sharper for the original's not having "hate"—*odium*—but "invidiam"—*envy.* . . . The case was still so well remembered after thirteen years that the translator, in providing a key to the characters, remarked of this pair that they "need no proper name in this edition."

William Browne of Tavistock, himself a pastoral poet, gazing "On the Countess of Somerset's Picture," found it all very hard to believe: "Yet I, if Misery did look as she,/Should quickly fall in love with Misery."

Aftermath

10

The crowd wanted their blood, which was fair enough considering what the law had meted out to the four others who had been found guilty. Surely there was not one justice for the common people, and another for the Lord and Lady. It would be a mockery if the great ones escaped. Outsiders flocked thirstily to Tower Hill, looking for activity at a scaffold, but those closer to the court noted cynically—and said, as Chamberlain did on June 8th—"they live yet and for aught I can learn so are like to do many a day." As the weeks slipped by and the murderess whom they had heard confess was neither hanged nor decapitated, it was no wonder if Londoners—there being a limit even to an Englishman's endurance and self-control—behaved like French rabble, surrounding her supposed coach "railing and reviling," terrifying their good dropsical Queen, who herself was not long for this world.

Having taught Overbury, and then having thoroughly experienced himself "the narrow space 'twixt a prison and a smile," the Earl of Somerset had no visitors. He was, however, given leave to write the King. Whether as a cunning bid for sympathy, or in simple manly dignity, he requested that the judgment of hanging be altered to beheading. Hanging was the common lot, and ignominious, even with a silken noose which nobles were entitled to. If a man did not have his codpiece, there was the embarrassment that hanging triggers an erection (see *Waiting for Godot* and *Naked Lunch*). The appropriateness of this for one who was dying because of his infatuation for a woman was a bit too much. One seventeenth-century meaning of *dying* was orgasm, what the French call *la petite mort*. Donne played on the ambiguity: "We can die by it, if not live by love." There was also the mean belief—which Carr seemed destined to illustrate—that orgasm shortened life. Arthur Wilson, in his 1653 history, offers a suggestive phrase for Carr: "swallowed up in this gulf of beauty." Carr wanted to depart as a lord, though he was not the son of a lord—to go out in the grand, clean-cut manner of, say, Essex's father or the King's mother (that is, it would have been clean-cut if the executioners had known their business). He also begged "that his daughter might have such of his lands as the King doth not resume and reserve in his own hands."

Fanny received frequent visits from her older sister, Elizabeth, Lady Knollys. Some friends came, too. The baby girl —now half a year old—was brought two or three times. It was not the worst apartment living, if one could forget why one was there. She had brought in sumptuously upholstered furniture, with carpets, tapestries, plate. She was making do with three maids, two others—one of them Toothless Margaret— being in the common jails on account of their connection with the case. She had a terrace, and below was a little garden with a henhouse that Ralegh had converted into a laboratory for his chemical experiments. He was conditionally free, after thirteen years, going up and down looking at all the changes. A nuisance was the hoary prison rule of not being allowed to be alone with visitors. But they kept coming and they stayed long. She tired out the "continual attendance" of Sir George More. Villiers sent word from Greenwich on June 18 that the Lieutenant could be spelled by his wife or his daughter-in-law.

She had told the court, "I desire mercy." She had virtually been promised that. Would the King keep his word? The question was, which word? He was given to swearing. When the case first broke he had got down on his knees before his councilors to attest to his personal innocence, "desired God to lay a curse upon him and his posterity forever, if he were consenting to Overbury's death." This is on the authority of Wilson, writing four years after the execution of Charles I. Another version is that he vowed "all lawful courses that . . . the innocent may be cleared, and the nocent may severely be punished." This did not sound good for Fanny (but of course she had not heard it). Still more drastic is Weldon's quotation for that occasion: "If you shall spare any guilty of this crime, God's curse light on you and your posterity. And if I spare any that are guilty, God's curse light on me and my posterity forever." This, published a few months after the beheading of James's son and successor, is terribly, suspiciously, neat. But it is clear that James did avow something that, if not true (his innocence) or kept (full punishment of the criminals), would fully explain—by the providential view of history—why his son lost a revolution that cost him his life and why his grandson, James II, was driven from the throne, and why the Stuart dynasty petered out with Anne, whose babies never lived.

July 13, 1616, the very day that the Queen's coach was mobbed on its way to Whitehall, Lady Somerset received a pardon. It was as if the crowd had had some clairvoyance. But she was not on the loose, as they thought. It was not a full pardon. It was a reprieve from the death sentence. Four reasons were given for the King's having exercised his prerogative of mercy: "The first respecteth her father, and friends, and family, and noble stock." Such a reason would never be admitted today, but James could hardly, for instance, keep looking into the eyes of a Lord Treasurer whose daughter he had executed. He was still greeting the mother with a kiss whenever he saw her, to the astonishment of the Spanish ambassador. The second reason "hath respect to herself, because she freely and willingly confessed her offence, submitting and prostrating herself at the altar of our mercy, not only during the time of her imprisonment, but also publicly, and in her trial." What a relief that open confession was, for all concerned! Thirdly, the Lord High Steward, with the Peers, had interceded for her. The fourth reason was added by Bacon under instruction by the King: "that she seemed to have begun by the procurement and wicked instigation of certain base persons." In other words, she had fallen in with bad company. That extenuation has a modern ring: the more or less juvenile delinquent so lured and tempted by elders that it was not really her fault: the social worker just did not get to her in time! But of course the bias was different: our humanitarian feeling is that the poor can do no wrong, while in that time and place the blue-blooded string-pullers were blatantly favored.

Still, Fanny was under "imprisonment at our royal pleasure" (*imprisonamentum ad arbitrium nostrum regium*). That could last for years, and in fact did.

And the sword still dangled over the head of her husband, because he had not confessed and was thus unregenerate and obstinately put in doubt the King's justice, instead of throwing himself entirely and humbly on his mercy. James got another stiff letter from him (if he was innocent he had a right to be aggrieved) in which he declared, "I fell rather for want of well defending than by the violence or force of any proofs." Since the King had created him it would be proper for the King to redeem him: an analogy with God that "I took from Dr. Donne his sermon" (one he must have heard the previous year sometime between April, when the newly ordained poet received, by royal mandate, a D.D. from Cambridge, and October, when the murder suspect was shut off from public preaching). Besides instructing the King as to his duty, the missive mumbles darkly against enemies, gives vent to threats so obscure that only the recipient—if he could have—understood them, and refuses "such way of intercession" as had been set forth as the prisoner's best hope—that is, suing to Villiers. *That* Sir George was definitely the one to reckon with now. Within a few months James, who took all divine comparisons in stride, announced complacently, "Christ had his John and I have my George." Still to come were some touching love notes, as when the aging and infatuated monarch urged this, his final beloved, to hasten to him that night that "his white teeth may shine upon him" (another blasphemous parody—"The Lord make His face shine upon thee, and be gracious unto thee"). He would be rewarded with some such reply as, "I kiss your dirty hands" (the King deemed it bad for his delicate skin to wash them). They were two spotted doves, with no room for a third except "Baby Charles." The son and heir was called that at sixteen, and for eight more years until the father died.

When, on July 7, 1616, Villiers with two others was installed at Windsor Castle as a Knight of the Garter, "there was a chapter held about taking down or continuing of the Earl of Somerset's hatchments or arms, but, after long dispute, by warrant under the King's own hand they were removed higher, as the manner is when new come in." Despite those who deemed this a disgraceful indulgence unendurable for other members of the order, technically it was correct, since that individual, though civilly dead, had not been convicted of high treason. He bore his Damoclean sword, as well as his bright ribbon, bravely, moved about freely in the Lieutenant's company, and before the month was out was glimpsed "walking and talking with the Earl of Northumberland, and he and his lady saluting at the window." Congratulations were certainly in order to her, the reprieved one.

Everything became very relaxed (or lax, depending on the point of view), with no one forbidding. They were harmless now. Their comforts gradually merged. By August the two were conversing day and night. We'd give the £156 of silver plate that he'd brought, or her figured satin chairs, to know what they said. Soon they had—shades of the Raleghs!—adjoining apartments. The first week of December, false rumor babbled that she was with child again.

They—and particularly she—became rather too involved with their fellow prisoner, Henry Percy, ninth Earl of Northumberland (a direct descendant of Hotspur and the other Percys of Shakespeare's histories). Apparently she could not keep away from magicians and Catholics. Northumberland was called "The Wizard Earl" on account of his dedication to the occult sciences, and, a Catholic sympathizer rather than a Catholic, he had been in the Tower since 1605 on the charge of complicity in the Gunpowder Plot. Intrigue never ceased to fascinate him. He had stepped forward as an intermediary in the 1602 case of Donne's elopement. He himself had married a sister of the father of Fanny's first husband—Dorothy Devereux—but they had not lived together much, nor cared to. They did have a daughter whom Lord Hay, once Carr's patron, was courting. Northumberland, however, was not on the side of love and marriage: he forced Lucy to reside in the Tower with him to preserve her from Hay. Meanwhile, at fifty-three, he warmed up to Fanny. To gain easier entree himself he encouraged his daughter to visit her. But Fanny encouraged the romance of Lord Hay and Lady Lucy to such an extent that the daughter had to be sent away.

Recent writers cite this against her. "She . . . embarked on a disgraceful intrigue with the Earl of Northumberland, was plotting at the same time with Lord Hay to get Lady Lucy Percy for him as a bride in the teeth of her father's opposition," states William McElwee. "Frances repaid him by strengthening Lady Lucy's determination to marry Lord Hay," complains Beatrice White. This is unfairly put, and falls into the same fallacy that has been put around Carr, that a person who was guilty of one reprehensible thing must have been guilty of another, that a woman who was "a bad lot" must be a wholly bad lot. There is no evidence nor any particular reason to believe that Fanny was playing her husband false, and she was being consistent in doing what she could to further a love match, repaying the libidinous, double-standard father in exactly the way she felt he deserved to be repaid. She had seen enough of parental arrangements in marriage. There would have been fewer ruined lives (to say nothing of murders) if more girls had been brave enough to go "in the teeth of . . . father's opposition." As for "a disgraceful intrigue with the Earl of Northumberland," all we know is that *he* flirted with *her*, disgracefully. Her reputation as a loose woman gave him fantasies of easy conquest. And this was the man who had once written an essay to his wife loftily informing her that scholarship and learning were infinitely preferable to female companionship. He was now acting like a character in *Love's Labour's Lost*.

While we are on the subject of fidelity, there is something like evidence that Carr deviated, and after having been married scarcely a year and a half. An enigmatic passage in Chamberlain's letter to Carleton of July 20, 1615 is quoted neither by McElwee nor White. "Young Gibb of the Bedchamber is willed to absent himself, which is taken for an ill sign and cross-blow to somebody else. All the reason I can hear is for carrying a scandalous message and some say a letter to Mistress Murray of the Queen's Bedchamber from the Lord Chamberlain." Miss White says nothing about this, and all that McElwee says is, "His friend and protégé, Henry Gibb, got into trouble and he could not prevent his banishment from Court." What could have been involved except advances to Mistress Murray or possibly (Overbury's bee in the bonnet) through her to the Queen? We have nothing outside this one reference.

Now, in the Tower in 1617, if Carr was jealous, it does not follow that his wife gave him reason; Northumberland did. But the husband began to have differences with the wife. He was outraged, perhaps as the father of a daughter about whose marriage he, if he lived long enough, intended to have some say. As one who had never lost his burr, he would normally have been expected to resist prejudice against his benefactor, Hay, the only reasoning Northumberland offered being "that he was a Percy and could not endure that his daughter should dance any Scottish jigs." When the hypocritical father found that Fanny was not on his side he denounced her as a bawd. But the thoroughly respectable Countess of Bedford had been in favor of the match. And Hay did the Somersets a favor worth £4000 per year. Carr had refused to unbend enough to ask for, in the proper tone, a portion of his estates, and they were being redistributed right and left when some of the Howards and his friends came and begged him "that he would take care, if not of himself, yet of his wife and child." He grudgingly gave permission for Fanny to write Hay to intercede with the King, and the result was a liberal, though of course greatly reduced, maintenance.

Nevertheless, having done two good deeds—assisted a girl in love and a husband dispossessed—Fanny began getting it on both sides. Just after the fiasco, when Lucy—having been dismissed by her father and refused by her mother—had no choice but to live in London on money provided by Hay (ultimately they married), there was an explosion so loud that it rumbled past the thick walls to the alert ears of Chamberlain. "There is a great falling out of late twixt the Earl of Somerset and his Lady in the Tower, but it is not yet so public that I can learn the original [cause] or particulars, but certainly there is a great jar, howsoever it will piece again or be smothered."

One quarrel bred another. The end, sad to tell, had begun, an end more deadly than disgrace or imprisonment, an end that lay between them like a corpse the rest of their lives together, not Overbury's corpse—though that was there too—but the body, the clay and ashes, of what had once been passion. The reports of their bickerings and their long silences are too persistent and too inherently plausible to be attributed merely to the wishful thinking of moralists. He had plenty to blame her for, and she was not one to forbear forever from striking back. There they were together, with creature comforts, even luxury, and great lenience on the part of the authorities. They could copulate as much as they liked; and they did not like, and they found they did not like each other. She lived for fifteen years more and never had another child, a good index, in that prolific era of no or poor birth control, of abstinence. He might just as well have been Essex. Unless, of course, she now really had an obstruction, which would be very ironical.

One thinks of the carnal sinners, Paolo and Francesca and

the others, in the second circle of Dante's Inferno, stuck together for all eternity. That is what lovers ask for, to be together. Those whom the gods wish to punish, they answer their prayers.

With the dragging out of another year she perhaps came to feel it would serve her husband right if she gave him something to be jealous for. Nor was Northumberland the only man available within those remarkably privileged bounds. In the fall of 1618, Chamberlain had "heard in the country of a great falling out twixt the Lord of Somerset and his Lady for that he had taken her tripping [that is, she was caught playing him false], and that they were upon parting, but I have had no time to learn any certainty." "Parting"—that was a good jest. But country rumors were admittedly less reliable than city rumors. Subsequent letters do not mention the matter again.

In any case, unbearably ironic now was Jonson's poem for their wedding day:

> . . . So, be there never discontent, or sorrow,
>   To rise with either of you on the morrow.
> So, be your concord still as deep, as mute,
>   And every joy in marriage turn a fruit.
> So may those marriage-pledges comforts prove:
>   And every birth increase the heat of love.
> So in their number may you never see
>   Mortality, till you immortal be.
> And when your years rise more than would be told,
>   Yet neither of you seem to th'other old,
> That all that view you then, and late, may say,
>   "Sure, this glad pair were married but this day!"

Was the poet an idealist, hopelessly out of touch with reality—or had he been sneering? Was *she* an idealist? Did that account for her ruined life? Before she had known what she wanted, she was an uncriticized, docile girl, doing, at thirteen, what her parents told her. Then she came to believe in love, and fought the good fight for it, though not exactly with St. Paul's, or any saint's, methods. But society, or the Church, should have made divorce possible without resort to chicanery, black magic, or murder. It was virtuous to have the goal that she had set before her and pursued so unswervingly. Blake was to say, "Those who restrain Desire, do so because theirs is weak enough to be restrained." She had nothing but contempt for people without will and without dedication. They were dead. She was endowed with the fanaticism of a saint, or a revolutionary. She had been love's martyr. And now "love" did not seem to be the right word at all. Blake also said, "The road of excess leads to the palace of wisdom." But the Tower of London was no longer a palace, and if wisdom was what she had arrived at, she did not want it. She was undesired—and reproached—by the man for whom she had done everything. She had not noticed his hideous weaknesses before, but she still wanted to be wanted. She had to test her attractions again, even as she had once flaunted her newly ripe breasts. Or was she old and finished, buried alive, and with a taint in her blood?

The observers, the students of history, the partisans who had *known* the Howards were incorrigibly tainted were soon able to point in a variety of current directions. In November of 1619 the father, the Earl of Suffolk, after having been brought before the Star Chamber on signal from Villiers, now Buckingham (already a marquis), was found guilty of peculation as Lord Treasurer and joined his daughter and son-in-law in the Tower. The mother went there too, for bribery. On top of that she had just been visited by the smallpox, the marks of which, it was cruelly said, "would have done her more harm forty years ago than they can do now."

James had become disgusted with her on learning the year before that persons wishing to do business with her husband had to grease her palm, and he swore that if she did not keep out of London he would have her wheeled away in a cart like a common whore. Their eldest son was also thrown into the Tower, along with the Howards's protégé as Secretary, Sir Thomas Lake. Although none of these except Lake was there longer than a week or ten days, the jest went around that they were holding a Privy Council meeting, "being provided with a Lord Treasurer [Suffolk], a Lord Chamberlain [Somerset], a captain of the pensioners [Theophilus Howard], and a Secretary [Lake]," to say nothing of the female powers that moved the men. The imprisonment was brief, but the fines were grievous, and the Howards, for all their remarkable bounce and push, seemed finished as forces to be reckoned with. Even old Charles Howard, Nottingham, who could not be convicted of anything else, was convicted of old age and obliged to hand over his post of Lord Admiral to Buckingham, who also profited from the Ralegh-Carr estate of Sherborne.

Neither of Fanny's sisters made a decent marriage. The younger, Katherine, got William Cecil in 1608. Politically he was a prize, as the only son of the great Secretary, Sir Robert Cecil, Earl of Salisbury. Personally he was a homosexual. Everybody knew he had had for years a "mignon," Will Lytton. As with Fanny's first husband, Katherine's left her *virgo intacta* to go abroad for years. When he got back, Will Lytton was still "his principal mignon."

As for Elizabeth, the sister who kept comforting Fanny, she, it will be recalled, had been handed over to a widower forty years her senior. This catch, eventually the Earl of Banbury, took part at Whitehall in a May conference representing Essex in 1613. He was, in fact, through his sister Lettice Knollys, Essex's great-uncle. But the passing years brought up the question of how potent was *he,* William Knollys. In 1627 and 1631 Elizabeth gave birth to sons that she passed off as her husband's. He should have acted to the hilt the proud father, since he was in his eighties: in 1631 he celebrated his eighty-fourth birthday. Gossips and biological skeptics noted that the son of that year was born at the residence of Edward, fourth Lord Vaux (the first son had actually been named Edward), and that a few months later, in 1632, when at last Banbury expired, Elizabeth lost no time in marrying her host. Banbury's will of May 19, 1630, failed to mention the son that had been born in 1627, nor was there any contingency for the second offspring that was already on the way. Banbury's funeral certificate declared that he died without issue. The legitimacy of the Banbury line became a nagging question that sputtered to an end in 1813, when, after the eighth Earl was denied a seat in the House of Lords, the family gave up pushing its claims.

It was the general conclusion that these daughters of Eve led their husbands by the nose and to their ruin. When James, yielding to Buckingham, took the lucrative Mastership of the Rolls away from Knollys in 1619, he absolved him of guilt, complaining only that he, like the others, "was altogether guided and overruled by an arch-wife." With reason, most people sympathized with Suffolk, the fallen Treasurer. "The Countess made use of her husband but as a seal-ring, with a man's head upon it, to confirm what before she had resolved to do."

In January 1622 the Somersets were released from the Tower, but still without a full pardon. In fact he was still formally under the death sentence. Although he probably by now felt reasonably safe from its ever being carried out, and was wrangling, rather, over lost property, there was the ominous and recent precedent of Ralegh, executed fifteen years after *his* sentence. True, Ralegh had never been loved by James. Still, out of touch, the fallen favorite had no way of gauging his successful enemies' intentions and poisonous influence. A fortune teller told him that if he could see the King once more all would be well. But he was distant from any such opportunity. His wife's reprieve had mentioned as a future possibility "restraint, confining to a certain place," and this was what was now spelled out in the Council Order from Whitehall, on January 18, 1622:

Whereas His Majesty is graciously pleased to enlarge and set at liberty the Earl of Somerset and his Lady, now prisoners in the Tower of London; and that nevertheless it is thought fit that both the said Earl and his Lady be confined to some convenient place: it is therefore, according to His Majesty's gracious pleasure and command, ordered, That the Earl of Somerset and his Lady do repair either to Greys or Cawsham, the Lord Wallingford's houses, in the county of Oxford, and remain confined to one or either of the said houses, and within three miles compass of either of the same, until further order be given by His Majesty.

Lord Wallingford was the current title of William Knollys. His wife, Fanny's favorite sister, may have been pulling the strings of a bargain. The Marquis of Buckingham wanted to buy the Knollys town house near Whitehall. He could have it in return for a favor or two, the second being the elevation of brother Sir Thomas Howard to a Viscount. All these changes happened with dizzying simultaneity. The Old Testament had said, A life for a life. Buckingham said, A life for a house.

But what sort of life was it? They spent the first night at Northampton House in Charing Cross, where seven and a half years ago her great-uncle had come to a literally rotten end, where she had resorted for undoubtedly too much advice, where once she cried she would make away with herself if she could not get free of Essex. Now, with the husband she *had* wanted, one of a like complexion with herself, she was borne to Greys, a once idyllic place, which had been the scene of a different sort of confinement in the summer of 1615, when she was expecting her baby, and Elizabeth and she had talked about the lying-in, and the first rumblings of discovery began to destroy the tranquility she needed, and her husband started frantically asking questions (just when she had at last won him thoroughly from the King), and spent good money to get back his letters to Overbury, and Anne Turner went hysterical, and they all prepared for the worst, the worst which was not a death sentence but a life sentence.

Based on the reports of such contemporaries as Arthur Wilson and Simonds D'Ewes on how "this glad pair," as Jonson had hailed them, "lived long after, though in one house, as strangers to one another," Philip Gibbs, himself a novelist, sketches a vivid and all too likely picture:

It must have been a living torture to both of them—to sit opposite to each other at the same table day by day, and to be forced to bear each other company in dreadful solitude, without society; to tire each other out with upbraidings and accusations; to suffer the horrible silence which afterwards followed when, as inmates of the same house, they lived entirely separate and estranged. It was a situation which would provide a psychological novelist with some powerful scenes; for if the King had been a fiend of cruelty, he could not have devised a more subtle punishment for two erring souls.

Unfortunately the only novel these two have received has been *The King's Minion* (1930) by Rafael Sabatini, which has 445 pages but a stultifying absence of "powerful scenes": that author did better with *Scaramouche* and *Captain Blood*. However, *The Scarlet Letter* twice refers to the case; Hawthorne borrowed materials on it from the Salem Athenaeum while he was writing his great study of sin, and Hester Prynne is something of an amalgam of Lady Frances and Anne Turner. (The latter, by the way, inspired Dame Ursula Saddlechop, milliner and secret agent in Scott's *The Fortunes of Nigel*. Sir Walter himself edited a *Secret History of the Court of James I*.) Professor Alfred S. Reid contends that Roger Chillingworth, the wronged and avenging husband, combines no fewer than five historical figures: Essex, Carr, Turner, Franklin, and Weston. That raffish personality, Richard Savage, whose biography Dr. Johnson wrote, acted the title role in his own tragedy *Sir Thomas Overbury* at Drury Lane in 1723, a feeble piece in blank—very blank—verse. Savage invents an orphan, Isabella, who is the reason for everybody's action. She and Overbury are in love, to the chagrin of Northampton, who has wanted her for himself. Frances has married, but does not love, Somerset, preferring Overbury, who has rebuffed her for Isabella. Frances makes Somerset jealous, accusing his friend of having attempted her, and Northampton aids the plot by presenting Overbury's unaddressed love letters to Isabella as proof. The passion-struck villainess weakens in her vengeful purpose in the end, "melts in a fit of softness," even to being caught by Somerset as she gropes for the prisoner's chamber, but it is too late: Elwes and Northampton have seen to the poisoning. An attempt to salvage the play by revising it was made by William Woodfall in 1777, a year that will continue to be better known for Burgoyne's surrender at Saratoga.

Carr's career probably influenced Chapman's tragedy *Chabot*. As Swinburne remarked, "An austere and stately moralist like Chapman could hardly have sought a stranger patron than Carr"; but having started with him, Chapman stayed with him. In that very year of transfer from the Tower the poet printed an "Epistle Dedicatory" that began, in typical clogged fashion, "All least Good, that but only aims at Great,/I know, best Earl, may boldly make retreat/To your retreat, from this World's open Ill." The dedication to the *Hymns of Homer* says with considerable exaggeration that the "retreat" was Carr's own choice, "Not forced by Fortune, but since your free mind/(Made by affliction) rests in choice resigned/To calm retreat, laid quite beneath the wind/Of grace and glory—." But this makes pleasant reading compared to such a libel as that found in *The Five Years of King James* (a pamphlet attributed wrongly to another poet, Fulke Greville), published while Carr was still alive, which tells the breathless reader, in the historical present, that the villain "sends into France to make away the apothecary that administered the physic that killed Sir Thomas." Chapman, in submitting books "to your Lordship's judicial perspective," was making one good point, namely that that Lord had plenty of time to read, even as Bacon, after his downfall in 1621 for corrupt practices as a judge, had plenty of time to write. When the Somersets weren't quarreling they were bored; as McElwee points out, "neither of them had the education or the resources within themselves for solitary, uneventful existence." We just do not imagine Fanny with a book in her hand or getting interested in sheep. For the English reader it is startling to come upon the cognate of *hausfrau* on the title page of a Dutch news pamphlet of 1616 on the sensational conviction of *"den Grave van Somerset en sijn huysvrou."* After all, she did not even prepare her own poisons.

Knollys was their jailer-host for nearly three years. On October 7, 1624, less than half a year before the King's death, Carr received a full pardon. The story goes that he and the King eluded their various watchers and had one secret meeting. They fell weeping into each other's arms. By then a considerable part of the kingdom, if not the King himself, realized that Buckingham, who fancied himself an administrator and stretched out tentacles everywhere, was a much bigger—more dangerous because more ambitious—mistake than the preceding favorite; but he ruled over James in his dotage and over Charles, and there was nothing to do about it—until, in 1628, an assassin's knife did something about it. The meeting of the old friends, if it took place, was doubtless close in time to the pardon, the Latin of which makes much mention of wicked Weston and none of Lady Somerset. It seemed to go without saying that she was as free as her husband now. The reason assigned for the relaxation of justice was Carr's past services and—mentioned first and at much greater length —those of his father, Sir Thomas Carr of Ferniehurst, who, it seems, had been more loyal to the King's mother than the King was, "underwent with steadfast mind and fidelity exile and the overturn and ruin of his fortunes."

The Somersets were now alone with each other with their child Anne and the servants. They took a house in Chiswick, a village tantalizingly close to London, and that was where they ended their days and their loveless nights. He still had enough money—and enough vanity—to write from Chiswick on November 20, 1624, offering "£400 or £500" for a diamond and gold sword. They were scarcely settled when the plague came, marking, as it had done in 1603, the accession of another Stuart. Charles I, who had not yet even seen his French bride Henrietta Maria (he had married her by proxy), had but one intimate, who "lay the first night of the reign in the King's bedchamber." Well, that was one of the Duke's pristine titles—Gentleman of the Bedchamber. The late Queen Anne had yielded her consent.

In earlier plagues Chiswick had proved a good refuge, but now some of those who had fled the city broke out with it there. There is no indication that the Somersets did anything but stick it out, but as the deaths soared alarmingly that August their neighbor, Francis, Lord Russell of Thornhaugh, retreated with his wife and ten children to Woburn Abbey in Bedfordshire. These and other patrician residents returned in the winter. Lord Russell, who inclined toward the Puritan party, looked down on that family of three who had settled all too near. He personally had been on the jury that heard Lady Somerset confess to murder. He would have had second thoughts about returning to Chiswick, pleasant as it was and within easy rowing or riding distance of Westminster (all his children had been born there), if he could have foreseen the passionate love that would eventually develop between the Somersets' little girl, now ten, and his eldest son William, now twelve.

Did Fanny ever leave her sullen home to venture into society again, London society, court society, so teasingly near? To so venture was not exactly illegal, but it took verve and it took nerve. There is only one record, a letter to Hay of November 28, 1628, from Archie Armstrong, the court fool, whose *Banquet of Jests* was a best-seller in 1630. Maybe it was his idea of a joke, but he said that the Duchess of Rich-mond and the Countess of Somerset stood as godmothers at the christening of his infant son (Philip—"for the King of Spain's sake"!). Or perhaps Archie's standards were the usual court ones—blood, not morals. For the Duchess of Richmond, whose maiden name was also Frances Howard, and her father, Thomas—Viscount Howard of Bindon, another branch of the family—had other things in common with Fanny. A great beauty in her day, she had worn out three husbands and been reputedly the mistress of the third while waiting for the elderly second to die. But the third marriage, to a genuine Stuart, cousin to the King—with the demise of Queen Anne she had been the first lady in the land—had not lasted long, that spouse having passed away (one hesitates to use so sexual a word as *died*) in his bed one morning from—so it was rumored—an overdose of an aphrodisiac. (It sounds like Spanish fly, which, for quite a different reason, had been served up to Overbury in place of pepper.) As the all-powerful Duke of Buckingham, that arch opponent of Howards and Somersets, had been stabbed on August 23, 1628, by a disgruntled lieutenant who (like Iago) had been denied promotion, Fanny may have felt that she could at last take a step away from rural exile. (Her husband was the dedicatee in 1629 of *The Tragedy of Albovine, King of the Lombards,* by William D'avenant, who was wont to say in his cups that he was Shakespeare's natural son. "My Lord," he now printed, "You read this tragedy, and smiled upon it, that it might live." Why would the young poet have looked hopefully in the direction of Chiswick? Did he think that, with Buckingham gone, Somerset might make a comeback?)

Less than four years later Fanny was dead. She died at thirty-nine, give or take some months. Who was it who said that no beautiful woman should reach forty? But as a reminder that there are other ravagers of fairness than the passing years is the story of her end. There are three ugly accounts, all similar, and no one saying nay except Bishop Goodman, who always contradicts Arthur Wilson, that former henchman of Essex. Wilson hated her, and his hatred reaches its pitch (pun intended) in this paragraph:

She died before him. Her death was infamous, his without fame, the obscurity of the rest of his life darkening the splendor of it. And though she died as it were in a corner—in so private a condition, the loathsomeness of her death made it as conspicuous as on the housetop. For that part of her body which had been the receptacle of most of her sin, grown rotten (though she never had but one child), the ligaments failing, it fell down, and was cut away in flakes, with a most nauseous and putrid savor, which, to augment, she would roll herself in her own ordure in her bed, took delight in it. Thus her affections varied—for nothing could be found sweet enough to augment her beauties at first, and nothing stinking enough to decipher her loathsomeness at last. Pardon the sharpness of these expressions, for they are for the glory of God, Who often makes His punishments (in the balance of His justice) of equal weight with our sins.

Was he perhaps overstating "for the glory of God"? What is the diagnosis, uterine cancer? William Lilly had published two years before Wilson: "She was incapable of coition at least a dozen years ere she died, having an impediment in that very member she had so much delighted in and abused; and this I had from the mouth of one who saw her when bowelled." Sir Simonds D'Ewes had heard it "credibly related that soon after the birth of her daughter she was disabled by the second punishment of a higher Providence from being capable, and that though she lived near upon twenty years after it, yet her husband the Earl of Somerset never knew her; but the said infirmity still increased more and more upon her, till at last she died of it in very great extremity." This may be an inference from her not having been a multipara like Lady Russell and all the other ladies, who had every year a child with some expectation that half of them might reach maturity.

It was a death to gladden the hearts of moralists. In the end was her beginning, the *impenetrable* woman. It was a poetically just death, like the loathsome but cautionary ends their creators gave Madame Bovary and Nana. We may suspect exaggeration, at the least, but it is certain she did not die of old age and perhaps would not have wanted to.

The date was August 13, 1632. Two weeks later (it took some arranging) her body was laid to rest in the yard of the parish church at Saffron Walden, not far from Audley End, that useless pile that gawkers with their two-and-six entrance fee give a dinosaur's life to in this democratized world where the remaining lords and ladies tend to preside over museums, and, if they are really in step with the times, zoos.

As for what Wilson with scant exaggeration calls "the obscurity of the rest of his life," Carr's destiny was thirteen more years of that. In James he had lost a former friend; in Charles he had never had one. Cotton got him into trouble again in 1630 by circulating to him and certain others "a pestilent tractate, . . . containing a project how a prince may make himself an absolute tyrant." The author and the several recipients were arrested, but the case was soon dropped. In 1633 Charles forced him to return a jewel that was declared to be the property of the Crown. Two years later the King started—but did not carry through—an inquiry as to whether the erstwhile favorite (whom he was measuring by Buckingham's rapaciousness) did not have a secret fortune amounting to 60,000 pounds. Around the end of 1641, when Charles was having manifold troubles of his own, the retired but persistent resident of Chiswick petitioned unheeded for property that he said King James had pledged him. By then he was a thorough anachronism: favorites were dead. The Earl of Strafford, the King's adviser in despotism, had been put to death that May by Parliament under a Bill of Attainder, and bigger upheavals were to come. With revolution swirling all around him, Carr breathed his last in 1645, the year that his lovely, romantic daughter reached thirty.

There is a portrait of Anne Carr by Van Dyck—one of his finest—in Woburn Abbey, done as she was entering upon her twenties. She stands in a gown of white silk, with a bow at her breast and a spaniel at her feet arching his head in admiration. It was as if she were getting ready for some sort of coming-out, stepping from a Persian carpet to what could be a ballroom floor. She has her parents' fairness, but a softer, shyer beauty than her mother's, and a vulnerable chin. Her mother looked every bit as bold as she actually was, and a little twisted. But this girl radiates virtue and innocence, and not less so for its being a fact that she was in love and her love had been answered. Although the Russells had moved from Chiswick in 1627, when the father succeeded as fourth Earl of Bedford, the oldest son never forgot the girl who had been his neighbor, and when he returned in 1634 from the Grand Tour abroad, "a handsome, genteel man," and had a choice of ladies, "the voice goes that he bends somewhat towards the Lady Anne Carr, though it is said that his father has given him the admonition to choose anywhere but there."

"All in a flame with love" though they were, their marriage was held up for three years and achieved only after the overcoming of difficulties ordinarily found insuperable. His father was opposed for obvious reasons, and her father did not have the required dowry. Thinking to quash the union once and for all, Bedford demanded of Somerset the crushing sum of 12,000 pounds. A surprising assent came, to the effect that, if he or his daughter was to be undone, better that it be he. He agreed to mortgage his house and furnishings in Chiswick and pledged the reversion of certain lands in Scotland and initiated an installment plan payment of 12,000 pounds with a thousand down. Finding his son still determined to have his heart's choice or none, and even pressed to consent by King Charles and Queen Henrietta Maria, Bedford allowed the wedding to take place. They were not children—they knew what they were doing, it being 1637, the year the bride became twenty-two, the groom twenty-four. Unfortunately, Somerset did not come through with the rest of the money and a lawsuit was instituted against him. The widower turned against his happy and prosperous daughter in envy and self-pity, which their early succession as Earl and Countess of Bedford—the father was carried away by smallpox in 1641—did nothing to alleviate. After his house was raided by Royalist troops in 1643 and some unique tapestries carried off, Carr wrote bitterly to relatives in Scotland that he believed his daughter and son-in-law had instigated the incursion and that those very hangings, which they had often cast greedy eyes upon, would end up in their home. He never did pay off the dowry.

As a consequence of nursing her father-in-law during his last sickness, Anne came down with the smallpox, too, a danger that her mother had carefully kept clear of when her first husband was stricken with the same disease. The result was that Anne ceased to sit for portraits. But at the ninety-room Woburn mansion, where the gallery was adorned with the fair, unblemished faces of her father and mother, Anne's reign was long and prolific in the old Howard way—six sons and three daughters, enough insurance for a straight line to the present Duke of Bedford, who, in his autobiography, *A Silver-Plated Spoon*, manifests surprise that love could persist despite an unpaid dowry: "William's marriage was an extraordinarily happy one, although his father-in-law defaulted on his daughter's dowry." Anne lived till 1684. There is a story that she developed a fatal illness from the shock of coming upon a pamphlet that told her who she was, that is, what her parents had done. But this is not very credible, since as a girl she could hardly have been protected from all inkling of why, for instance, there were difficulties in the way of her marriage. She would well have remembered her mother, whom she had till she was almost seventeen, and her father was the sort who would talk of the slings and arrows of his outrageous fortune. A likelier variant of the story is that at some point in her life the reading about the case (and from the prosecution point of view) caused her to drop in a swoon. Wilson's 1653 *History* was worth that, and there were several others in similar vein. (For a modern equivalent, Stalin's daughter learned only on browsing through an English-language magazine that her mother's death, ten years before, was a suicide.) A terrible shock Anne did have in 1683, before her last, her sixty-eighth, birthday. Her son and heir, William, Lord Russell, a prominent Whig and rabidly anti-Catholic statesman, was convicted—on perjured evidence—in the Rye House Plot, a plan to assassinate Charles II and his brother. His head was cut off on the scaffold that his grandparents never had to climb.

As for Essex, whom Carr had won the bride from (but he who laughs last laughs best), that Robert had to decide whether to venture into matrimony again. Egging him on was his honor, besides the normal wish to perpetuate a noble family. There was a little matter to be proved to all and sundry. Still, he hesitated—he hesitated five years, ten, fifteen, until he reached forty, an age which many, Fanny, for instance, did not attain and by which others—with no need to apologize—were impotent. Then he took the plunge with young Elizabeth, daughter of Sir William Paulet of Edington. It cannot be said that the experiment was an unequivocal success. He went off to the country, leaving his wife (a habit of his) in the city. There, at Essex House, she was accused of adultery. It is true that the charge was made by servants with whom she did not get along (Wilson left the Earl's service on account of her) and by Sir Walter Devereux, Robert's bastard brother, who, if Robert died without issue, would become Viscount of Hereford. In any case, the lady was pregnant. Robert, alone at Chartley, pondered the problem, made a calculation, and announced that if the child was born before

November 5th (the anniversary of the Gunpowder Plot!), he would acknowledge it as his. But if it was born after that day, he would declare it a bastard. The infant was born on the day itself! But this son, the only offspring ever claimed for Essex, died, sparing him an agonizing decision. He and Elizabeth separated, and she remarried after his death.

He and James had got along less and less well. He was on a committee that objected to the creation of Scotch and Irish Earls and Viscounts, whereupon the old king singled him out with the remarkable and prophetic words, "I fear thee not, Essex, if thou wert as well beloved as thy father, and hadst 40,000 men at thy heels." By the end of 1639 the Earl, whose feelings were never difficult to ruffle, became convinced he had been slighted by Charles I, "which," says Clarendon, "wrought very much upon his rough, proud nature, and made him susceptible to some impressions afterwards which otherwise would not have found such easy admission." In the Civil War that broke out in 1642, Essex was one of the few lords that opted with Parliament against the son of that King that had sanctioned the divorce fiasco and the brother of that prince that had once stigmatized him on the tennis court as the "son of a traitor." In view of his martial experience in the Palatinate and Holland, the Earl was appointed commander in chief of the Parliamentary forces. But "Old Robin," as the citizen soldiers called him—he was now white-haired and round as a tun—proved an ineffectual and indecisive leader, lost his infantry in Cornwall, got sick ("an impostume in his back parts"), and resigned, dying without office in 1646 while Cromwell (a general who never lost a battle) brought the war to a smashing end. Macaulay points to a lifelong temperament when he writes: "The military errors of Essex were probably in some degree produced by political timidity. He was honestly, but not warmly, attached to the cause of the Parliament; and next to a great defeat he dreaded a great victory." Or we may take as a sexual comment that in the *Dictionary of National Biography*: "There was always a want of initiative in Essex which prevented him from making the best of adverse circumstances."

Fanny's two husbands died in ignominy within fourteen months of each other. The Jacobean house at Chiswick, which no longer exists, changed owners frequently. We do not hear, exactly, of ghosts but a superstition that bad luck went with it.

Samuel Rawson Gardiner, whose many-volumed history of the period, begun a century ago, is still standard, commented on the Lady herself: "If that unhallowed marriage had not stood in the way, she might have become his [Carr's] wife innocently enough, and have left no records of her butterfly existence with which history would have cared to meddle." This is reminiscent of the belated wisdom of James, when in 1613, that year of murder and divorce, he inveighed against "the marrying of young couples before they be acquainted one with another."

Which brings us to Bishop Goodman's account of her last days. Contrary to Wilson, he has her perfectly approachable, visited, as Christians were supposed to be, by the local minister. That worthy, either out of a burning curiosity widely shared or a desire to help in her purgation, brought up the question of what had really happened in that first marriage— or what had not happened. "She did then protest upon her soul and salvation that the Earl of Essex was never her husband." It is a legal maxim that the dying do not lie.

She was an exemplar here of modern freedom, and, in the poisoning, of doing what Freud says we all want to do. The Master's "Thoughts for the Times on War and Death" (1915) are uncomfortably relevant:

...for strangers and for enemies, we do acknowledge death, and consign them to it quite as readily and unthinkingly as did primitive man. Here there does, indeed, appear a distinction which in practice shows for a decisive one. Our unconscious does not carry out the killing; it merely thinks it and wishes it. But it would be wrong entirely to depreciate this psychical reality as compared with actual reality. It is significant and pregnant enough. In our unconscious we daily and hourly deport all who stand in our way, all who have offended or injured us. The expression: "Devil take him!" which so frequently comes to our lips in joking anger, and which really means "Death take him!" is in our unconscious an earnest deliberate death-wish. Indeed, our unconscious will murder even for trifles; like the ancient Athenian law of Draco, it knows no other punishment for crime than death; and this has a certain consistency, for every injury to our almighty and autocratic ego is at bottom a crime of *lèse-majesté*.

And so, if we are to be judged by the wishes in our unconscious, we are, like primitive man, simply a gang of murderers. It is well that all these wishes do not possess the potency which was attributed to them by primitive man [and Dr. Forman or his clients]; in the cross-fire of mutual maledictions mankind would long since have perished, the best and wisest of men and the loveliest and fairest of women with the rest.

Finally, it should be kept in mind how young Fanny was, not a woman—a girl, a teen-ager, right up to the poisoning. She was not more than thirteen when, nominally a wife, she was left adrift at a corrupt court. Her mother and her father turned out to be thieves. Her great-uncle and, in some sort, fellow-conspirator was a treacherous scoundrel. There were no paragons of virtue or wisdom anywhere among her relatives and her associates. People of a lower class were interested in her money and her jewels. Prince Henry and Carr became aware of her body, and she had a strong drive to make them so. Originally other-directed—and directed extremely badly—she became impassioned and inner-directed, with a vengeance. Her life was set and over before she came of age. Only it took some more months before that was apparent—to her and to the world. Reaching forty would have been utterly pointless; reaching twenty-five was, unless that pretty daughter kept her going.

She, Frances Howard, successively Countess of Essex and Countess of Somerset, not having troubled to justify herself before posterity, we can look to that line, in Latin though it is, provided her by that gallant Scot, Sir Robert Aytoun:

Denique quidquid erat, magni fuit error amoris.
"Summing it up, whatever it was that I did, it was the error of a great love."

A NOTE ON AUTHORITIES

The three most recent books have been: William McElwee, *The Murder of Sir Thomas Overbury* (London, 1952; New York, 1952); Miriam Allen deFord, *The Overbury Affair: The Murder Trial that Rocked the Court of King James I* (Philadelphia, 1960); Beatrice White, *Cast of Ravens: The Strange Case of Sir Thomas Overbury* (London, 1965; New York, 1967).

McElwee gives the best running account. It is hard to say whether he made any use of his best predecessor, Gibbs (see below); he seems to have started from scratch, winding his way with aplomb through intricate and contradictory and chronologically confused material. A British schoolmaster and and the author also of a good biography of James, *The Wisest Fool in Christendom*, McElwee has an easygoing style appropriate to his "conviction that a piece of history, if it is properly written, is a better story than any novel which can be written about it." Though never dodging names or details or quotations, seldom can he be caught in a mistake, as when he goes wrong on the chronology of Sir John Harington (p. 150), or dates the Somersets' release from the Tower a year too early because of Old Style/New Style difference (p. 265), or neglects to notice that Carr's petition printed in the State

Trials cannot be 1625 (p. 266), since it postdates the daughter's marriage. And who can get all the Howards straight? McElwee's index confounds Admiral Charles with William (p. 277). I doubt if the "tablet" Carr was given with the King's picture was "a golden table" (p. 26; see *Oxford English Dictionary*). Those following McElwee's instruction to look in the appendix to Vol. II of Gardiner's *History of England, 1603–42* for Overbury's letters from the Tower (printed from MS Harl. 7002) will be disappointed at most libraries, since the appendix was dropped after the first edition (1863), and there is the further complication that the long, last tirade is printed only in Sir Ralph Winwood's *Memorials of Affairs of State* (London, 1725), III, 478.

Mrs. deFord, veteran author of mystery stories and that engaging study of famous bastards, *Love Children,* whirls through "the Overbury affair" in 137 pages. She makes an analogy with a scandal in the White House. (One could work out some parallels with Harding.) Her essay is a triumph of lucidity, of cutting Gordian knots, and for those in a hurry it is to be recommended (with a correction of errors), along with one of her sources, the 41-page article by that canny Scot with many fans, William Roughead, "The Fatal Countess" (in his *Nothing But Murder*, New York, 1945). For a non-specialist Mrs. deFord's errors could easily have been more numerous. Following Roughead, she assigns Overbury a "character" entitled "The Mistress Made a Wife"—which is too much of a good thing (p. 30), and she also dates the release from the Tower as 1621 instead of 1622 (p. 127). Cotton received, did not write, the letter quoted on page 17; the State Papers do not say that Mary Woods was "hanged" (p. 31); the couplet on page 42 is not from a Jonson masque; there was no scheme to smother the Countess's testimony with cloaks (p. 95); there has never been such a word as "tam-

mel" (p. 97—a misprint in Howell's State Trials for "stammel": McElwee went down this false path too, p. 239.). Not
all the peers were on the jury (p. 98): Essex was not—and
therefore the following speculation is baseless: "It would be
interesting to know if the Earl of Essex voted or abstained
from voting, but there is no record" (p. 123). The Somersets
could and did have visitors in the Tower (p. 126). Ellesmere,
being long since dead, did not seal the pardon of 1624 (p.
127). Knollys was not "the uncle of the Earl of Essex" (p.
128). What basis is there for saying "that in her confession
Frances had insisted her husband knew what she had done"
(p. 104)? Somerset did not sell Chiswick (pp. 128, 133), but
mortgaged it, and the Star Chamber proceedings were not as
described (p. 131). The statement, which is wrong, that Somerset went to Chiswick unpardoned (p. 130) contradicts the
inaccurate description on page 127 of his being "formally
pardoned." I am very doubtful that "keep the Lord still to
me" in Fanny's admittedly confusing letter refers to Essex
(p. 23): she is asking Forman to keep her beloved Carr interested. "Ryde" House Plot (p. 134) should read "Rye." But
Mrs. deFord's unpretentious bibliography contains useful
items not mentioned by White.

Miss White, of the University of London and author of
Mary Tudor, does not waste words either, her main text con-
sisting of 187 pages as against 256 by McElwee (whose
name turns up as "MacElwee" in her bibliography). Even so,
her specialty is to call attention to discrepant accounts, instead of smoothing out or giving a favorite version to the sup-
pression of others. She alone has "been careful to give chapter
and verse throughout": the footnotes, placed in back, amount
to 13 pages. Most valuable of all, to serious students, is
her 8-page Select Bibliography, especially its identification
of pertinent manuscripts at the British Museum and the

Bodleian Library, Oxford. I did research in England in 1965, but after Miss White's book came out I could request photo reproductions of whatever manuscripts she had made sound interesting and have them sent across the Atlantic to me in Albany, New York. Manuscript versions are often worth following: Andrew Amos partly founded his pioneering book, *The Great Oyer of Poisoning* (London, 1846) on them, as regards the murder trials. When, in the fourth sentence of my third paragraph, I quote the richly ironic phrase "a pure virgin untouched," I am not giving my translation of "virgo intacta" but extracting from a seventeenth-century manuscript inserted in the pocket (marked CS 439*/H 84/p. 204) of the Ohio State University Library copy of Henry Howard's *Indication of Memorials . . . of the Howard Family* (Corby Castle, 1834), a book I had sent for in the (vain) hope of getting a date for Fanny's birth: the manuscript that came along was a surprise bonus. White is not given to errors, though as a biographer of Donne I should point out that he was not married in 1600 (pp. 193, 203), nor is 1573 (p. 203) any longer regarded as the year of his birth. The couplet quoted on page 187 as from Savage's play is not in the original, but from Woodfall's revision a generation after Savage's death; nor is the quotation from Aubrey on p. 45 accurate. One should pay White's excellent bibliography the compliment of noting its significant omissions. Omitting de-Ford and Gibbs, presumably on the grounds that they are not scholarly enough, she strangely includes Edward Abbott Parry, *The Overbury Mystery* (London, 1925), who quotes Browning on his title page, "Fancy with fact is just one fact the more" and indulges in imaginary conversations and other novelistic embroideries that make the book a better romance—it is better written—than Sabatini's. Judge Parry's is a book with personality and flavor, rather like an old wine.

King's Favourite: The Love Story of Robert Carr and Lady Essex (London, 1909; Philadelphia, n.d.), by Philip Gibbs—Sir Philip Hamilton Gibbs (1877–1962), of a well-known writing family—should not be left off anyone's reading list. It is the only biography of Carr we have, even as W. B. Devereux's *Lives and Letters of the Devereux, Earls of Essex* (London, 1853) will have to serve for the third Earl of Essex until something better—much needed—comes along. (The most scholarly biography of James has been D. Harris Willson's *King James VI and I*, New York, 1956, but David Mathew's *James I*, London, 1967, has now to be reckoned with; an independent work that taught me much is G. P. V. Akrigg, *Jacobean Pageant*, Cambridge, Mass., 1962.) A journalist, novelist, World War I memorialist, and author of two books on Buckingham, Gibbs did a good deal of research—although his footnotes have no page numbers—and his 315 pages (American edition) bring out the moral and dramatic features of what he clearly recognizes as a stunning story. True, he does not always handle dates well. His footnote on page 48 shows that Fanny's first marriage took place in January 1606; page 47 declares she was born in 1593, but the same page asks us to believe "she had reached sixteen years of age [when] her father and mother arranged" that marriage. Nor are Gibbs's quotations invariably trustworthy. On page 128 he has Overbury writing, "I pray you keep my Letters that they may see how much I forgot your Lordship in my Exyle." But the next page quotes this as, "I pray you keep my letters, that they may see how much I forgot your Lordship in my style!" (the correct reading). A politically sophisticated biography of Carr is needed. Lacking it, we have entertained in Maurice Ashley's Pelican history, *England in the Seventeenth Century* (revision of 1958) the incredible theory that Carr himself brought the future Buckingham "to the King's attention, arguing that if the King were known to have English favourites, as well as a Scottish favourite, those who disliked him mainly because he was a Scot might be mollified. Unfortunately for him, matters worked out badly." Indeed they did, and Carr was not quite *that* stupid. (Present-day historians have shown little interest in or knowledge of this material. The usually impeccable C. V. Wedgwood makes Essex twenty-four, instead of twenty-two, at the time of his divorce—*The King's Peace,* New York, p. 129—besides being disappointingly terse on him in her subsequent volume, *The King's War.*) I hasten to add that I have otherwise long admired Mr. Ashley's paperback guide, and that I found particularly useful the same author's bold *The Stuarts in Love: With Some Reflections on Love and Marriage in the Sixteenth and Seventeenth Centuries* (New York, 1963). I might also mention, for its sinister bearings, R. E. L. Masters' recent *Eros and Evil: The Sexual Psychopathology of Witchcraft* (New York, 1962).

Pushing further back, we get the seventeenth-century accounts, variant in their opinions and their facts, of Sir Anthony Weldon, Sir William Sanderson, Godfrey Goodman, Arthur Wilson, Sir Simonds D'Ewes, Francis Osborne, Sir Edward Peyton, Roger Coke, and *Truth Brought to Light,* attributed to Fulke Greville, Lord Brooke. John Chamberlain's Letters are indispensable and have been completely available since 1939, edited by Norman E. McClure (Philadelphia). Basic both for the annulment and the murder is Vol. II of T. B. Howell's *A Complete Collection of State Trials* (London, 1816). A useful compilation is *"Sir Thomas Overbury's Vision" (1616) by Richard Niccols, and Other English Sources of Nathaniel Hawthorne's "The Scarlet Letter,"* Facsimile Reproductions with an Introduction by Alfred S. Reid (Gainesville, Florida, 1957), which reprints, besides other pertinent material, the Loseley Manuscripts. John Nichols, *The Progresses, Processions, and Magnificent Festivities of King James the First* (4 vols., London, 1828), has lately been phototyped by Burt Franklin in New York. Probably the most grievous omission from Miss White's bibliography and book is Anna Maria Crinò, "Il Processo a Lord e Lady Somerset per l'Assassinio di Sir Thomas Overbury nelle Relazioni di Francesco Quaratesi e di Pompilio Gaetani," *English Miscellany*, VIII (1957), 251–88, which furnishes a dozen important points not to be found elsewhere, including Fanny's remarkable dialogue with Coke when he came around to question her and she turned him away. Another item that deserves mention is William Addison's resplendent monograph, *Audley End* (London, 1953).

Recent articles of literary interest include: Thomas Kranídas, "Possible Revisions or Additions in Jonson's *Epicoene*," *Anglia*, LXXXIII (1965), 451–53; James L. Sanderson, "Poems on an Affair of State—The Marriage of Somerset and Lady Essex," *Review of English Studies*, XVII (1966), 57–61; Raymond B. Waddington, "Chapman's *Andromeda Liberata*: Mythology and Meaning," *PMLA*, LXXXI (1966), 34–44. As a reminder that the remarkable submissiveness of Coke's victims was traditional, there is Lacey Baldwin Smith's article, "English Treason Trials and Confessions in the Sixteenth Century," which, having originally appeared in the *Journal of the History of Ideas*, XV (1954), 471–98, has been reprinted in *The Elizabethan Age*, edited by David L. Stevenson (New York, Fawcett paperback, 1966). As Professor Stevenson comments (pp. 18–19):

If the Elizabethan aristocrat was willing to die for the hierarchical order which sustained him, men of lower rank often demonstrated equal loyalty to it, equally convinced of its divine necessity. John Stubbs, as an example, had personally outraged Queen

Elizabeth by publishing a book, in 1581, which argued against her marriage to the Duke of Anjou. Stubbs was apprehended for merely having had opinions about those above him. A lawyer, Dalton, who defended his right, was committed to the Tower; his lenient judge, in the Court of Common Pleas, was forced to resign from the bench. And Stubbs (and Page, who had distributed the book) were punished, as Camden reports it, by having "their right hands cut off with a cleaver, driven through the wrist by the force of a mallet, upon a scaffold in the marketplace at Westminster."

But Stubbs publicly accepted his punishment by a show of allegiance to the system as "honorable" as that of an Essex at the block. As Camden describes it, "I remember (being there present) that when Stubbs, after his right hand was cut off, put off his hat with his left; and said with a loud voice 'God save the Queen'; the multitude standing about was deeply silent." Stubbs was to die in loyal service to the Queen, eight years later, as part of the English expeditionary force which she had sent to aid the King of Navarre.